The Psychotherapist

The Psychotherapist

Use and Abuse of Psychological Influence

Gordon Warme, M.D.

JASON ARONSON INC.
Northvale, New Jersey
London

Production Editor Judith D. Cohen

This book was set in 10 pt. New Century Schoolbook by Alpha Graphics of Pittsfield, New Hampshire and printed and bound by Book-mart Press of North Bergen, New Jersey.

10 9 8 7 6 5 4 3 2 1

The author gratefully acknowledges permission to reprint excerpts from the following sources:

Let's Do It, words and music by Cole Porter. Copyright © (renewed) Warner Bros. Inc. All rights reserved. Used by permission. "The Witnesses" by W. H. Auden, from *Collected Poems* by W. H. Auden. Copyright © 1945 by W. H. Auden. Reprinted by permission of Random House, Inc. Also in *W. H. Auden: The Collected Shorter Poems 1927–1957*. Copyright © 1966 Faber and Faber Ltd. and used by permission.

Library of Congress Cataloging-in-Publication Data

Warme, Gordon.
The psychotherapist : use and abuse of psychological influence / by Gordon Warme.
p. cm.
Includes bibliographical references and index.
ISBN 1-56821-736-6 (alk. paper)
1. Psychotherapy—Philosophy. 2. Psychotherapists. I. Title.
[DNLM: 1. Psychotherapy. WM 420 W277p 1996]
RC437.5.W37 1996
616.89'14—dc20
DNLM/DLC
for Library of Congress 95-24831

Manufactured in the United States of America. Jason Aronson Inc. offers books and cassettes. For information and catalog write to Jason Aronson Inc., 230 Livingston Street, Northvale, New Jersey 07647.

Whatever is profound loves masks . . .
Might not nothing less than the
opposite be the proper disguise for
the shame of a God?

—Nietzsche

Audi partem alterum.

Hear the other side.

—Augustine

There are shallow truths and deep
truths. The opposite of a shallow
truth is false. The opposite of a
deep truth is, somehow, also true.

—Werner Heisenberg

Contents

Introduction

This book is an introduction to the genre "psychotherapist," a lively and prominent figure in the modern Western world that appears in many guises. I have no opinion on whether the abundance of psychotherapists in our culture is a good thing. But, in view of their ever-increasing presence, it seems to me wise to address the question of who these creatures are and who seeks their counsel. And when some do, indeed, consult with them, what is it that they do, and what is their rationale for doing so?

I am dissatisfied with the way many psychotherapists practice and with the theoretical models that they use as their guides. At times you may even conclude that I have decided to complain about *everything* that psychotherapists do! Partly, the inadequate practices that I complain about are an inevitable result—never completely correctable—of the personal arousals and disturbances that result from looking very closely into any human soul. But many examples of poor psychotherapeutic practice stem simply from the failure of practitioners to think, to study, and to know their own foibles.

Ordinarily, one would hope that such a critique would appear in professional journals. And, in all fairness, there is, in the professional literature, much worthwhile critical thought. But I aim my critique not only at practitioners, but also over their heads and address the intelligent public and the users of psychotherapeutic services. Since psychotherapy and the opinion of psychotherapists have assumed a position of great social power, the critique should reach as wide an audience as possible. There is nothing in this book that I consider to be a washing of dirty linen in public. Instead, it is a serious attempt at pointing out problems and abuses.

I will adopt the practice of referring to the psychotherapist as "she." I began to do this in a previous publication and to my chagrin—and amusement—the overwhelming first reaction to the book was my use of the feminine pronoun. Some were annoyed, some shared my amusement, and many teased me for being "politically correct." My actual intent had been to silently illustrate that language is profoundly important, that a simple change of gender in a pronoun will alter one's sense of what is going on, and that this should be a more centrally acknowledged truth for those who are practicing the "talking cure." It may even be true that, at least in North America, the majority of practicing psychotherapists are women.

Obviously, a consistent gender pronoun is necessary if the reader is not to be thrown into a hopeless muddle, especially since most of the "live action" is between two people—a patient and a therapist. Therefore, just as I did in the earlier book, I have opted to make the patient male and the psychotherapist female—at least when the clinical material permits.

My practice is to speak for "The Psychotherapist" and for how she should think her psychology and practice her craft. It will quickly be clear to the reader that, were I more honest, I would spell out that I am speaking for myself and for how I think the psychotherapist should think and act. In other words, I hide behind the more abstract figure of the generalized psychotherapist figure. This is a rhetorical strategy since, in the world of psychotherapists, there are many who will disagree with me.

Disagreeable though some will find my admonitions, I stand by what I say. *This book is about what I think the psychotherapist should be.*

In the pages that follow, I bolster my arguments with favorite quotations. Despite what one might expect, those whose words I have chosen to quote are not usually psychotherapists; instead, I have gone to literary sources. As I consider who it is that I have most often chosen to help me with my arguments, I see that they are, without a doubt, four of the truly great psychologists of the Western tradition: Shakespeare, Mann, Nietzsche, and Freud.

There is nobody like Shakespeare. If we all could learn his psychological lessons, there would be no need for psychotherapists. Of course, without saying so explicitly, Shakespeare would have known that some form of psychotherapist—shaman, priest, counselor—will always be needed, and that learning and savoring the psychology in plays, novels, and poems does not immunize us against suffering, nor does it lead us away from tomfoolery.

Psychological wisdom springs from the mouths of Shakespeare's characters and, on many occasions in this book, I will quote the words of these philosopher-psychologists. But his wisdom is just as often embedded in the actions of the characters. I think, for the moment, of three kinds of love (surely love—and sex—are great psychological puzzlers) that appear in *Romeo and Juliet*.

First of all there is the courtly love that Romeo has for Rosaline when the play begins. That passionate and painful courtly love—a sort of institutionalized masochism—possesses him and, as it is supposed to do, transforms him into a poet. Is it a psychological insight to note that frustrated sex and love can lead one into poetry? But then, as fate would have it, Romeo spies Juliet. Instantly, the love for Rosaline vanishes:

> The fresh-crowned hero fell without firing a shot. A certain Amy Lawrence vanished out of his heart and left not even a memory of herself behind. . . . He had been months winning

> her; she had confessed hardly a week ago; he had been the happiest boy in the world only seven short days.

No, not Romeo, but Tom Sawyer, who, at the sight of a blue-eyed creature, Becky Thatcher, forgets his past love instantly. Mark Twain, too, recognized the psychological genius of Shakespeare.

The love of Juliet is central, but, in order to keep things psychologically complex, Shakespeare lets us in on a third love, a love less visible to modern eyes. When Tybalt kills Mercutio, Romeo, in turn, kills Tybalt. This act inflames the feud between the families of Romeo and Juliet. Indeed, it puts in jeopardy the future of their love. In short, Romeo's love for Mercutio overrides his love for Juliet. It is the love of a man for a man—a love nowadays unknown or unacknowledged. Because it is nonsexual, such love between men was considered to be a higher and purer form of love than was heterosexual love. Thus Shakespeare, a psychologist of love. He will be heard from further.

Thomas Mann is a much more explicit and wordy (but what wonderful words!) psychologist than is Shakespeare. He is more like the psychotherapist in her expository and theoretical moments. His characters are analyzed and explicated with an artistry available to few. Over and over again, these expositions name the favored posture of the psychotherapist, namely, the position of never committing to final opinion. Like the psychotherapist, Mann stands for this adage: there are many ways to skin a cat, and many ways to live a life. Who is to judge and who is to advise? Certainly not the psychotherapist!

Shakespeare is polychromatic; Mann is a sort of Johnny-one-note. He has a number of psychological ideas that he flogs over and over again. His most precious idea has to do with the eternal conflict between art and life or, in the language of the psychotherapist, the conflict between seeing through the falsity of the world and getting on with life. These are not conflicts to be resolved, at least not resolved in the sense of making conflict go away. These are the conflicts, says Mann, that awaken and enrich, and that torment and inspire. The psychotherapist can only agree.

That theme is enlisted in Mann's discussions of sexuality, both homosexual and heterosexual. It is remarkable that, in *Death in Venice* (written as early as 1911), he was able to write paradoxically yet sympathetically of Gustav Aschenbach's homosexual love for a boy and get away with it. In that story, homosexual love is part and parcel of an ambiguous transformation in Aschenbach. On the one hand he is ill, degenerate, and dying. On the other hand he sees truths never before recognized, and is possessed of love never before known.

The same psychological conflict appears in many of Mann's short stories and novels. *Tonio Kröger, Tristan, Doctor Faustus,* and *Buddenbrooks*, among others, are works that echo the theme of art versus life. Idealized loves are bound up with illness, death, and insight. Plenty of food for thought for the psychotherapist and Mann's words are therefore plentifully quoted in the pages to come.

I came upon Mann by accident. Through a misunderstanding, I had been volunteered to give a short talk on one of Mann's short stories. It was supposed that I had some expertise in the subject. When I remonstrated to the organizer of the meeting, she begged me to try to do the job, and, reluctantly, I did so. As I prepared myself, I was taken aback to find in Mann a psychologist par excellence—and found him to be a witty and literary prodigy to boot. It did not take long before I found myself reading everything that he wrote and considering myself to be a minor expert on Mann.

The woman who persuaded me, Florence Rosberg, is one of those great souls who, on occasion, one is privileged to meet and who can alter and inspire the course of a life. Although she is far too young for the analogy to be perfect, she is a reincarnation of my grandmother, Line Reichwein Warme, who, with her love and her fiery intelligence, stirred me into thought in my early adult life. I acknowledge these splendid women as contributors to this book.

If Mann is notable for his cool psychotherapist-style disinterest, Nietzsche is, in that respect, as unlike a psychotherapist as one could imagine. When he titled a chapter "How to Philosophize with a Hammer," he was not talking through his hat. He is blunt, furious, and insulting toward those who do not see his truths. Nevertheless, Nietzsche was a psychologist par excellence and, with plenty of truth, he announced himself as "the first psychologist." But he is a philosopher-psychologist and, in his hands, the two disciplines become one.

His great psychological point, and perhaps my main point in this book, is that final truths can never be known. There are, he says, an infinitude of roads to truth; there is no end to interpreting; description and redescription go on forever. Nietzsche's Zarathustra is the God-man who sees through the world; "the Blonde Beast" (the lion—*not* the aryan, as the Nazis would have had it) is that person who is strong enough and brave enough to know that all the trumpeted truths are merely the crutches of those who will not stand alone; the "*Übermensch*" (the translation of this as the "Superman" does not work; the "Overman" of Walter Kaufmann—Nietzsche's chief translator—is even worse) is that person who can lead us into a new vision upon which to build a life, without the baggage of outworn moralities.

These are terrible words. They convey terrible truths, uttered by terrifying characters. All of the simple and accepted beliefs—especially moral beliefs—that we live by are subject to Nietzsche's wrathful critique. Our every "obvious" morality can only be shaken by his diatribes. Unlike Shakespeare, Mann, and Freud, he had little to say about sex. Tellingly, there is a story—perhaps apocryphal—that is told of him in Thomas Mann's *Doctor Faustus*. In that novel, the protagonist, Adrian Leverkühn, is a screen for a number of real people. Most of all, he represents Arnold Schönberg, the inventor of the twelve-tone row in music. Although he was a close friend of Thomas Mann, Schönberg was mightily annoyed by his portrayal in the novel. But Adrian Leverkühn also stands in for Gustav Mahler, for Richard Wagner, and for Nietzsche.

One evening, it is said, Nietzsche took a cab and asked the

driver to take him to a good restaurant. As a joke, the driver took him instead to a brothel. When Nietzsche entered the brothel he was taken aback, but covered his confusion by walking across the room to the piano. He was an accomplished pianist, and, let us say, he played brilliant classical music. The prostitutes, painted and bedecked, bare-breasted and giggling, watched. Shortly, one of the whores or, perhaps, one of the resident butterflies, Hetaera Esmeralda, walked over to where Nietzsche was and briefly, perhaps inadvertently, touched his cheek with her arm. After a short time, he stood up and left.

The story says that Nietzsche could not forget the touch on his cheek and later—perhaps months later—he returned to the brothel and asked for Esmeralda. She had moved to another city, he was told. In his state of inflamed desire, he pursued her. When he found her, she remonstrated and said that she was sick, that is to say, sexually and venereally sick. Nietzsche, possessed by the satanic, the poetic, and the carnal, did not care. He insisted on knowing her love and her poison and, touched by his suit, she surrendered to him. Subsequently, he succumbed to the spirochete and, eventually, died of syphilitic paresis. It was, the story says, the only sexual experience of Nietzsche's life. He did, of course, die of a brain disorder that could well have been syphilis.

Why does this story matter? Only because, once again, genius, sex, and death come together. Is this cheap romanticism? Is it a psychology that is out of date? My answer is that, in the hands of my master psychologists, it is as profound and as revealing of our species as it ever was.

To which of Freud's theories, hunches, speculations, and dogmatics, should we attend? I say that it all boils down to his observation that our conscious thought is not reliable. More than that, he taught that our conscious thought is unreliable *in principle*, that is to say, it is forever deceiving and self-serving. The psychotherapeutic cure is no return to reality, nor is it a discovery of the real truth about oneself. The "cure," if we dare to call it a cure, is modest. Perhaps a shift or a change.

Hopefully less suffering. Probably a wistful awareness of one's own arbitrariness.

He certainly talked a lot about sex, and much more explicitly than did either Shakespeare or Mann. By choosing a technical as well as a literary language, he could write more coolly about a hot subject. Sex (or, rather, anxiety about sex), he said, is all too often the motive that lies behind self-deception. He was surely correct in this assumption and no psychotherapist can do her job properly if she does not keep this in mind. But in other respects, I suspect that Freud was off the track with regard to sex. The novelists and the playwrights, by way of their literary poetics, have all too often outflanked him.

One of Freud's projects was to try to develop a biological model of sexual behavior, and to establish patterns of normality. Attempts to nail down a psychosexual schedule are always doomed to failure because, as we all know, human behavior—especially sexual behavior—is endlessly plastic and packed with symbolic intent. Besides, when he veered into biology, Freud was off topic. It is surely more accurate to emphasize that psychoanalysis is about the unconscious and about self-deception. In his fervor to be scientific, he pursued the false lead of biology. In his clinical (as opposed to theoretical) writings about sex, he stayed right on topic.

If Nietzsche neglected sex, and Shakespeare, Mann, and Freud did not, then we must also note that Freud, compared to my other three, neglected music. Music? What has music got to do with psychology? To those who love music, no answer is necessary. And for those who care little about music, I do not know how to answer. But for Nietzsche, Mann, and, I think, for Shakespeare, music is central. Thomas Mann has written of this more explicitly than have the others and, if the reader is inclined to pursue the topic, his writings are the place to go. The topic must, I fear, also be neglected by me.

My account of Freud is as skimpy as my commentary on music. My only excuse is that an adequate appraisal of him requires a book, or several books. The only comfort that I can offer is that my personal sense of him will become somewhat clearer in the following pages.

In Chapters 1 and 2 I outline my vision of the psychotherapist and, in complement, my vision of the patient. That account is not a matter of demographics but, instead, is a portrayal of the cultural and symbolic significance of these two indispensable social roles. I decline, in that account, to reduce them to mere personifications of their respective curative and sickness functions. Instead I insist that both the position of helper and of unwellness are unendingly complex and subject to no final definition.

Chapters 3 and 4 spell out the nature of the primary psychotherapeutic act, that is to say, the unexpected form and quality of the psychotherapist's stance of listening. As she carries out this function, she declines to do so according to the ordinary standards of human propriety. Instead she listens with *impropriety*, and with an odd artistic interpretiveness that Thomas Mann once described as "positively indecent." These chapters also spell out how that privileged attitude of listening transforms the patient by teaching him to join in, and to listen to himself in new and surprising ways. He can thereby come to adopt new and less humiliating psychological attitudes toward himself.

In Chapters 5 and 6, I suggest that being or becoming a psychotherapist is not for everyone. It is truly puzzling to think about why some people feel that they are to become the psychological listeners, the hearers of secrets, and the locale toward which the fumes of life are to be directed. It depends, I argue, on a peculiar psychological readiness in certain students, a readiness that must be polished and refined by way of a life of serious study. Those who think themselves to be "naturals" (whatever that might be) are almost always wrong. I recommend in these chapters that the awful responsibility of being a psychotherapist is partly achieved through formal training, but insist also that there are, in every life, countless nooks and crannies wherein the psychological can be discovered in all its freshness, complexity, and obscurity.

I hope that Chapters 7 through 10 on theory have in them enough of real life to prevent them from being too theoretically dry. I have tried to keep unhelpful jargon to a minimum. The point that I make is that the psychological is always and only a matter of interpretation. I hope that I will be found convincing when I argue that a world of interpretation is magically enlightening—even as it disappoints us. Why disappoints? Because it renders us more modest in our sureness about what we know and what we can know.

Chapters 11 and 12 take the form of a complaint, perhaps not as warranted as my critical style might suggest. Surely in a field as fraught with practical pitfalls as is the practice of psychotherapy, one ought to know in advance that problems will be eternal and that no correct or perfectable system can ever be put into place. Nevertheless, I make my critique with plenty of heat. For that I apologize. But, in the tradition of the ironically inclined psychotherapist, I make no apology for my critique. People's lives are at stake in our offices, and this means that questionable practice should be forever under the gun.

The patients and the psychotherapists who appear in the following pages have all been given fictitious names. The stories, when possible, have been disguised so that privacy will prevail. Since the clinical stories are true, some patients and students may well recognize themselves. Inevitably, they will have their own interpretations of the events that I have recorded.

I owe thanks to many persons above and beyond the two women whom I have already named. Like all psychotherapists, I know that we learn most from our patients. They themselves cannot help but know this. I also acknowledge my friend and colleague, Shmuel Hazanowich of Jerusalem, who has examined and criticized the manuscript for me. Like all friends, he has been kinder in his comments than he should have been. The same goes for Norman Doidge and Barry Simon, who have discussed these ideas with me on many occasions, and who have made explicit comments about my venture into cultural theory in Chapter 9. A less-technical critic, Diana Hartmann, has helped me to restrain my overenthusiastic style, and has insisted that I speak in the plain English that theoreticians all too often neglect.

Once again, my editor—by now my friend—is Judith Cohen, who has soothed and comforted me while I fretted over the final form which the book would take. Jason Aronson, as always, gave editorial help that reflected his serious interest in, and knowledge of, psychoanalysis and psychotherapy. With their help, this passionate book, on a topic that is of mighty importance, is put into your hands.

1

The Psychotherapist

> What he offered was a tone—crusty bemusement eventually resolving itself into a kind of wistful poetic insight. That was enough. If you could hit that note, it seemed, you could charm your way around any obstacle life threw up. It sounded like the voice of sanity, because it took failure as a given and confusion as an absolute.
>
> —Adam Gopnik, 1994 (said of James Thurber)

At a recent student seminar, I asked that someone present to the group a difficult psychotherapy case. A resident psychiatrist offered to present but, she said, she had not seen the patient for more than a year and believed that she had discarded her notes.

I watched ruefully as the student, with great passion and enthusiasm, recalled the story of the patient's difficult and complicated life. Her eyes flashed with excitement and, in the group in general, there was a complementary excitement. At other times one sensed how hopeful she was and, in counterpoint, how disappointed, how chagrined, and how frustrated she was with the difficult young woman she had chosen to treat. The frowns, the groans, the delighted laughter, and the nervous giggles of the group, all contributed to what, at the time, struck me as a remarkable spectacle. How could these students possibly understand this as science, I wondered? What did this have to do with objectivity and determinism, criteria almost synonymous with science in our technological, product-oriented society?

Such thoughts make one realize how felicitous is Kaufmann's (1980) appreciation of Freud as the creator of a "poetic science" (p. 9). To me, the roots of any worthwhile conception of psychology lie in Shakespeare—especially Shakespeare—Dostoyevski, Goethe, Nietzsche, and, ultimately, in Freud. Harold Bloom, in his "elitist" (I admit that I love its elitism) tract, *The Western Canon* (1994), goes so far as to claim that Shakespeare all but invented psychoanalysis and that all of Freud's ideas that count, were first to be found in the work of the great Bard. But what do I mean by this? In fact, my claim is intended to be a radical critique of the positivism that still confounds modern thinking but that cripples psychology and the humanities more severely than it does, say, physics.

My eager students are an equal rebuke to any narrow understanding of the scientific status of psychotherapy and of psychology. Their audience behavior has little resemblance to that of traditional students of science and, for better or for worse, is the behavior of theatergoers. But we psychotherapists, in our lingering self-doubts about our scientific status, still cling nervously to theories analogous to Newtonian materialism and determinism, whereas physics, for example, has gone on to structure its theories in terms of relativity, indeterminism, flux, and process.

Freud remains the best introduction to the role of psychotherapist. He himself acknowledges that psychotherapy, "compared with our physico-chemical remedies . . . appears positively unscientific and unworthy of the attention of a serious investigator" (1905, p. 258). Despite the prejudices that Freud anticipated, there is no escaping the fact that psychotherapy is the most ancient of medical methods.

Furthermore, he points out, we could not discard psychotherapy even if we wished to do so. Our patients, he says, would not permit it. For better or for worse, those of us who are physicians (psychologists, social workers) do, and must, practice the psychotherapeutic art, even when we have no intention of doing so. Our every word, our every gesture, our every glance has influence on the patient and, since this is so, it behooves us to study and perfect this art as well as we can.

Why is it that our patients will not permit us to stop being psychotherapists? There are, to this question, bad answers and good. First the bad. Patients come to us because we are mother figures, father figures, or because they are dependent, sick, damaged, and needy. Perhaps they are unconscious psychic exhibitionists? Or, perhaps, a deteriorating Western culture drives people to come to see us. Or is it those nonnurturing nonempathic parents? These are the bad answers—not necessarily completely wrong, but reductionistic and judgmental in the extreme. They are the explanations of the blamers, the ideologically naive, and the simplifiers.

The second set of answers is very different. It is so grand a generalization that many will be as dissatisfied with it as I am with the first group of bad explanations. People go to psychotherapists because it is something that we, in this culture, do. Just as we all go to films, to concerts, and to plays, and just as we ritually celebrate birthdays and Christmas, so do persons in every culture have their analogous celebrations. We marry and have children as a participation in our cultural heritage. Other cultures celebrate their totems, their Gods, and their harvests, and, just as we do, they visit their soul doctors—be they called shamans, witch doctors, or medicine men. Such practices are deeply embedded in every culture, and are just as honorable in their practice in Zimbabwe as they are in Toronto.

> Transference to a shaman is an ancient, worldwide technique of healing, widely studied by anthropologists and scholars of the history of religion. Shamanism preceded psychoanalysis and will survive it; it is the purest form of dynamic psychia-

> try. Freud's work, which is the description to the totality of human nature, far transcends the faded Freudian therapy. If there is an essence of Freud, it must be found in his vision of civil war within the psyche. [Bloom 1994, p. 376]

I am not so sure that Freudian psychotherapy is yet "faded," but Bloom is quite right when he places us, the psychotherapists, in our geographic and historical context. He is also quite right when he uses the word *description* for what we do. I will have much more to say about description and "thick description" later. For now, note that the "bad" theories that I have invoked propose to be *explanations,* whereas the "good" theories claim only to be *descriptions.* Since I am in the description camp, the modesty of my claim ("claim only to be") is a false humility.

This method is an example of what has been called "thick description," a theorizing strategy with fine credentials, taken up years ago by luminaries such as Edmund Husserl (1929), Clifford Geertz (1973), and Stanley Leavy (1980). Freud made the same description-affirming avowal in *The Question of Lay Analysis* (1926) where he said, "In psychology we can describe things by way of analogies. There is nothing peculiar in this; it is the case elsewhere as well. But we have constantly to keep changing these analogies, for none of them lasts us long enough" (p. 195).

The distinction that I draw between explanation and description is crucial in how we are to understand psychological theorizing. In this instance, the explanations that I have cited are superficial and, by suggesting closure, all invite us to stop thinking. The descriptions, which I prefer, invite further thought and further description. There is, here, a serious additional problem of which one must take note. How can one describe that which is unconscious? That puzzler I will address in Chapter 7, "Description and Redescription."

Our forebears were not all medical healers. In an address to the American Psychiatric Association, Karl Menninger (1959) said this:

> It should be remembered that there were once many different kinds of competing healers. There were the apothecaries who in 1617 were granted a charter permitting them to sever their 200-year association with the grocers. There were the various trade guilds: the barber-surgeons, midwives and bone setters; and then there were the physicians, with their plasters and clysters. All were busy "treating."

Until recently, we have been under the illusion that we have become more modern, and that our culture has relinquished its old-fashioned belief in quacks. Hopefully, we say, scientific medicine has prevailed. A vain hope. Legions of naturopaths, herbalists, and acupuncturists have thriving practices. The same holds for psychotherapy, which is practiced by legions of enthusiasts of many stripes. The difference is that, in biological medicine, at least some effective treatments can be differentiated from the ineffective ones. The unorthodox treatments may survive, but the demonstrably effective ones will always tend to prevail.

In the field of psychotherapy, the story is less sanguine. Our best research efforts demonstrate that all forms of psychotherapy are effective and that the degree of effectiveness is high with all the diagnostic categories (Luborsky et al. 1975, Lipsey and Wilson 1993). Unfortunately, it has turned out that in the field of psychotherapy, we do not have the definitive effective methods that, as in biological medicine, would tend to limit the practice of charlatans, of the misinformed, and of the evangelical enthusiasts.

For those with high hopes for science, this must be a dreadful affront. But couldn't this be a worthwhile reminder to us? Could we respond to such news with a renewed and vigorous struggle with the fascinating fact that we psychotherapists have at our disposal a power that we do not understand well?

When at her best, the psychotherapist does, indeed, find herself inspired by this challenge. But such inspiration must be leavened by other, more sober, considerations. If we have at our disposal a power that is so great, how is this power to be harnessed? It is not easy to fault the host of practitioners who claim success, even though we would like to scorn and denounce many of them. Whether we like it or not, they have a clientele that is as sophisticated and conventional as is that of those of us who count ourselves as the orthodox.

About all that the psychotherapist can do is to submit her own theories to the harshest possible critique, and to humbly consult with the great thinkers of Western tradition. With luck, the psychotherapist will find among that lot some ideas that will help her on her therapeutic and theoretical way. Most great thinkers worth studying are dead white males, even though we are now encouraged to look for truth elsewhere. It is an obvious truth that whether a thinker is black, female, or alive doesn't add a trace of additional worth to what he or she thinks.

Nor do those of us with medical degrees have any special warrant to decide what is to count as a good therapy or as a bad therapy. The only special task assigned to the medical doctors is the practice of diagnosis. This practice, so essential in general medicine, is of questionable value in the field of psychotherapy and may well have undesirable by-products.

> It is the privilege of some of us to be *called* doctors. And if the peculiar phases of existence which Jones and Smith are experiencing lead them to approach us in the belief that we can help them, they can then be called patients and their afflictions may be *called* disease. But we cannot discharge our responsibility by "calling."...
>
> Today there is a trend away from names, states and entities and toward dynamics, relativity and process. Just as the nature of matter has assumed a new aspect, so the nature of disease has come to be understood differently. . . .
>
> Words like *non compos mentis* or "responsible" and "irresponsible" really indicate only whether or not we think an accused person is able to appreciate being executed. "Psychotic" and "neurotic" cannot be competently defined, since what they mean at any one moment depends upon who is using them to describe whom. Many of us have urged their abolition, but they persist as weapons in scientific name-calling. [Menninger 1959, pp. 487–488]

We psychotherapists are terribly hampered by our shortage of facts. Like all who are short of facts, we are inclined, instead, to unwittingly embrace a variety of meta-religions, antitheologies, and surrogate creeds (Steiner 1974). Such "beliefs" are best called mythologies that, characteristically, claim to be complete pictures of man's estate. In and of themselves, such mythologies are to be judged neutrally since, for better or for worse, all of us have mythologies to which we cling. Science, for example, despite its claims of objectivity and discovery, is merely a way of making the world coherent; that is to say, it is another mythology. If I may be forgiven for saying so, the psychoanalytic creed, too, is merely another mythology. That mythological status in no way implies a negative judgment upon these disciplines. Indeed, their splendor is only enhanced when we, the adherents, recognize our field as just one more breed of mythopoetics.

Mythologies all have, as Steiner points out, three major characteristics. First, they suggest a total comprehension or analysis of man's place in the world. Second, there are canonic texts—in the case of psychotherapy, largely the works of Freud. Third, mythologies all have a set of identifying symbols, gestures, and metaphors. None of this, in and of itself, matters very much, except that the totalization, the canonic, and the symbols join together to form a language. Such a language limits—dangerously limits—the possibility of new thought and new ideas. Therefore, the defining feature of the psychotherapeutic mythology is that it systematically doubts its own claims. This claim will, again and again, be the central theme in this book.

The eternal danger faced by that multifaceted creature, the psychotherapist, is that she will betray her humane model of what should go on between her and her patient. If she is a psychiatrist, she is at risk of retreating to a naive and reductionistic biology; if a psychologist, to a moralistic and authoritarian behavioral advocacy or behavioral engineering. Those who live in a language world—simply put, all of us—are at risk of remaining subject to "the paternalism, the jealous, outworn authority of the speech system into which, unchoosing, we are born" (Steiner 1989, p. 108). Steiner is not condemning paternalism (although he may well do so), but is critiquing the paternalistic tyranny of any and all language systems. Even as language illuminates for us the wonders of the world, it also imprisons us in the language world we are using.

Part of our task is to decide upon the nature of the psychotherapist, the modern soul-doctor. I like to think of her as a benign worrier. Rather than having strong opinions about her patients, she is wary of conviction, fearful of strong belief, and appalled by ideology. When her competitors announce that they know the cause of psychic suffering and its proper cure, she is saddened by such naïveté, but, more important, she tries to summon up her courage. To what end? Well, she summons up her courage because she knows that, in her public life (she *never* does this with her patients!), one of her duties is to stand against tyrannical belief. Beliefs count as tyrannical when they are simplistic (in psychology, two plus two *never* equals four, and the half may well be greater than the whole), when they lead to blame of the other, and when they are enthusiasms or intoxications.

It is always more likely true that the psychologist will be interested in the cool, inward look, and in the pondering of this and that. Recently, a patient stormed into a colleague's office, sat on the edge of her couch and bellowed, "What the hell have you got that look on your face for! What are you trying to tell me?"

That colleague and I had just discussed that wonderful word *ponder*, that is, wonderful to the psychotherapist. Our conversation, God, and her own native wit, had therefore granted her a fine response to the challenging young patient. "I am pondering the presence here today," she said "of a man who is of great interest to us—a man who does not ponder his own speeches. I pray that he will not leave us too quickly, so that we may come to know him better." What a wonderful piece of wisdom for a young student to display. Contrary to every instinct that we indulge in our day-to-day life, this psychotherapist knew that the ornery character in her office was welcome—a precious creature who was not to be squelched, banished, or invited to be "realistic."

When I characterize the psychotherapist as a benign worrier, I do not mean that she is obsessive and thereby paralyzed. I mean only that she is worried by the obvious, by that which is taken for granted, and by slogans and pronouncements. That is why she is uneasy about the various pitfalls into which her parent discipline might lead her. She never wants to ask, "What is it?" because that question presupposes a final answer. Instead, she wants to ask, "Which *one* is it?" In other words, for every question there are many answers, many interpretations, depending on a host of interpretive circumstances. All that counts is what answer is clung to dogmatically and blindly by the patient.

This idea is invoked by Bloom (1994) to explain the greatness of Shakespeare:

> Part of the secret of Shakespeare's canonical centrality is his *disinterestedness;* despite all the flailings of New Historicists and other Resenters, Shakespeare is almost as free of ideology as are his heroic wits: Hamlet, Rosalind, Falstaff. He has no theology, no metaphysics, no ethics and rather less political theory than is brought to him by his current critics. [p. 56]

The word *disinterest* is important to the psychotherapist. By *disinterest* she does not mean that she is uninterested. Unfortunately, the word *disinterest* has now lost its purchase and carries with it connotations of neglect. It ought to mean putting aside one's own interests to view a situation dispassionately. Perhaps only professors of English use the word properly, for example when they point out Shakespeare's remarkable disinterest as he portrays (not judges) his characters. The psychotherapist cannot really be disinterested in her patient and yet this word must always haunt her because disinterest is precisely what helps her to not judge his way of life.

Because the word is worrisome, the psychotherapist struggles to find other words that, although they may not be better, would add different dimensions and insights to the vocabularies that she has used up to now. She is also aware of the word *neutrality* that Freud used. She has no major objection to it, but, nevertheless, she is convinced that the quest for more words and more metaphors can only help her improve her theories and her work.

Words like *reserved, constrained*, and *reluctant*, come to mind. Is the psychotherapist reluctant? Indeed she is. She may even be obstinate. In her silence she is always "obstinately" suggesting that there must be more to the matter at hand than has been said, and more to the matter at hand than meets the eye. Tell me more, she is saying, and more and more. And is she resolute? Indeed she is. She is absolutely resolute that she will remain reluctant to come to final conclusions about the ways of life of her patients. Could she be found to be wistful or wistfully amused? Quietly ironic about the unending problematics of every life? She is also horrified by life and by the tragic destinies into which her patients, like Hamlet and Lady Macbeth, are led by their own characters.

Must one be concerned about the health of such a person's soul—that psychotherapist-person who, in her ironic remoteness, is horrified yet near to mockery and to laughter? Is it not dishonorable to afford more honor to her patient's freedom than to the "truth" or the "reality" of what he actually says? To always keep her distance and to give privilege and hearty acceptance to the odd, the profane, and the uncanny?

If she has disinterest, how does that jibe with kinder words? Does the psychotherapist, for example, care? By *care*, I mean what Heidegger refers to as *Sorge,* the care that is sorrowful and full of human concern. Does the psychotherapist care in this sense?

I say that she does not. If she loves her patients and cares for them, then she must rise up, enter their lives, and participate in their woes. If I care for the starving child in Africa, I must sell my house and go there. I would, if I cared, walk over forty miles of broken glass as I would for my own child. Ivan Illich (Cayley 1992) has taught the same idea this way:

> [When my friend] asks me, "But don't you care for the bloated-belly children on their stick-legs, for those afflicted with

> kwashiorkor in the Sahel?" My immediate reaction is, I will do everything I can to eliminate from my heart any sense of *care* for them. I want to experience horror. I want to really *taste* this reality about which you report to me. I do not want to escape my sense of helplessness and fall into a pretense that I care and that I do or have done all that is possible of me. I want to live with the *inescapable* horror of these children, of these persons, in my heart and know that I cannot actively, really, love them. [p. 216]

The psychotherapist that I am evoking is a most attractive figure. However, some readers will be troubled by the qualities that I am describing in her. Disinterest and lack of care: how could these be essential and defining qualities for a person concerned with the psychological suffering of others? Also, I grant her only weak scientific status and no fundamental virtue beyond that of any shaman. The case on her behalf is to be made only tortuously, largely because her role is so central and yet, is so unspecified. I hope, nevertheless, to make a convincing rationale for my version of who she is.

She is not a warrior although, in many previous incarnations, in many cultures, she has been a warrior. She is also not a sage or, if we must conceive her as such, in our culture she is a sage who thinks at great length and with great caution. The unique version of the soul doctor that has been born into our culture does not presume to know the way. Her wisdom is not that of the sage unless the sage is granted wisdom precisely because she does not know the way for another. Nor is she the objective scientist.

Great comedians are disturbingly pessimistic about the human condition. In their humor, they zero in on our foibles, hypocrisies, and vanities. Jackie Mason, to cite only one of these master psychologists, is to be acknowledged as an honorary psychotherapist. But can we allow even hypothetical entry to our ranks to a man who mocks and satirizes and confronts? Isn't the psychotherapist sober and respectful? Is humor the proper method of she-who-helps-her-fellow-man with the torments of life and death, of sex and love?

My answer is yes. Shakespeare's fools, the comedian, and the clown, are all psychologists par excellence. The stuffy fellows who taught me that humor is out of place in psychotherapy were off base. Humor is not absolutely essential but, without it, the psychotherapist is robbed of one of her most potent therapeutic instruments. In keeping with my definition of the psychotherapist by way of metaphors, I now say she is the fool, but a special fool, akin to those of Shakespeare, and therefore the inhabiter of an honorable estate.

The fools in the plays of Shakespeare are, like the psychotherapist, solitaries. They comment on the world as outsiders, having no personal life and being without a past. The great fool of *King Lear* mocks and, more than that, confronts Lear with his folly again and again. Like the psychotherapeutic device of confrontation, his aim is to awaken in Lear an awareness of what he, Lear, is up to. Like the psychotherapist, he is not blunt and cruel; rather, he is subtle, and sprinkles his words with wit.

That tricky word *confrontation* is one of the technical injunctions that psychotherapy training may deliver to students and, like most formalized injunctions, is liable to be misused. It is not meant to suggest that the psychotherapist is demanding or insistent—although she may be—but, instead, means that the psychotherapist is to use her native wit to draw to the patient's attention what he is inclined not to know about himself. Lear's fool is a cornucopia of native wit, and, in that state of intelligent wit he is Lear's therapist (later on, Edgar, disguised as "Poor Tom" becomes Lear's psychotherapist as well). Any practitioner can profit from the vivacity, variety, and subtlety of the fool's confrontations, which are variants on interpretation.

The fool's psychological skills are apparent in speeches of other kinds. They are the envy of any aspiring psychotherapist:

> *Lear*. Dost thou call me fool, boy?
> *Fool*. All thy other titles thou hast given away, that thou wast born with.

Kent. This is not altogether fool, my lord. [I, iv, 148]

. . .

Fool. I have us'd it, nuncle, e'er since thou mad'st thy daughters thy mothers, for when thou gav'st them the rod, and put'st down thine own breeches,

[Sings] "Then they for sudden joy did weep,
And I for sorrow sung,
That such a king should play bo-peep,
And go the [fools] among."

Prithee, nuncle, keep a schoolmaster that can teach thy Fool to lie—I would fain learn to lie. [I, iv, 178]

More psychological tips for the psychotherapist—this time from the clown, Touchstone, of *As You Like It*:

Touch. Art thou wise?

Will. Ay, sir, I have a pretty wit.

Touch. Why, thou say'st well. I do now remember a saying, "The fool doth think he is wise, but the wise man knows himself to be a fool." The heathen philosopher, when he had a desire to eat a grape, would open his lips when he put it into his mouth, meaning thereby that grapes were made to eat and lips to open. [V, i, 27]

Like many of Shakespeare's fools, Feste, in *Twelfth Night*, is enamored of the play on words, just as Freud was and, I hope, as is every psychotherapist. The fool is psychologically wise and, in complement, the wise therapist will not neglect to know himself as fool:

Viola. 'Save thee, friend, and thy music! Dost thou live by thy tabor [drum]?

Clown. No, sir, I live by the church.

Vio. Art thou a churchman?

Clo. No such matter, sir. I do live by the church; for I do live at my house, and my house doth stand by the church.

Vio. So thou sayst say the [king] lies by a beggar, if a beggar dwells near him; or the church stands by thy tabor, if thy tabor stand by the church.

Clo. You have said, sir. To see this age! A sentence is but a chev'ril [kidskin] glove to a good wit. How quickly the wrong side may be turn'd outward!

Vio. Nay, that's certain. They that dally nicely with words may quickly make them wanton.

Clo. I would therefore my sister had had no name, sir.

Vio. Why, man?

Clo. Why, sir, her name's a word, and to dally with that word might make my sister wanton. But indeed, words are very rascals since bonds disgrac'd them.

Vio. Thy reason, man?

Clo. Troth, sir, I can yield you none without words, and words are grown so false, I am loath to prove reason with them. [III, i, 1]

In our Western tradition, the first psychotherapist was the serpent from the biblical book of Genesis. For my purposes I propose to call her—the serpent—Lucifer. She will bear that name because she is, indeed, "the Carrier of the Light." The story goes like this. The Garden of Eden is populated by Adam and Eve. Their suffering is not spelled out in the biblical rendition of their story but they take counsel from the serpent-psychotherapist, Lucifer. She, as is required of her by her professional responsibilities, seeks to impart wisdom— knowledge—to these consultees. Like all patients, Adam and Eve become informed by love and sex and knowledge.

I mean this fable more seriously than might at first be thought. The psychotherapist is truly a Lucifer, a devilish tempter who invites her patients to know what they have not dared to know before. Not only that but, just as the two citizens of Eden violate the law of God, so the patient violates the laws of convention. Succumbing to the temptations of his psychotherapist, he investigates the darkness and ambiguity of his own nether world. Like Faust, he is an eager seeker for forbidden knowledge. Unlike Faust, who made no secret of his desires, many patients protest and avoid, thereby claiming that they do not wish to know. But, if they come, does this not give away their kinship with Faust? After all, the psychotherapist offers for sale her assistance in the pursuit of knowledge.

Faust wants to know about the darker arts: about alchemy, black magic, necromancy, and all that has been forbidden by the church and by God. He is the best of patients; Mephistopheles, his therapist, does not have to draw a reluctant patient into the tricky mysteries of language. Faust eagerly embraces that world on his own. Like Feste in *Twelfth Night*, and like the psychotherapist, he understands that words create worlds and realities. His central struggle centers on the Greek word *logos*. As he attempts to understand the biblical texts, he is not content with its traditional interpretation as "word," in the opening line of the Gospel according to Saint John: "In the beginning was the word."

For every possible interpretation he can give to the word *logos*, he creates a new world of meaning or discourse. What if it were translated as force, as striving, or as deed, he wonders? With the help of his serpent psychotherapist, smelling of cinders and of sulfur, he explores the known and the unknown worlds. With his power over words, he creates universes never before dreamed of. Before he names them they do not exist. Like every patient, he discovers that, with the magic of language, he can change even the past. Have we not all known the patient whose "perfect" family was, after treatment (after biting the apple, after consorting with the devil), no longer so perfect?

A potent metaphor. Within the safety of her professional stance, the psychotherapist is a tempter and a subverter of the appropriate, the typical, and the proper. She does not do the decent thing and is better described as being positively *in*decent.

Bloom's idea of the "strong poet," an image or metaphor that he evokes in *The Anxiety of Influence* (1973), is she who dreads the possibility that she may not be unique. She is horrified by the possibility that she may be a mere duplicator of what came before—that she might be just a copycat. The psychotherapist dreads the possibility that she is not discovering the uniqueness in her patient but, instead, is imposing upon him a dead idea that she has come upon elsewhere. She is terrified of mouthing clichés and mere conventionalities. Worse, she hesitates to repeat to her patient anything that she has said to him before. She suspects that, having said it once, her interpretation, no matter how wise or novel, will have been transformed into a cliché. Saying it twice means she has flubbed it, she fears.

But I am only *tempted* by the image of the psychotherapist as the strong poet. I cannot say that she *is* the strong poet. But that image is more valuable than are many others and it should be kept in mind. However, the therapist never is any particular thing. She is always many things depending upon circumstances, and upon who is conjuring up her image. Perhaps she is the midwife who attends the patient as he gives birth to the strong poet.

In this final thought experiment, the patient becomes uniquely himself, is no longer a mere cipher and is no longer he-who-apes-convention. This metaphor suggests that the midwife/psychotherapist delivers the patient from his neurotic enslavement (which mostly just means that he is human), and that in doing his part, the patient gives birth to . . . himself.

A patient, chairman of a breast cancer support group, told of a remarkable meeting the previous evening. As usual, a member was reporting on the problems encountered when one is a sufferer from breast cancer. When her doctor told her that she had the cancer, she said, she had slapped his face. The group responded with whoops of delight and applauded loudly. My patient was taken aback. And at first, so was I. But is it not true that the bearer of bad news is to be killed? The doctor was the messenger who delivered the news, ergo, he is to be punished, because the messenger is regularly punished. Economic circumstances may dictate that taxes must be raised but woe betide the politician who delivers the message.

The psychotherapist is one of those unfortunates. Her job is to deliver news that her patient would rather not know. When she, through careful work, reveals that a lifelong hatred is misplaced, she can expect that she will be hated imminently. She is one of the messengers. She is Hermes, the messenger of the Gods, and the psychotherapeutic school of hermeneutics is named in her honor.

My rhetorical strategy is to kill all stereotypes of what, or who, the psychotherapist might be, first, by demonstrating that even helpful metaphors can mislead us (medicine, science, sage, and, not helpful at all, the "blamer"), and, second, by emphasizing that there are other helpful metaphors that we can turn to. One metaphor—the midwife who helps the strong poet to be born—has great aesthetic appeal but must not be treated as an exclusive or better metaphor.

This descriptive tactic is the strategy used by lovers: "How do I love thee? Let me count the ways." Lovers struggle to tell of their love over and over again.

> I'm so happy that God sent you to me.
>
> Your eyes are magical.
>
> You are more beautiful than the most beautiful poem about a butterfly.
>
> I ache for you and then my soul and my heart ache, too. I am bedeviled and besotted and possessed, my darling.
>
> How can it be that you are my sweet, my angel, my life, my love . . . my very breath.

Not exactly Elizabeth Barrett Browning, but lovers feel *compelled* to talk in this way. For their love-mission—obligatory and insistent—they have recourse only to metaphors. The satiation of physical desire does not stem the torrential outpouring of love that, in the heat of such love-madness, must be spoken. So much for drives and biological needs capable of satisfaction! Such circumstances are an occasion for words and more words or, in the language of semiotics, chains of signification. The language of desire is always endless, as is every attempt to convey important information about human affairs. My strategy of describing and redescribing the psychotherapist is the only vehicle available for explaining who she is.

In Lawrence Durrell's *Alexandria Quartet*, the city is evoked polyphonically, by a profusion of images, each of which is colored by metaphors. It is in that tradition that the psychotherapist works. The fear of the psychotherapist is that you will understand her, the archetypal psychotherapist, unidimensionally.

To some, this may sound like an exercise in "anything goes." But there are rules and intellectual grounds for designating some metaphors as legitimate and others as illegitimate. Much more will follow about the rules of interpretation and about the aesthetics and legitimacy of metaphors.

My ideal psychotherapist has become the outsider, the social isolate who, because she is without illusions, has become the commentator par excellence. But, lest she has become an image too extreme in her psychological posturing, I add a caution that can be directed against Shakespeare's fools: the psychotherapist—or anyone—who is totally without illusions is only a figment of the imagination. In our very nature ("in our very nature" is one of the illusions) we register and present things to ourselves concretely even as we try not to. She who thinks otherwise is as much a fool as are the romantics who the psychotherapist is trying to undermine. She must never forget that she is a helper of the unhappy.

Jürgen Habermas (McCarthy 1981) has hopes that psychotherapists can achieve—indeed, may come to be defined by—"dominance-free communication." In a world poisoned by authoritarianism, his hopes are laudable. Such psychotherapeutic methods could, he argues, result in the emancipatory goals that any humane citizen must desire. To illuminate his point he enlists words such as *intersubjectivity*, *empathy*, and *unconstrained communication*, all of which reinforce the equality of the dialectic that he has in mind.

Mirroring, repetition, and reflection lead us into greater wisdom and into greater knowledge of ourselves and of others. Why else would artists paint and repaint what their predecessors have painted? Why else would a film be remade or a play revived? Why ponder the fate of Hamlet over and over again? Doesn't every mirroring lead to a rethinking, a rearrangement, a renewal?

The hope for egalitarian reflection and mirroring is undermined by noting that rethinking is not mere repetition after all. Once rethought, an idea is new and different. The Romantics, not wanting to know this, were convinced that they could achieve such transparency, such spiritual bliss. In short, they believed that the sublime was attainable, even if always just around the corner. Megill (1985) explains the dilemma:

> Any such reproduction is simply impossible; for however much we try, we cannot place ourselves back into the context within which the original production took place. The task of the interpreter, then, is not the recovery of something that cannot be recovered. Rather, his task is to make the object of his interpretation intelligible to himself and to the audience for whom he intends that interpretation. He accomplishes this task by looking at the object in the light of his own knowledge and concerns. In so doing, he quite legitimately gives new meanings to the object—meanings that may go far beyond anything [of which] . . . the original textual authors or historical actors could have conceived. . . . Thus, the Romantic notion of empathetic understanding, with its concern for mere reproduction, gives way to a notion of "active" or "productive" interpretation. [pp. 23–24]

The fate of every metaphor is to be both enlightening and limiting. To conjure the psychotherapist as teacher, sage, or as priest will, upon analysis, yield the same sort of result. All of these metaphors, and others, will have the same fate. This is not to be regretted. Psychology has few or no facts, and therefore its favored formulations are by way of the exhaustive or the thorough. The thorough is now much out of favor, even though it is only in thoroughness that we can discover what is of high interest. We are stuck with our metaphors or, since paradox is a psychological touchstone, we are blessed with our metaphors.

The longing for true understanding tends to blind us to the agonistic nature of persons. In other words, dominance-free communication is fundamentally contradicted by human experience. For example, in a dialogue, if I speak and then you respond to me, you will say something different. Your response can never be a pure agreement because, should you and I totally agree, there would be nothing to say. Perhaps you could just say "Amen." But even if you agree, you are still differing since you are never me, and are saying only that you, an Amener, an agreer, are present, albeit different. No conversation is possible without difference.

Everyone adds his two cents' worth, even if the difference is slight. If I say, "It is a fine day," and you respond, "Yes, indeed it is a fine day," then our dialogue is close to being a non-dialogue. Any worthy exchange is spicier, livelier, and agonistic. The play of differing opinions is what keeps us talking. If we all totally agreed, life would come to a standstill, and we would be boring robots. Here is a dialogue between two 6-year-old boys, sitting in the back seat of my car. They are best friends:

Orin. Street cars don't have to stop at red lights.
Alex. They can turn left where cars can't.
Or. But they don't have to stop.
Al. There is no difference.
Or. They don't turn there.
Al. Cars *can't* turn there.
Or. You don't get it.
Al. I get it. I just don't believe it.
Or. Yeah, but you don't get it.
Al. Yes I do. I just don't believe it.

These best friends spoke this way for the whole thirty-minute car ride. They also had plenty to say about that night's planned sleep-over and whether or not Orin's mother would see

Alexander's "dinky." They were, however, permitted to see one another's dinkies because, "We are both boys." These conversations were conducted in a boisterous, yet affectionate, manner. Ergo, persons as agonists.

> We are so made, that we can only derive intense enjoyment from a contrast, and only very little from a state of things. [Freud 1930, p. 76]

For many, the gentler metaphors are to be preferred. But more is expected of the psychotherapist than is comfortably encompassed by her preferences. She is not a god, but godlike demands are placed upon her. She is required to be at home with multiple and contradictory metaphors for the psychotherapeutic act and, even if she is drawn to gentle metaphors, she must painfully encompass agonistic metaphors as well. The opposite holds for her feistier colleagues. They must abide the world of gentleness despite their preference for images that bristle.

The privilegers of the agon will find terms like the following to be pallid metaphors for the psychotherapeutic interaction: dialectic, communication, fine conversation, lovemaking, and dancing. They might even have trouble with spicy variants on lovemaking (such as *soixante-neuf*) as a metaphor for psychotherapy. Their gentler colleagues, although equally determined to encompass all sorts of metaphoric representations, will be made uneasy when psychotherapy is thought of as war, critique of a life, struggle, a boxing match, or as a homosexual punch-up.

Hegel introduced us to the topic of struggle by elaborating on the characteristics of dialectic. If you propose an idea, you have announced a *thesis*. My response is the *antithesis*. The product of this exchange between agons is the *synthesis*. Out of opposition, Hegel claims, comes a new idea. This is the metaphor of life as struggle, a fruitful conception that reminds us of something that we often prefer to forget. People are fighters and strugglers. To aim for dominance-free communication is a Romantic denial of the obvious. And, in the context of the Romantic, let us not ignore Hegel's naive belief in progressive synthesis, progress, and, in its Marxist version, the expectation that Utopia is on its way. For those, remedial training is indicated for their unresolved Utopian strivings.

The psychotherapist knows of the dangers of her own agonistic positions. She tries to minimize her own power attempts by thinking like Richard Rorty (1994):

> It's one thing to say "we want you to consider the possibility that your tribal, religious or other form of life may be rendered obsolete in the course of this conversation," and another thing to say, "you are irrational and primitive." The first suggestion is perfectly reasonable. [p. 14]

The accusation "You are irrational and primitive" is the kind of statement that spouses make to one another when in the throes of an argument. Each, convinced that his or her personal reality has priority, denounces the psychological world of the other. This is what the psychotherapist is doing when she talks of the "irrational and primitive" in her patients. This is non-psychotherapeutic talk—allowed only as a countertransference reaction—and never to be believed. If she succumbs to belief in this countertransference reaction, she, herself, is being "irrational and primitive."

Here is one more metaphor, one more likeness, for the psychotherapist. She is a troubling figure and, in that troubling guise, she reveals an unsettling and insoluble problem. Whatever costume she is wearing, the psychotherapist is a *blamer*. This is easy enough to see in those who universally and simplistically blame psychic suffering on unempathic parents, on paternalistic oppression, or on bad spouses. To this list can be added bad (but not yet discovered) chemical disorders and a bad culture. The blamer is also easy to see in the shamanic incarnation of the psychotherapist. The shaman typically finds an offensive worm, a spell caster, or a "swear" that must be exorcised.

More subtle, but still easy to see, is our tendency to diagnostic name calling. The problem from which a patient suffers, it can be said, is that he is "borderline." The ostensible purpose of such a label is to make a medical diagnosis but, for "borderlines" and "narcissists," it really means that the patient is a form of damaged goods and is eligible for referral elsewhere. Such patients are often consigned to less ambitious treatments, which means that they are denied what they deserve as much as anyone else.

The most subtle blaming is done by me and by the model psychotherapist that I have invented here. She and I are dreadful elitists. We pride ourselves on our industrious examination of great thinkers, on our serious and exhaustive analyses of theory, and on our attempts to improve both theory and practice. We are proud of our nonelitist attitudes, especially when we say things like, "All ways of life are honorable," and "We have no advice to give, since we will never pretend that we have better opinions than do our patients about how they should live their lives."

How, then, can we be failures in our quest for the status of "elite" when we are so fair, so egalitarian, so nonhierarchical? It is precisely in our pride that our participation in the world of "blaming" appears. To us, those who do not join in on our thinking are—dare I say it?—the "rabble."

So far, our patients, except for having to put up with us, are spared the world of contempt for the other. Or are they? Our patients, like the patients of all psychotherapists, are enlisted into our blaming of, and scorn for, some convenient other. But, in addition, my model psychotherapist and I are devilishly clever in keeping this blaming attitude obscured.

How do we draw our patients in? We seem subtly able to entice our patients into joining our elitist club. They are to become egalitarian in the extreme, especially with regard to their own foibles. What they once considered to be stupidity and neurosis in themselves is now to be ironically perceived as just another facet of life. Their new perception of their symptoms becomes, peculiarly, a fading and vanishing of symptoms.

At the same time, they come to shun the less enlightened attitudes of the mere masses and the masses of lesser therapists, patients, and colleagues—their literalness, their naive belief in progress, in sickness, and in cure. Words like *scorn*, *contumely*, and *contempt* come to mind. Contempt for the rabble. For the other. They have joined in on the all-too-human blaming of the other fellow.

This "arrogance of disenchanted insight" and "stoic condescension" (Steiner 1958, p. 240) is the fate of all who pretend to be thinkers. And is psychotherapy not about thinking? The impossible alternative is the benign worrier. This is not the obsessionally paralyzed worrier. Rather, I am invoking the psychotherapist who does not judge.

Her eternal pride is a terminal disease. Her patients will forever aid and abet her in her project of believing in her own special powers, be it cleverness, supposed humility, or, as I illustrate, my prideful self-mockery. *The greatest problem faced by the psychotherapist, no matter how skilled, and no matter how experienced, is the belief in her own superior powers and the acceptance of her patient's aggrandizement of her.*

I have now had my fill—almost—of metaphors, imagoes, and archetypes that can define the psychotherapist. There are a few other titles that she must bear, albeit titles that are borne only in the consulting room. Publicly, she is, in one guise or another, a figure of potency. In the privacy of the professional office, secretly, and only cautiously acknowledged, she is finally to be found out in all her mortality. Publicly, the titles of potency are necessary because, otherwise, the psychotherapist as a genre could not survive. In the privacy of the clinic, she must eventually become the bitch, the coward, the jokester, the seductress, and the patronizing maternal caretaker. In her masculine incarnation, she will become the brute, the sissy, the rapist, and the naive, "Prince Charming," rescuer. These forbidden images will, if things go well, come to be realities and truths (realer and truer than most of us would wish) about the psychotherapist during the course of the treatment.

In our Western world, psychotherapists fall into three large categories. First, there are the highly trained and professionalized doctors, psychologists, and social workers. Many, like me, are analytically oriented and will find this book to be right up their alley.

The second group, usually well trained, deals with various kinds of offenders such as drug abusers, criminals, and other miscreants. These psychotherapists try to harness the power of groups to promote behavior less damaging to self, to family, and to society. They also rely heavily on the training and education of their patients. Some use psychological information—like that in this book—to augment their more inspirational and encouraging types of activity.

We cannot do without these heroes who do the psychotherapeutic dog work. Regrettably, their work is less acknowledged than it should be. Furthermore, they have been rendered tired and depleted by work carried out with less training than they need, and a professional identity not yet well enough developed. Certainly the formal psychotherapists are inclined to neglect the patients that, instead, go to the educational psychotherapists.

The third group of psychotherapists is comprised of the self-appointed who, all too often, have an ax to grind. They have urgent health goals that they press upon their patients and, in general, they are ideological enthusiasts. They typically have "found the way" and wish to convert others to their cause. They feel that they are on the side of the angels; in truth, they are insufferably sanctimonious.

Their unwitting patients are exhorted to "get in touch with your feelings," to "express" themselves, to "confront" wicked parents, and to "share," "communicate," and to "trust." Their reserves of banality are unlimited and, with great talent, they are blamers and, more worrisome, believers in their own cause and in their own virtue.

The standards of training set up by these blamers have more to do with adopting the point of view of the movement than with placing any serious intellectual demand upon the student. Intellectual types find these therapists to be acutely embarrassing and heap scorn upon them and their methods. Most frightening is their determination that they, like the leaders of every tyranny, *know* the way to go. Those who "know" are always to be feared.

A good motto to keep in mind is that *belief is a sure sign of error.*

The authentic Western shaman, the magical, poetic, and oddball psychotherapist that I am recommending to you, is a fascinating creature but, unharnessed, would be a loose cannon. But in fact the psychotherapist is two people. As a private figure, she enjoys the same conventional system of values as anyone else. As a professional, she thinks in unexpected ways. Some of you will love her for her prickly and intimate way of thinking; others of you will find her ridiculous.

In her private life, the psychotherapist will be conservative, might be liberal, or have left-wing leanings. In her business arrangements with her patients she is perfectly bourgeoise. Typically, she sells her time in strict fifty-minute blocks. The patient pays for that time whether he uses it or not, which is the only responsibility that the patient has.

In contrast to her psychological thinking, the psychotherapist is a conventional, business-minded professional. I recommend to students that, in their demeanor and their dress, they should clearly indicate their professional status and their professional intent. For example, men should wear a jacket and necktie.

The exploration of a patient's secrets—his villainy, sex, and every filth and glory that can be imagined—is best carried out in an atmosphere that keeps clear the professional nature of what is going on (Warme 1994). The psychotherapy situation is not a relationship between lovers, enemies, or friends. That contract, duly agreed upon by both parties, is between equals, albeit demanding from them radically different contributions.

The patient is permitted as much leeway as is possible within the bounds of common sense. He can horse around, snooze, or ply insults upon the therapist. He does not have to "try," to be industrious, or to do anything else—except that he is responsible for payment of the contracted fee. The psychotherapist, in contrast, is required to take a psychological position with regard to all that goes on. She listens, thinks, and speaks only in that psychological vein. She does not make any small talk *whatsoever*. Nor does she answer questions except with the intent of communicating a psychological observation. Within these guidelines, both parties to the psychotherapeutic contract may well love, hate, be bored, or feel friendly. Although perfectly bourgeoise in her professional behavior, the psychotherapist is, paradoxically, postmodern in her psychological thinking.

I end now with a definition: The psychotherapist is the culturally validated figure to whom people turn with their psychological woes. She has three defining attributes: first, she maintains a once removed, and therefore peculiarly reflective, posture vis-à-vis her patients; second, she declines to believe the idealizations and, less commonly, the depreciations, with which she is plied by her patients, including their claims of improvement; and third, she responds to all of her patients' communications with interpretations—interpretations that have the strategic intent of coming to know the feared and the radically disavowed, that is to say, the unconscious. Around this ideal image are clustered only some of the psychiatric, psychological, and social work psychotherapists, and only some of the frontline educational psychotherapists.

Undoubtedly, some will object to this set of practices. There is no solid justification for the psychotherapist practicing as she does, except to respond to objections as well as she can, whenever they arise. This book may be seen as one such response. As Rorty (1994) says,

> There are lots of things you can't justify that are important. Your mother, for example. There are things that are so basic to one's identity that one wouldn't know who one was if one stopped cherishing them. John Dewey felt that way about democratic institutions and I suppose I do, too. [p. 14]

2

The Patient

> Nothing happens to anybody which he is not fitted by nature to bear.
>
> —Marcus Aurelius

Every person, from time to time, consults with someone about personal sorrows, anxieties, and dilemmas. Ordinarily these are informal conversations that have the character of friendliness and of benign human concern. Apart from consultations with psychotherapists, such encounters carry only a small burden of responsibility for either the sufferer or the advisor. Nowadays the elders of a family are afforded no greater status as counselors beyond what is granted to a friend. Warriors and priests fare little better than do families in the soul doctor stakes since psychotherapists have cornered the market.

Whether or not this is a positive development is beside the point. It is simply a fact that the healing of the soul is now delegated to the three groups of psychotherapists described in Chapter 1.

Every culture offers access to a species—or a number of species—of psychotherapist. Typically, the option to consult the psychotherapist is left in the hands of the prospective customer and any soul illness qualifies one for this form of consultation. The psychotherapist then validates or does not validate, the claim of illness or, in other circumstances, the claim of demonic, astrological, or circumstantial influence.

Our Western culture is thought by some to have gone overboard in this regard. These critics say that too many seek therapy and this excessive demand bespeaks a peculiar cultural stupidity. Psychotherapists might wonder about this modern turn of events. Ivan Illich, in *Limits to Medicine*, proposes that the medicalization of health beyond a certain intensity increases suffering by reducing the capacity to suffer and destroying "the community setting in which suffering can become a dignified performance" (Cayley 1992, p. 19).

The psychotherapist is unwilling to come to a final judgment. She believes that psychotherapists have now been designated to carry out tasks previously done by families, community leaders, priests, and other culture heroes. She also knows that in the past she might have been a medicine man, a witch doctor, or a shaman, and in the future her quasi-scientific methods may be superseded, and that other, perhaps poetic, and perhaps sacrificial, counselors will do her job. She minds not at all that her work is designated by some to be based on human suggestibility. Her great concern is that she practice her profession responsibly. That act of responsibility is, to her, best achieved by studying the great writers of the Western tradition (psychotherapists are, willy-nilly, creatures of the Western tradition) and, most of all, by her resistance to the faddish and the banal.

Those who come for psychotherapy do so with a well-known set of rules. They suffer, they say, from symptoms: phobias, obsessions, sexual dysfunctions, anxieties, and depression. Some describe relationships that are unsatisfactory. They repeatedly act, they say, against their own interests, and their own careers. Their bodies and their *joie de vivre* are, we are told, unsatisfactory. Conventional symptoms all, and the required entry ticket for getting into the therapeutic arena.

Also conventional, although less satisfying to the psychotherapist, is the situation of mandated psychotherapy. A frightened spouse presents himself because his wife has laid down an ultimatum: "Either you get some help or else!" Psychotherapists are often leery about such a turn of events and say things such as, "Psychotherapy is a very personal matter and the decision cannot be made by any other person, be he an interested party or not." I share this sentiment but I do not believe it to be legitimate, nor do I agree with the rationale. We simply do not know whether people are less likely to profit from psychotherapy when it has been mandated or urged by another.

Why, then, do we psychotherapists complain in such a circumstance? Although I am now wise enough not to openly object, I can still track a certain negative twitch in myself when a prospective patient says he is here because his wife/brother/doctor/parole officer has instructed him to do so. Even worse is the situation in which an offender is sent for psychotherapy by his lawyer in a clear attempt to favorably influence a judge. And yet, one must be extremely cautious about declining to treat such persons. Only a god, I assume, could adequately make such a decision.

Many years ago, Hellmuth Kaiser (1962) published in *Psychiatry* a short story called "Emergency." Using a literary vehicle, he argues that psychotherapy requires for its success only the opportunity for two persons to speak with one another. In this remarkable story he tells of a therapist, masquerading as a patient, who successfully treats a doctor who believes that *he* is the psychotherapist. If Kaiser is right—and I believe that he is—any person who comes to us, the psychotherapists, can benefit from our labors. This is not a strong reading of psychotherapy as being magically effective; rather, it is an announcement of influence that any person can have upon another. The degree of that influence may be less than we might wish but, on the other hand, the influence may be far beyond what we had ever imagined to be possible.

Arthur Koestler, too, has written of an unwitting or unacknowledged psychotherapy. In *Arrival and Departure* (1968), the protagonist, Peter Slavek, meets regularly with Sonia Bolgar, a friend who is his only slightly disguised psychotherapist. The point is that the only requirement is that two people should have an opportunity to meet with one another. Koestler's wisdom permits him to portray a nonromanticized ending in which it is unclear whether the changes in Peter Slavek are a cure or a failure—whether he is better or worse.

I once read of a case in which a distraught mother brought to a psychiatrist her flamboyantly psychotic daughter. Her complaint was that her daughter had a sore throat. This despite the fact that she had come with her complaint to a psychiatrist. On each occasion upon which the psychiatrist attempted to speak of the child's psychosis, the mother threatened to leave. The wise doctor realized that this mother could speak of her child's unwellness only in the language of an ostensible sore throat and that her language of safety must be honored by him. He spoke then of his determination to diagnose the sore throat properly; he did not wish to rush his decision-making process, and he had no intention of making treatment decisions quickly. Surely, he argued, the mother must agree that medical decisions must be carefully thought out and accurate. Did she not wish to make further appointments to further pursue diagnostic and treatment possibilities?

In Chapter 11 I will discuss the case of Mrs. Allan, an elderly woman who was not offered psychotherapeutic help despite the urging of her family. Her age, and a concurrent convulsive episode, distracted her psychiatrists from the psychological crisis with which she was struggling. Neither age nor neurophysiological insult should deflect us from a patient's psychotherapeutic need.

Troubling and problematic patients are those who have suffered, or who claim to have suffered, some form of abuse. Often these persons have predetermined that there is a noxious villain who has perpetrated injuries upon them (be that villain a parent, a psychotherapist, or an employer), and that this evildoer's acts are a full and exhaustive explanation of the patient's suffering. The psychotherapist is inclined to think psychologically, that is to say, inclined to try to understand the patient's personal interpretation of hurtful events. Her working assumption is that neurosis—and the service that she provides is the treatment of neurosis—has to do with internal conflicts that shape and can make into unbearable torment both the enormities and the trivialities of day-to-day life. Cruel life events are not, says the psychotherapist, to be seen as exceptions to this psychological truth. Besides, she knows that there is nothing that, as a psychotherapist, she can do about hurtful life events.

Patients who report abuse often have other ideas on this score. They cannot or do not wish to look inward—the defining activity encouraged by the psychotherapist. Instead, they wish to denounce and, furthermore, to find allies who will join forces with them against those who have, or are said to have, injured them. Not for them the sober second look.

The concerned psychotherapist is typically chagrined that her prospective patient wishes not to look inward. Furthermore, she fears that, in his mounting rage, the patient will manage to find an unsophisticated therapist who will join him in an orgy of hatred against an increasingly denounced villain. To the psychotherapist, the patient is at risk of feeling better by way of a psychologically expensive "trick cure." To her, the cure by rage or by hatred raises fears that the patient is achieving well-being through membership in a virtue claiming minority. The achieved state of wellness resembles the extreme forms of tribal, racial, and religious exclusivity.

Such a patient is to be worked with as is any other. The poor psychotherapist is often in despair because it appears to her that she has, outside of the treatment situation, enemies ranked against her and against what she is attempting to do. But she should take what comfort she can from the fact that every case, even the ostensibly easy case, is difficult. One cannot easily change people; change is always difficult, and we are usually deceived when we think some of our patients are easier than others.

The Case of Martin Lebahn

The following case is a rather strange one. I record it to illustrate the uncertain ground upon which we stand as we evaluate who should be a patient and what criteria we should use in making such a decision. This psychotherapeutic venture illustrates what, for rhetorical purposes, I call a "perfect" beginning. Neither the therapist nor the patient expects or demands explicit indications or criteria for the work they will do together.

> My first contact with Martin Lebahn had been in 1959, when he was 23 years old. That consultative meeting was brief—perhaps abortive—and he did not begin his psychotherapeutic work with me until eight years later. Later he became an able, perhaps talented, psychotherapist. He was also able to indulge in the kind of self-scrutiny that is demanded by any adequate practice of the psychotherapeutic art. It seemed clear that the price of his eventual talents was a complementary dedication to self-examination.
>
> When he first consulted me, Dr. Lebahn was a medical student. His concern was that, although he knew and associated with young women, he seemed never to love them. Additionally, after many brief enthrallments with various of the medical specialties, he was much disillusioned with medicine. Although already interested in psychiatry and psychoanalysis, he was also skeptical of those darker arts and even more skeptical of the introverted hopefuls who entered those fields.
>
> In the summer immediately prior to consulting me, he had traveled to Europe and had been shaken by an incident that, ordinarily, would seem innocent. He had walked past Maxim's in Paris and when he paused to look, a man had accosted him. The man was obviously American and, as was typical in those times, was dressed in gaudy clothes (a Hawaiian shirt, perhaps?). He spoke to Lebahn in a loud, incautious manner. "Hey, son, they won't let me into this darn restaurant without a tie. Would you sell me yours?"

Lebahn happily agreed to sell the tie since his accoster was clearly willing to pay generously for the tie and, since he was still a student, he was chronically short of money.

However, the noisy American had more requests. "I am going to Egypt tomorrow, young man. If you have no other plans you could come along since I need someone to assist me. I would be prepared to pay a reasonable fee." Lebahn considered the offer carefully. He had no fixed schedule, his own finances could not have accommodated a trip to a place as exotic as Egypt, and an adventure seemed appealing. But a surge of oppressive uneasiness led him to draw back and he refused the offer, then quickly retreated from his encounter with the garishly dressed American. That uneasiness had plagued him for the remainder of his stay in Europe and its continuing presence still puzzled him when, in late October 1959, he decided to make an appointment to get help for himself.

In September, upon his return to Toronto, another troubling incident had taken place. A young woman had invited Lebahn to visit her in her apartment. He, somewhat hesitant to go to her home, had suggested that, instead, they should go to a party at one of the local medical fraternities. But when young Lebahn arrived to pick up his young lady, he was shocked at her appearance. Her hair, jet black, was swept upward with, to him, inappropriate severity. Its flat blackness led him to have a disturbingly offensive thought. "Has she colored her hair" he wondered, "with shoe polish?" In contrast, the skin of her face, neck, and arms (too exposed for a cool autumn night) was dead white. With his medical student eyes, he could see the dark, depressed tracks of collapsed veins under the unwelcome transparency of her skin. The young woman's dress was too scant, too tight, too revealing of her tall, thin frame. Her bizarrely erotic presentation of herself unnerved Lebahn. He was ashamed and filled with loathing for himself since he feared that he might be taking advantage of a psychologically disabled person. He was additionally ashamed to realize that he dared not take this woman to a place where his friends would meet her. He lied and explained that they would go to a movie instead. His face burned as he walked down the aisle of the movie house with the young woman and as he imagined the stares of the other moviegoers when his partner came into view. He was relieved when the lights dimmed.

Later they had coffee and when they returned to her home, she invited him in. He had embraced her inexpertly and fumblingly caressed her stiff but accepting body. Although still filled with shame, he touched her further, her sex, her dry sexuality. Her passionless embrace repelled him yet he had tried unsuccessfully to awaken her. He had found an excuse to leave and returned to his residence shuddering at what he had done.

"Is this normal, or do I need some help?" he asked me. But this all-too-orthodox question did not ring true. I suspected that this intense young student did not simply wonder about his unwellness or his health. Orthodox notions such as these did not fit a young man who, as he later revealed, had chosen to consult with me because he had heard that I had an "unusual way of thinking about things."

Since I think like a psychotherapist, I doubt that this quality was the only reason why Lebahn chose to consult me. The selection of a personal therapist is always based on a multitude of elusive motivations. Typically, medical students and psychiatric residents make contact with therapists in the hospitals and clinics to which they are assigned and, when they wish for a personal consultation, make a decision based on various nebulous factors. Their personal observations of psychotherapists in lectures and in clinical situations plays a role in their choice, as does the information that they get from fellow students. But such statements neglect the factors that may be most important of all, namely, those of which they are unconscious.

And now, in our first appointment, Martin Lebahn wondered whether he was "normal." I did not, of course, take his questions literally and therefore responded in a manner intended to deepen the discussion, to demonstrate the extent of his zest for the uncanny, and to tempt him into thinking further about what he had said.

"You are uneasy as you ponder the darker side of medicine, the revelations of psychology, the inner purposes of a garishly dressed man, and the secrets of a madwoman. You are unnerved, perhaps, by what you may dare to know? And additionally, you wonder what temptations you may yet taste?"

Should a psychotherapist speak this way to a patient? What could have possessed me to address such words to a man who, obviously, came because of a suffering of the soul and of the spirit? In truth, I do not think such actions are untoward.

Here is another example of a psychotherapist attempting to elicit novel thinking in the person she is interviewing. A colleague and I were interviewing prospective residents for our psychiatric service. I had found one candidate to be worrisome because of his stiff, intellectual, and remarkably formulistic thinking. I spoke of my worried thoughts about the candidate to my colleague who, by then, had also interviewed the young man. "Yes," she said, "I found him to be without imagination and without spirit. After about twenty minutes, in desperation, I tried to get him to reveal just a bit of his inner life to me by telling him that I now wanted to hear something different about him. Now, I said, I want you to speak to me of sex, of Wagner, and of bum-sniffing."

I doubt that my colleague truly said such words to our prospective student but her idea is, nevertheless, sound. With students, just as with patients, we are the encouragers of the unusual and the unexpected, and of the sacred and the profane. This is never done idly, but only in the context of teaching our student and in the context of helping our patient. To think in these ways is a witty, literate, and subversive action, valuable in many contexts, but permitted the psychotherapist only as part of her respectful illumination of the patient's inner world.

The great danger is that wit will be used to impress, as an act of vanity.

My actual recollection of the encounter with Lebahn is not of specific words but of possibilities held out by me—offerings of help, perhaps of love, and of knowledge. No therapist can promise to a potential patient that any particular outcome will come to pass, although it is expected that there will be an increase in knowledge—including the knowledge of sex and love. What else is there that could be had from a psychotherapeutic experience?

Lebahn seemed to have got what he came for. He thanked me for meeting with him and took his leave. I did not see him again until 1967, eight years later. My patient was by then only 31 years old. When he called me again, I remembered him immediately, even though we had met only once. In the intervening years I had become a seasoned psychotherapist and was a training analyst, conducting the analyses of young analytic aspirants. I assumed, therefore, that Lebahn aimed at training to become a psychoanalyst and that this was part of his motivation for coming to see me.

Since 1959 Dr. Lebahn had completed medical school, trained in psychiatry, and, for the past two years, had practiced as a private psychiatrist. For one half day each week he taught psychiatric students at a university hospital. He wished to enter therapy (therapy, not analysis, is what he said, even though it was clear that analysis or formal psychoanalytic treatment was what he wanted), in order "to pursue further what we discussed when we spoke eight years ago." Once again I sensed that he was demanding an intense psychological posture between us in which both of us were to look into the shadows or, perhaps, into the abyss. Not for Lebahn the easy entrée to analysis via studenthood, that is, by requesting a "training analysis." Nor did he this time claim medical inferiority by listing symptoms that might have afforded him the status of neurotic disability, of patienthood, of the afflicted one. No, this aspirant asked only that we should talk and think and know. He asked for no cure, for no counsel, for no guidance.

Lebahn was unmarried and did those things that young professional men do, although he imagined himself a loner and an outsider. He said that his supposed state of aloneness was both a fact and an affectation, an adolescent self-indulgence. Like all who affect loneliness, he longed to be gregarious. "Is it possible" he asked, "to feel like a loner without craving the state of belonging?" Most of all he disliked groups because, since they require organization and a community of beliefs, the lowest common denominator prevails. In Lebahn's opinion this meant that mediocrity is required of the members of any group.

In this non-illness mode, Lebahn began the psychotherapeutic dialogue. And, in analogous fashion, so do most other patients—at least after a few days or weeks. They are patients despite the fact that they speak mainly of the vicissitudes of life and, in short order, give up talk of symptoms and of unwellness. Instead, and unbidden, they talk of dreams, of love and sex, and create for the therapist their image—their version—of the world.

Not unexpectedly, he who consults the psychotherapist is in a state of suffering. Some would say that he is ill, has a disease or disorder, or that he has mental pathology. Apart from suffering (a safe term), these words, for one reason or another, are problematic.

The psychotherapist knows what is meant when psychic "illness" is spoken of, and she frequently uses that and related sickness terms herself. But she does so cautiously and worries that she is contributing to a language that judges certain persons to be inferior. The danger springs from the lulling effects of the cool and sober language of illness.

Disease and illness terms, when used properly, have great value since they permit access to help for those in a state of psychic anguish. But, in the world of diagnosis, the element of suffering is all too often overshadowed by a connotation of inferiority. Consequently, patients are referred to as immature, infantile, or as functioning psychopathologically. Such words deviate from the neutral descriptive phenomenology that is warranted, because—without warrant—they assign value to one behavior over another. This situation is most troubling when patients are announced to be "borderline" or "narcissistic" because, no matter how hard one tries to avoid it, the terms affirm that certain ways of life are of lesser worth.

Those who use these terms will insist that they imply no such thing. But years of experience have made me exquisitely sensitive to the scornful intent when, for example, a patient is said to be "narcissistic." The idea to be conveyed is that such persons are tainted or damaged, that this damage is fundamental and bespeaks a certain primitiveness, and that such persons are unlikely candidates for psychotherapeutic help. Students are cautioned not to take on such cases or, worse, forbidden to do so. It is unbecoming to a psychotherapist to speak and think in this way.

The attitude that I recommend is much more simpleminded and, I hope, more wholesome. Any unhappy person who wishes to speak to a psychotherapist deserves the service, provided that financial and administrative circumstances permit. Despite much comment that patients must be selected, we are not good at predicting who will do well in psychotherapy. Neither diagnosis nor type of therapy is of help to us in our predictive attempts (Luborsky et al. 1975, Lipsey and Wilson 1993).

No figure of this century has had as dramatic and transformative effect on the psychological thought of the Western world as has Freud. And yet many serious thinkers are cautious about criticizing Freud, even though thoughtful scrutiny of his psychological (and literary) contributions are central to any psychotherapist's work. In contrast to serious thinkers, the know-nothings are free in their criticisms of Freud, most often attempting to abuse him by way of weak misreadings and gossip.

Like Shakespeare, Plato, and Kant (and that small host who constitute the "Western canon"), Freud has revolutionized our view of man. Like Shakespeare, he influences or restructures every film, every book, every work of art to which our culture gives birth. This is in addition to our twentieth-century understanding of our fellow man, which would be considered mundane if not informed by Freudian ideas.

What, you may ask, is the central idea which, in Western culture, we now cannot do without? It is that man is a deeply disturbing creature, possessed of enigmatic, unsavory, and magical splendors. His psychology is infinitely various and unendingly innovative. You will note that, in order to make my point, I resort—I must resort—to a poetic language.

Freud's significance depends on more than these key, but abstracted, ideas. It depends also upon the body of Freud's work: his controversial case histories, his convoluted and infuriating theories, and his poetic and inspiring literary style. Analogously, to say that the plays of Tennessee Williams are about the self-deceptions and secret hatreds to be found in families is a moderately important truth; profound truths are only to be found in the study of the texts or of the performances of the plays themselves.

Like Shakespeare's *Romeo and Juliet*, Freud's writings inform us poetically about the vital and eternal truths of love and sex. Such truths are magical and aesthetic. They are absent from noncanonical works like self-help and how-to-do-it books. Youth will best learn about love and sex by reading *Romeo and Juliet, Madame Bovary*, and the biblical story of Jacob and Rachel. The mere mechanics of love and sex, they can figure out for themselves, just as we did.

Freudian thought has little to do with trivialities such as concretized egos, ids, drives, and pleasure principles. Nor does it have to do with, for example, Freud's undoubted sexism, nor with his ignorance of the female orgasm. May I prophesy that, in the next year or so, you and I will be found to have been ignorant of some fact? Note that I use the word *fact* with a touch of scorn to emphasize that, compared to great "truths"—such as the paradoxes of human existence—mere facts are, at best, of only modest importance.

Freud's successors sometimes misread him. Some swallow his work like scripture and thoughtlessly proclaim and promote his every banality, thereby diluting or missing the nature of the Freudian offering.

A second group, perhaps best illustrated by Lacan, blithely affirms that Freud's banalities are, in truth, nonexistent and that his (and their) work only addresses profundities. By suggesting this they miss one of Freud's central points: stupidity and self-deception are in all of us. Freud is not excepted.

A third group of commentators—those who find only banal truths to be interesting—searches for and finds errors and biases in Freud's corpus, and denounces these faults as decisive demonstrations that his work is worthless or destructive. Some of these denouncers are gossip mongers. Who in the world (except as a matter of fun or of sympathy) cares if Freud had sex with his sister-in-law? It has always been true that:

> Birds do it, bees do it,
> Even educated fleas do it,
> Let's do it, let's fall in love.

Such charmingly naughty gossip is, to my astonishment, used as an argument to discredit Freud's ideas. There is plenty to criticize but these writers have not found the points of vulnerability.

Psychotherapy is performed by persons from many walks of life. The most professional practitioners tend to be much influenced by medical custom, largely, I assume, because the illness model dominates psychotherapeutic circles. But this does not explain why medical tradition is so unabashedly triumphant. Since I am a medical practitioner, this turn of events suits me very well. Nevertheless, there are problems. My chief concern is that patients, before they are to be considered suitable candidates for psychotherapeutic treatment, must successfully negotiate an array of obstacles. Just as there are indications for surgery, for antibiotics, and for bronchodilators, so, the argument goes, there must be clear indications for psychotherapy.

These criteria, like all medical or psychotherapeutic dogmas, ought to be subjected to severe tests and criticisms—as are all scientific hypotheses. In science, such severe critiques are accepted as necessary, although probably not welcomed as much as they should be. In the psychiatric and psychological disciplines, critique of established rhetorical positions tends to be abhorred. The fact that psychological theorists are rhetoricians makes for plenty of trouble.

First, almost any position can be subversively critiqued. Second, every critique has a very personal flavor, since the proponents of various propositions, are putting forward valued ideas rather than objective facts. There is lots of room for trouble in this. In making a harsh and subversive critique I am asking for trouble. But the notion of "indications" for psychotherapy is deeply and irremediably flawed, and my hope is that my scolding behavior will encourage others to rethink their opinions on this matter.

Here are some important complaints about Freud's comments on the indications for psychotherapy. Freud (1905) listed four contraindications to psychotherapy. Briefly summarized they are:

1. Lack of a reasonable degree of education and of a fairly reliable character.
2. Psychosis.
3. More than 50 years of age.
4. Necessity for the speedy removal of dangerous symptoms.

Most psychotherapists, being highly educated, have an easier time speaking of the complex with persons with similar educational backgrounds. But this does not mean that psychotherapy will go less well under circumstances in which the patient has little education. A century of psychotherapeutic experience has changed our thinking, and few would now exclude patients on the grounds of education.

I also disagree with Freud's requirement that prospective patients have a reliable character. Unreliable patients will soon stop or have themselves expelled from treatment, such as those who do not pay their bills. Any other unreliable behavior is only of analytic interest to the psychotherapist.

If this unreliable soul opts to come late, to not come at all, or to remain silent during his appointments, this is to be understood as merely another worthwhile display of himself and of his personal madness. The therapist can only *applaud* what appears in the treatment situation, even if the conventional reactions to such behavior would be personal offense or indignation. If the patient has insurance to pay for his psychotherapeutic treatment, keeping his insurance current and paying for missed appointments are his only obligations. Whatever else he does, even if odd and obnoxious under other life circumstances, is welcome and revelatory.

Freud's second contraindication is difficult to critique. Certainly, my experience is that persons with psychosis usually will not come to psychotherapy. But some claim that such persons benefit. I would therefore disagree with Freud—albeit weakly—since in most circumstances, he is correct on this score. Nevertheless, in my view, those in a state of psychological suffering, even if psychotic, deserve a trial of psychotherapy. I have no sense that psychotic persons are made worse by *in-depth* psychotherapy, even though many disagree strongly with me on this point.

My own experience, and the experience of many colleagues, demonstrates that Freud is also incorrect about patients over the age of 50. The older patient, in contrast to the rigidity that Freud anticipated, is often wise and reflective. This, in my experience, makes the older patient an attractive candidate for treatment. The crucial factor, as is always the case, is the patient's suffering.

The final contraindication named by Freud is that treatment should not be attempted when the speedy removal of dangerous symptoms is required as, for example, in a case of hysterical anorexia. Effective drugs and other directive medical maneuvers must not be withheld. But psychotherapy is not contraindicated. The patient with dangerous symptoms can have a psychotherapeutic experience even though other measures are indicated as well.

There are more modern criteria that have been laid down. They are, in my opinion, no better and perhaps are of less value than those that Freud had to offer. Their codification has come to make them even more vulnerable to critique than are the criteria laid down by Freud. Judd Marmor (1979 p. 152) has summarized the typically demanded expectations as well as anyone:

1. evidences of ego strength (e.g., intelligence, level of educational achievement, sexual adjustment, type of work, ability to assume responsibility),
2. at least one meaningful interpersonal relationship in the past, indicating a capacity for basic trust, which is essential in the psychotherapeutic process,
3. the ability to interact with the therapist in the first session (i.e., the capacity to form a positive transference),
4. the ability to think in psychological terms (i.e., the ability to accept interpretation or, as it is sometimes called, the capacity for insight, which is usually tested in the initial interviews by making a tentative interpretation and evaluating the patient's response to it),
5. the ability to experience feelings (i.e., the degree to which the individual seems to be in touch with his own emotions).

I have a strong distaste for such formulas, because they are a scheme for keeping out of psychotherapy those who are suffering the most and who therefore need it the most. Also, I find these criteria, in some respects, incomprehensible.

Does Marmor's demand that prospective patients show evidence of ego strength mean that "intelligence" is a definable category of behavior above and beyond what was preferred by the psychology professors who developed IQ tests? And, even if there were an objectively ascertainable thing called "intelligence" apart from what is conventionally valued, who has demonstrated that persons who do not have that "intelligence" do poorly in psychotherapy? My experience belies any such claim.

Do we really require of our patients that they be sexually "adjusted"? What does sexually adjusted mean anyway? Heterosexuality? Some kind of mandated frequency or method of orgasm? Although Marmor is known to be a refreshing antidote to much smug conventionality, on this topic he has fallen into a trap. Here he is unreflectively recording slogans and lists that aim to rid us of problematic patients. Marmor's professional stature makes him the best possible object of my critique because the sinister power of rhetoric is all the more starkly revealed.

What does he mean when he says that the patient's type of work is a criterion of suitability for psychotherapy? Could he mean that a working-class person is not suitable? Is laziness a contradiction? Or is the enormous work schedule taken on by a nation's prime minister or president an indication of unsuitability?

Marmor, like Freud, states as a further ego strength requirement that the applicant for psychotherapy must be able to assume responsibility. How moralistic! Why does he say this? We are not behaviorists, are we? Isn't one of the prime requirements of the psychotherapist that she does not advocate for her patients any particular way of life? Does she not believe that, within the therapy situation, all ways of life are honorable?

Marmor's next requirement is that patients should have had at least one meaningful relationship in the past. The key word in this statement—*meaningful*—is meaningless. All human behavior is meaning-laden, including all relationships. Whether these are bourgeois, rebellious, or unorthodox matters not a whit. All are meaning-rich, meaning-saturated, and meaning-full. Hermits relate to people very intensely insofar as they avoid people with great intensity. To have never had an enduring friend or an enduring love is, to some of us, a sad state of affairs. But it is, nevertheless, full of complex meaning, is meaningful, and is legitimate and nonpathological.

Everyone has relationships and to say so is merely banal. We can describe the nature of a person's relationships, but only at her peril does the psychotherapist judge. She assiduously avoids assigning differential value to one way of having a relationship over another.

I suppose that, by *meaningful*, Marmor means relationships that resemble the conventional values of our culture. In the language of psychoanalysis we might call this living and loving according to the cultural law—that is to say, according to the oedipal law. When we psychoanalyze (and I do not differentiate sharply between psychoanalysis and psychotherapy) we have no intention of leading our patients into conformity with the oedipal law. On the contrary, we hope that, by way of our labors, our patients will be freed from their enslavement by violent superego strictures that urgently demand compliance with the oedipal law. I am biased in favor of marriage and children, of hearth and home, but professionally, and as a member of the passionate tribe of psychotherapists, I heartily disagree with any position that aims to shape or direct patients in one direction or another. Most of us are already too much in thrall to conformity and to the unimaginative.

Such a meaningful relationship, says Marmor, indicates a capacity for basic trust. Advocacy of "trust" strikes me as a behavioral expectation that smacks of naïveté. We should not be routinely trusting. Mistrustfulness is simply another way of being in the world. And if a person complains that his mistrustfulness causes him anguish of one sort or another, then surely we would not turn the patient away.

As for "the ability to interact with the therapist in the first session (positive transference)," I think that any behavior is an interaction. The demand for a positive transference narrows down what is wanted but, unfortunately, that narrowing down is also of little help. Does Marmor mean that those who are suspicious, crabby, and disagreeable are to be disqualified? Some persons who are "negative" eventually decline to come, but this does not mean that they are to be excluded.

Persons who present themselves as difficult do, indeed, aggravate the psychotherapist. She is, after all, just as vain and judgmental as are other people. I hope, however, that the psychotherapist is wise enough to know that some aspiring patients begin with a storm of obnoxiousness and then, after beginning treatment, settle into a pattern of traditional patient behaviors. Contrariwise, there is a cohort of trusting patients that we examine who, after an initial positiveness, become ferocious and perverse. This indicator of psychotherapeutic suitability is, nowadays, commonly referred to as the patient's ability to develop a *therapeutic alliance*. The new term is, for me, no improvement over the language used by Marmor.

Psychotherapists are pleased if patients are insightful and show a psychological bent. But this does not mean, as Marmor's fourth point suggests, that this is a requirement for acceptance as a patient. All persons think psychologically. There is no *lack* of psychological mindedness but only different *kinds* of psychological thinking.

Earlier I mentioned patients who are inclined to explain their distress only in terms of external villainous persons, villainous events, and villainous circumstances. This type of psychologizing is disappointing to the psychotherapist because she prefers to think in terms of *motives* for unhappy behavior, especially unconscious motives. She is equally disappointed when patients use a psychology that explains their behavior in biochemical terms or who find their behavior inexplicable, and who are without interest beyond that supposed inexplicability. Others find social inequities to be explanatory and, for still others, the will of God is at work.

The psychotherapist, despite her own prejudices, is at great pains not to judge a patient's explanatory habits. The type of psychological thinking used by patients is motivated and (at least potentially) explicable, as are the therapist's own preferred ways of thinking psychologically. Take, for example, my requirements that persons are always to be seen as being evil as well as good, and that they must be understood as complex, enigmatic, and poetic. To the psychotherapeutic community, my demands for the psychological mind may well be seen as laudatory and insightful. Indeed, in a later theoretical chapter, I will argue for my own psychological views.

My views are a product of my own shadowy motives, are a vanity and a tyranny, even though they may also be shrewd and illuminating. The same goes for every prospective patient's psychological intuitions. Those patients who I judge to be psychologically obtuse—and this is a judgment and not an observation—may be my theoretical allies after a few weeks or years. The psychological sophisticates—that is to say, those who think like me—may soon be judged by me to be recalcitrant and obtuse.

I disagree with Marmor's fifth point. The reader will already have noticed a certain pugnacity in me. Those of you with an analytic bent will have your suspicions: could this tough mindedness be a mask—a cloak for softness and gullibility? Am I, perhaps, tempted to passively submit to the ideas of a senior colleague, that is to say, am I unconsciously inclined to accept, believe, surrender, and give in? These analytic readers will be correct and will be addressing important truths about me.

But I am oblivious to this side of myself except in an intellectual and unconvincing way. Was my personal analytic treatment a failure? And am I out of touch with my feelings? If this is true, does this mean that I am not a candidate for psychotherapy? This is the point of which I am now complaining. Marmor claims that those who, like me, are out of touch with their feelings, are not suitable for psychotherapy. He is, I fear, quite wrong.

The expectation that all should "express" and "be in touch with" their feelings is silly in the extreme. It suggests that the person of calm character is flawed, but worse is the tyrannical idea that emotionality is healthier or more virtuous than is coolness of mind. To these promoters, I presume, an intellectualizing style is akin to a capital crime. Does this mean that histrionics should be encouraged?

Kaplan and colleagues (1994) recommend additional indications for intensive psychotherapy:

1. "High motivation" (p. 825). "High" because they mean, specifically, formal psychoanalysis. But if patients come,

they are motivated. If they come and talk of the weather, remain silent, read a book, eat their lunch, or give political sermons, this is only of psychological interest to the perfectly balanced psychotherapist that I am conjuring for you. She does not exist, but, for us, the psychotherapists, she is our exemplary model and our necessary heroine. If the patient wants to come and can manage the various administrative arrangements, that is motive enough for the psychotherapist.

2. "Ego strength." Kaplan and colleagues define ego strength differently from Marmor. By ego strength they mean

> the ability to oscillate between two types of ego functioning that are antithetical to one another: the capacity to regress, and to relinquish fantasy for reality, and to be dependent and passive; second, the ability to obey analytic rules, to integrate interpretations, to defer important decisions, to shift perspectives so as to become an observer of integrative processes, and to function in a sustained relationship responsibly. [p. 825]

Such hopes for a patient are very attractive. They are the kinds of psychological abilities that intellectuals and psychotherapists value for themselves. They are, however, merely the aesthetic preference of people like me, and only at my peril do I grant them objective health or "ego strength" status. Such intellectual standards can be demanded by us of our students or of colleagues, should we wish it, but this is not true of our patients. They live in worlds of their preference and for us to claim such worlds to be pathological, or that such psychological worlds render them unfit for psychotherapy, is plainly improper.

Two more objections pertain. First, to require complex ego skills of the patient smacks of asking the unwell to be well in order to qualify for treatment. Second, the demand for such forms of ego behavior is another inappropriate demand for the nonmoralizing and nonbehavioral psychotherapist.

3. "Primarily oedipal conflict" (Kaplan et al. 1991, p. 572). Aren't all of us merely creatures struggling to keep our moral balance in a culture that dictates to us a congeries of values, expectations, and "correctness" demands? Chapter 8 spells out a theory of culture, of the cultural—the oedipal—law.
4. "Patient experiences internal conflict." Surely there are persons who, without any experience of conflict, claim that life is good. Indeed, it is not uncommon to meet patients who think in this head-in-the-sand way. Contrariwise, there are some who, without any experience of internal conflict, claim that they must forever fight off the world, who disparage all ways of life, or who passively submit to every demand. They perceive, at first glance, no internal conflict, but are they not well-known actors in our psychotherapeutic practices? We cannot predict how patients will act after two or after ten meetings. After a period of time, those who experience themselves to be in a state of conflict may, to our very great interest, have become oblivious to it; the non-aware may, in the same length of time, have become psychological sophisticates.

   Internal conflict refers to a theoretical notion and not to anything manifest or experienced by the patient. This renders the point logically impossible. If the authors mean a conscious sense of conflict, then they are merely pointing to a manifest behavior that is subject to analysis just like any other psychological phenomenon.
5. "Obtains symptom relief through understanding." Any therapist who wants symptom relief for her patients has lost her therapeutic poise. The therapist is neutral. Her aim is only to promote self-knowledge. Every form of therapy gives symptom relief but, to the psychotherapist of whom I speak, the hope that an interpretation will lead to change makes her feel at best like a behaviorist and at worst like a moralist.
6. "Able to experience and observe strong affects without acting out." If I am a man of great calm, am I thereby

certified to be a patient? If I shout at my child, am I disqualified? If I feel powerful waves of love for my wife during my psychotherapy appointment and then return home and make love with her, am I an acting-out psychotherapy reject? Is this criterion a piece of nonsense?

7. "Supportive relationships available both in the present and the past." What a patient tells the psychotherapist of his life is viewed by her as a psychologically important narrative. We do not take such narratives at face value. If he tells her of absent figures of support (and the notion of support is a tricky one), she continues with her psychological problem-solving attitude. It never crosses her mind to take the patient literally. Patients who talk of absent support figures—past or present—are making a psychological point: "You, my audience, are to understand me as being without figures of support in my life, just as I understand myself that way." The psychotherapist treats this only as a psychologically analyzable narrative. Since this literal hearing of the patient's narrative is such a pervasive psychological error, I am disinclined to admit that the psychotherapist ever does otherwise, for fear that my words will be used to legitimate nonpsychological listening. But sometimes the literal is to be drawn to the patient's attention, especially with those patients who live largely in the world of the abstract, of the hypothetical, and the world of theory. They repress and deny the concrete.

   Even if it were true that a patient has no support figures in his life, why would the therapist so patronizingly undervalue the ability of the patient to stand alone? And is there not equal honor to be afforded to those who stand alone and to those who stand in dependency? The psychotherapist has no interest in judging. As a widower once said to me about his hovering family, "Just because I'm lonely doesn't mean I don't want to be alone."

One of the things that these contributors are worrying about is that certain patients stop coming. In and of itself, this may not matter. But for academics who have students to worry about, the patient who stops early on is a training nightmare. Students are required to see patients for a certain length of time, at a certain frequency, during a prescribed training period. Often, a demonstration of psychotherapeutic improvement is also demanded. If the patient stops, such training requirements may be seriously jeopardized. This is a powerful motivator for teachers to find a way of predicting how a patient will progress.

But wishing to find predictors is a false goal. The academics who pursue this vain hope would do better with simpler, perhaps better, tactics. Students are usually expected to do a diagnostic study of a patient in one hour. Doing assessments this way is bound to lead to many patients stopping after a short time, simply because, in one hour, one can only inadequately test a person's interest in the self-reflective enterprise called psychotherapy.

When I was a student, we were much better predictors because patients were seriously challenged by the examinational procedure, which took about twenty hours. The psychiatrist saw the patient for five hours over the course of a week; the psychologist saw him for six to seven hours; a social worker saw the family of every patient for three hours; and an EKG, chest x-ray, skull x-ray, and neurological examination were required. Any person willing to undergo such an onslaught is likely to stick it out in a psychotherapy situation. We had few dropouts.

The lesson is simple. If stick-with-it patients are required for training purposes, then do a trial of therapy or a prolonged assessment. Those practicing psychotherapy, on the other hand, will continue to do what I do: almost anyone who wants psychotherapy is offered a trial of treatment. If it does not work out, nothing is lost, and the patient may well have learned something. Having thought it over, the patient who stops may some day want to return, and that, too, is as it should be. When a patient stops, the psychotherapist should accept the decision as one upon which no judgment is to be made. That nonjudgmental reaction on the part of the psychotherapist may well pave the way for a guilt-free return to therapy at a later date. The psychotherapist does not want the patient to feel guilty about having stopped, since that might deflect him from later requesting a treatment that he badly needs.

In summary, any person who suffers psychologically, and who wishes to deal with this by knowing himself better, deserves at least a trial of psychotherapy. A key word in this assertion is *person*. The psychological theory used by the psychotherapist is always a personology, a statement that demands that, when thinking about patients, all human activities are to be referred to the person. The person (not his body) is in a certain physiological state; the person (not his self) is inflated and grandiose; the person (not his ego) defends, resists, and is self-deceptive; the person (not his id, his impulses, or his instincts) strikes out, shrieks, and passionately loves; the person (not his superego) judges his own behavior and inflicts punishment upon himself.

The personological demand guarantees that we not be misled by notions of brain injury or mental retardation as contraindications for psychotherapy. The damaged brain does not mean that our patient is to be denied the status of being a person. We can also imagine an extraterrestrial to be a person and can imagine such a person to be amenable to psychotherapy. Clifford Scott of Montreal, perhaps the ranking child psychoanalyst in the world, tells me that he has psychoanalyzed retarded adults and found that activity to be straightforward, and to resemble the analysis of a child. I have analyzed a child under 3 years of age and found her to be a complex and bedeviled "person."

Certain schizophrenic persons (persons, not "schizophrenics") are entitled to the benefits of psychotherapy, should they want it. I recently interviewed a man who had suffered a schizophrenic catastrophe years ago. He is considered now to be in a state of remission but, on his own initiative, he had come to the psychotherapy clinic. But the interview had little resemblance to what I typically conduct with patients asking for psychotherapy, and I am sure there is no chance that I will find anyone who will take him on.

He recited for me a litany of conventional banalities: he wants to get married, he wants to find a job, he wants to upgrade his education. When I asked about important and interesting thoughts that he had, the patient was momentarily hesitant and then, quite smoothly, responded with more well-rehearsed banalities. Does he have poetry in his soul? Banalities. Is there music that moves him to tears? Puzzlement, and then banalities. Can you tell me about love and hurt? More clichés and, so to speak, evidence of his shocking determination to reside in the world of surface. Life on the surface. But this man is a person. He is a suffering person. He deserves to be in psychotherapy.

3

Listening to Susan Wever

> When you are philosophizing you have to descend into primaeval chaos and feel at home there.
>
> —Wittgenstein

The tension between intimacy and distance bedevils the psychotherapeutic relationship. The psychotherapist must be acutely aware of a vital and eternal contradictoriness that characterizes the therapeutic situation. On the one hand, the psychotherapist maintains with her patient a strangely austere yet passionate professionalism. On the other hand, and in peculiar opposition to her professional stance, she and her patient are located in a close and constant physical proximity, dancing and warring with one another, debating, healing, and loving, but always as part of the therapeutic demand. She is always and only Dr. X. He, her patient, is always and only Mr., Mrs., or Ms. so-and-so. No small talk, no chatter, only "Good morning," and "Our time is up," and an unfaltering therapeutic labor. She talks with him of his swollen succulent sexuality, of revolting bodily discharges, of murder and of joy, of the banal, and of selfishness and love. What is the detail, she wonders, of how these matters appear in the theater of his life?

She most of all talks of how these passions appear in the theater of their own life together, that is, the life of the therapist and patient. They are always therapist and patient and live their radically contradictory theater in her quiet office. She is safely and unswervingly defined as a professional by that office, by her demeanor, and by her attire. In a certain sense, the psychotherapist is obsessed by both the psychological *Sturm und Drang* of her patients and by their stillness and tenderness.

Most of all, the psychotherapist listens. That listening takes a complex form and is not easy to explain. Sometimes, in order to teach her how to listen well, the psychotherapist is mandated to be empathic. But that mandate makes me a little uneasy. The word *empathy* has come to be abused and misused. In a strict sense it refers to a kind of vicarious introspection by way of which we can imagine what another soul may be feeling; in practice it has come to mean a kind of pallid kindness that inevitably leads us away from the pomp and spice of life.

The enthusiasm for the word *empathy* has led to neglect of another good word—*sympathy*. I suspect that it is now a better word than empathy since the latter has been appropriated to the sterile habits of the sloganeering enthusiasts.

> The rise of empathy is indeed the most egregious example of the moral self-indulgence and importance we have all become heir to. It is a way of saying, "Well, enough about you. This is what I'm going through; what I'm feeling. Anything you can feel, I can feel better." [Bhabra 1995, p. A20]

We cannot know what our patients are going through unless we can become them—and that we cannot do. It is grandiose folly to think that we can know the mind of another, although we can have informed hunches. To be more technical, we can only make interpretations, and the number of possible interpretations is infinite. As a psychotherapist, I want to know about what my patients think but, nevertheless, an inner demon persuades me that feeling *for* somebody is more worthy than feeling *with* them. *Sympathy* makes me into a caregiver; *empathy* is a tool that I use in the service of my sympathetic care.

There are other problems. If I am to imagine what my patient is thinking and experiencing, do I empathize with what is obvious to him or, in contrast, do I empathize with what I suspect he does not see? For example, when I speak to the inept lover do I simply echo back to him his longing and his ardor? Empathy, after all, aims to capture the patient's experience, and his love dominates and suffuses my patient-lover's mind. As a shrewd and helpful listener, might I, rather, empathize with an obvious strategy of self-defeat that I can see, or, second, with a guilt-inducing state of suffering with which my patient aims to coerce and manipulate? And, third, does he see, and should I empathize with, the voluptuousness by way of which he secretly indulges a masochistic humiliation?

Used correctly, the word *empathy* can encompass all of the above possibilities. The only proviso is that the psychotherapist empathizes with different elements in the patient's behavior at different times, depending on the needs of timing, the current interpretive strategy, and the limits of her tact and wit. Unfortunately, that possibility has in recent years been foreclosed to us. To be empathetic now means that we are to be kind, and to avoid the horrible, the repellent, and the evil that is to be found in every person and in every patient.

It is not that the psychotherapist wants to rub her patient's nose in the unsavory; by her very nature, the psychotherapist is likely to be soft-hearted. She aims to be as honest as possible. She wants to talk about everything, even though this may well only be accomplished at great emotional expense to herself. This is not to say that she speaks bluntly. After a few years of experience she is more likely to be a master of tact and respectfulness. That skill at speaking comfortably also becomes problematic because, being human, she wants to be loved. Her wish that her patient think well of her will chronically cause her to misuse her tact and to spare her patient the full impact of what she sees.

Ultimately, the aim is to illuminate the unconscious, which is both a radically necessary theoretical construct and, at the same time, merely shorthand for behaviors that are subtly present but hard to see, even by the careful observer. A more thorough discussion of this matter is to be found in Chapter 8.

The marvelous ability of persons to understand one another—to empathize—is well illustrated by the example of the lover. When boy meets girl, their dialogue with one another is miraculous in its mutual transparency. They can almost read one another's minds. Even when the boy first telephones the girl, he is usually aware ahead of time of whether his suit will or will not be accepted. An elaborate nonverbal exchange has already taken place by way of metaphoric hints and body language. The even more dramatic eventuality is that, later, both he and she will have a near-magical knowledge of when the time has come to touch fingers and hands, and when the kiss can—and must—take place. In an era of supposed sexual liberty, this may sound like the rantings of an outdated romantic. But the balcony scene from *Romeo and Juliet* is not at risk of losing its popularity.

What about the lover whose kiss is spurned? As she listens, the psychotherapist is determined that he, the spurned lover, has not simply failed to understand. Instead, and with great resolution, she assumes that he is as astute a psychologist in the game of love as is his more successful colleague. In fact, she assumes that he is just as shrewd a psychologist as she is. After all, a professional psychologist is merely a person who has been trained to speak about psychological matters; every person, whether he realizes it or not, is the shrewdest of psychologists. This means that the ungainly lover is shrewd for a particular purpose and that his "failure" is actually a success.

How could this be? The psychotherapist's assumption is that the failure is as ardently pursued as is the triumphant love-suit of the more elegant and successful lover. The failure is sought. The patient in question understands perfectly well the give and take of silent love-speech and uses that knowledge for the purposes of losing. The motives for such self-injurious actions are as various as there are persons in the world but, except for the brief example that follows, a thorough discussion of self-defeat will have to await the later chapters on theory.

This anecdote illustrates the fine line that can distinguish joy from pain, and adds further meaning to joyous love on the one hand and exquisitely painful love on the other. This ambiguity is what the psychotherapist listens for. When I was a young man—a young swain—I loved a fair maiden (I use the word *love* advisedly, although the unimaginative might have preferred to call it puppy love or a "crush"). That teenage love was both wondrously thrilling and, at the very same time, fraught with doubt, longing, and (to use an embarrassing word often associated with masochism) humiliation. At one moment I was sure that she had the same love for me that I had for her but, in the next moment, I doubted.

It seemed to me that she gave me double messages. When I doubted her, I told myself to give up on her, both to save my pride, and to spare myself further suffering. But this was easier said than done. I seemed bound to her even though I was sure that she was toying with me and, perhaps, even cruelly toying with me. In the next moment, when I believed my love to be reciprocated, I was happy, happy. But, curiously, that passionate happy love had almost the same quality as did my masochistic suffering. The important point to be made here is that, in a peculiar way, love has the quality of suffering; contrariwise, masochistic enthrallment is thrilling. Love, "le désir," and "la demande," are not such purebreds as they first appear to be.

The clearest way to illustrate the listening habits of the psychotherapist is by way of an actual case. This report is from my own files and therefore the gender of the psychotherapist will deviate from what has been my usual practice in this book. My aim is to illustrate the unusual psychological postures that can eventuate from a proper adoption of the psychotherapeutic attitude. The patient in question had been referred by a one-time student.

Why had my student Gryfe written to me, I wondered? I had just written an affectionate letter to a woman friend and, it seemed, my conscience did not approve. Did he know that I had become a correspondent, or a sinful and adulterous correspondent? Did he know that I corresponded with women; that my letters were too intimate, too incestuous? Since Gryfe wished me to see someone in consultation, this meant that to Gryfe I was still the fatherly teacher. And I did, at that stage in my career, indeed think of myself as the father. In an incorrigible analytic way, I speculated to myself that a deeper truth about Gryfe was that he wrote because I was the archetypal father and because he was the archetypal student. Finally, I noted that Gryfe was sending his—Gryfe's—patient, *his* woman . . . his *woman*?

As I try to tell this story of myself as a "psychotherapist" I find myself distracted by little fears and doubts. The fretful image of myself, described on the written page, seems ridiculous. The endless associating, connecting, linking; always pursuing what conventional thought ignores, claiming that magical ideas are powerful and worthwhile truths; believing that the patient, Gryfe, and I truly are Oedipus, Lady Macbeth, the Madonna, and Faust. And what is the current distraction? It is the awareness of you, the reader, who will discover me to be vain and foolish. Perhaps most of all I worry that my impatience with the world will be too apparent and that my complaints about a world ever tempted by cliché, by eclecticism, and by compromise are too strident.

Are not psychotherapists, you might ask, kinder and gentler than the skeptical critic who appears in these pages? My defensive answer to that question is to quote Nietzsche: "This is the hardest of all: to close the open hand out of love, and keep modest as a giver" (1884, prologue, ch. 2). But back to Gryfe's letter.

> Gryfe's patient was a 40-year-old television interviewer. Could I see her and give him an opinion? Mrs. Wever was heavy and rusty-haired. She fiddled with her purse, looked into her lap, and the words *crushed* and *crumpled* came to my mind as I looked at her. A few months ago she had been interviewing a well-known politician. He had been bombas-

tic and patronizing and her first reaction had been, "If he insists on being a fool, then that's his funeral." Funeral . . . ?

But shortly she found herself filled with anxiety. According to other observers, her interviewing performance had been adequate but she herself had been so panic stricken that she was amnesic for the last half of the interview. Now she was terrified that she might not be able to continue her work and therefore, a few days later, she had consulted Gryfe. She praised him profusely—perhaps too profusely—for his kindness. She had been, he told her, in a state of dissociation. Both her father and her husband had also been available, supportive, and wise. So . . . a powerful man, a politician, suddenly was transformed into a fool, a weakling. This competent successful woman, with equal suddenness, returned the courtesy and was transformed into a picture of equal weakness.

Was it forbidden that a man should ever be weak in her presence? And then her psychiatrist, her husband, and her father enter the story. They were available, supportive, and wise. She, correspondingly, defined herself as needing support, as finding wisdom not in herself, but in reincarnated, reinstated men. Men reinstated as wise and strong. But why "reincarnated"?

Her forefinger supported her right temple with knuckles to her cheek. Right leg crossed over left. I suddenly realized that my forefinger supported my left temple, my knuckles curled on my cheek, my left leg was over my right. So common and yet so wonderful. Was I mirroring her, I wondered, or was she mirroring me?

"Mrs. Wever," I said somewhat brusquely, "are you imitating me or am I imitating you?" Why brusquely? Was it a requirement that I be tough and strong for her?

"I was sitting this way first, so you must be copying me," she responded. Did she smirk slightly as she said these words? This lady, I observed, was at that moment quite strong enough. Was her condition for strength that I should speak brusquely and provocatively, that is, that I become strength incarnate? Incarnate again . . . alive . . . alive in the flesh . . . and perhaps a link to carnality and carnal knowledge . . . knowledge of the flesh? If I spoke to her of such thoughts would she think "that's your funeral"?

Whereupon I went ahead and told her my preliminary hypotheses about her requirement that men be seen as strong and her self-sacrificing readiness to adopt weakness, anxiety, and panic lest she be seen as stronger than a man. I gave to her all the evidence that had led to my hunch.

With eyes like slits she scrutinized my face and told me of her mother's power over the family and especially over her father. Through illness, depression, and nagging she had made the father submit to her every whim until he came to be seen as an impotent weakling, and her brother, who had congenital heart disease, had been the pale and hollow-cheeked antithesis of her own robustness—her heftiness. Her robustness was, in her view, an unbridled and pornographic selfishness. Her mother's illness after Mrs. Wever's birth was consequent upon a theft of life and health by her, the new child.

As Joseph and Benjamin in the Bible had torn away Rachel's strength and life so that they might live, so Mrs. Wever had stolen life and strength from those dear to her. By imitating me had she stolen my life and my identity? Did she look at me with her slit eyes to see whether her quick psychological abilities would be at the expense of my life, mind, strength?

And are we humans endlessly fated to believe that we steal the lives and identities of others? I believe that my manner was wistful as I spoke to Mrs. Wever of how Isaac stole the life blessing from Ishmael and, I added, did not Jacob steal it from Esau? And is it not said that Christ lived and died for us?

"Why," said Mrs. Wever, "did Dr. Gryfe not tell me these things?"

I responded with irony. "Because you have rendered him a castrate. Think of the psychological acuity of your remarks.

Who could be your psychological equal? Think of how I bullied you when I asked if you were imitating me. Was I already aware and afraid of your strength? And my clever talk about Joseph, Jacob and Isaac: was that, too, my uneasy determination to keep you at bay?"

"Can we meet a few more times?"

"You are weak, of course, and need my help, or . . . no . . . you are strong and wish to steal my powers?"

I was somewhat taken aback by my own boldness and as I report these events I want to apologize. "What kind of psychotherapist's talk is this? I mocked my patient, I penetrated her, I tempted her to be strong."

Coming to talk again seemed wise since our discussion had been heady and evocative. But like every human act, it was also, to use the psychotherapeutic patois, a compromise formation. In other words, coming again would also be a reenactment of her madness.

What had Gryfe said about her? Something about Mrs. Wever having an unstable identity. I suppose that he meant that she had some sort of developmental defect and that this idea of his is similar to what some refer to as a weak ego or a fragmented self. I had despaired when I read this. It is precisely at those points where people think of weakness, of deficits, or of fragmentation that Freud wished us to reconsider. Think instead, Freud argued, of the unconscious—of hidden and unexpected purposes at work. Gryfe had been a bright student and I recall teasing him about carrying the intellectual banner for the unconscious. Often, when speaking to students, I speculate about whether they really understand the profundity of Freud's revolutionary notion of the ubiquitous contradictory repressed, and Gryfe, I thought, had understood.

In our local psychoanalytic training institute we teachers sometimes say to one another that a particular candidate does not grasp the full significance of the repressed unconscious but, because she is conscientious and sensible, we allow training to continue. This is done with the full knowledge that she will practice a form of supportive psychotherapy rather than analytic therapy. What we really mean is that the candidate will be a *mere* supportive psychotherapist, and does not have that intellectual spark that qualifies one to do "real" analytic work. I cannot overemphasize how difficult it is to be exclusively skeptical and to be single-mindedly focused on what is hidden. And yet, that is the requirement placed on those who do in-depth psychotherapy.

When patients speak, great emphasis is placed on the truth of their manifest statements. Simultaneously, proper psychotherapists search for the hidden truths that are logically forbidden by the patient's proclaimed and manifest statements. About his discovery of the hidden meaning of dreams, Freud (1900) said that "insight such as this falls to one's lot but once in a lifetime" (p. xxxii). He knew perfectly well that this was his great discovery. Even the most banal of remarks must, he said, be listened to in a way radically different from ordinary listening.

There are, I would say, three ways of listening to another person. Under ordinary conditions we take people's statements more or less at face value. All of us know, understand, and live with a set of shared conventions, and within those conventions we assume that literal listening is adequate.

That ordinary and typical way of listening takes place, for instance, if an acquaintance says to us that the weather is unpleasant. We do not respond with an interpretive remark that might, for example, raise the question of whether the person is depressed. Typically, we respond in kind and acknowledge that the weather is indeed unpleasant. We might well exchange further banalities even if our friend makes several further complaining remarks. But if this continues even longer, we eventually begin to think differently. At a certain point we ask ourselves why someone would persist so long on such a topic? Is there something else going on? Is he depressed? In other words, we begin to listen psychologically.

The psychotherapist aims not to listen in the usual literal way. Ideally she listens exclusively for hidden meanings and purposes. Talk of the weather, the description of a spouse—everything is listened to in the less usual complex and psychological way. A remark about the fine weather is listened to very seriously since, it is assumed, such a remark is as psychologically significant as any other. Could things be going badly for the patient at home and, in speaking this way, is he attempting to lighten his own mood? Is he resentful about my bill but, out of respect for me, determines that he will speak in a friendly way? Is he struggling with an unruly fragment of homosexual love for me that he dare not speak about in any other way? Although a remark about fine weather may well not be commented on explicitly, it will be added to the repertoire of information that the therapist is collecting.

There are some occasions in our day-to-day life when we expect to listen in the ordinary way and yet, suddenly, shift to psychological listening. If, for instance, someone tells us that, during the night, he has been transformed into a god, we will instantly raise psychological questions to ourselves. We will wonder why our friend speaks in this way, what his motive is, whether he is making fun, or whether he has become mad. In other words there are occasions when we determine in advance that we will listen psychologically, and other occasions when we will automatically listen psychologically.

Psychological listening is difficult, largely because we live within a cultural code that has great power over us. That code insists that we are to take at face value what is said to us. If a patient tells us of his spouse's sadistic behavior and his complementary passive submission, we are powerfully driven to listen literally and to urge our patient to stand up for himself.

Often we listen literally to such a story and, at the same time, deceive ourselves into thinking that we are actually behaving psychologically. We may, for example, talk to our patient of his inhibition against anger, thereby subtly urging him to revolt against his oppressor. In its most banal version, patients are urged to "express your feelings." It is extraordinarily difficult simply to discuss with the patient the details of his masochistic universe and to work with him toward illuminating why he chooses or is driven to live in that world. The most we can hope for is that on a few inspired occasions we can live up to the ideal of real psychological listening.

In addition to ordinary listening and psychological listening, a third way of listening, strongly advocated by some teachers, relies on intuition. Such intuitions come upon one unexpectedly and without (conscious) rational effort. When we admit that we work in this way, our enemies chortle happily, assuming that they can finally denounce us as fools or charlatans.

A common way in which such intuitions come to us is in the form of a countertransference experience. A cynical and embittered refugee saw the world—even the new "free world" in which he now lived—as universally organized in fascist forms. He mocked his therapist when this was discussed as his preferred psychological place of residence. One day the psychotherapist had the sudden fear that the patient would leap up and kill her. Upon reflection she remembered that just prior to her sudden episode of fear, the patient had said that "realistically" he simply had to take over the management of a minor domestic situation. The therapist realized that to "take over the management" was a revelation of the patient's own fascism. She feared that should she mention this fascism to her patient, he might (fascistically) kill her. The psychotherapist then spoke of this matter to her patient.

In other words, an intuitive countertransference experience led to understanding and therapeutic work. The example of the weather, banal though it may be, usefully illustrates the technique of psychotherapeutic listening, and how it helps the therapist and patient to reappropriate repressed unconscious contents.

This is the faith of the psychotherapist. It is also the faith that all psychotherapists are endlessly at risk of losing. Why should this be? The answer is probably very simple and very human. Who of us wants to know the hidden motives of another person in all his or her nakedness? Typically none of us wishes to know too much and, therefore, it seems safer to listen to patients' statements as simply true and to ignore the oppressiveness of what is warded off.

Suddenly I want to ask why I say all this so patiently? Have I not already announced my outrage at the lapses from orthodoxy that are so common? Why, for example, did Gryfe not want to know that Mrs. Wever, when she proclaimed herself to be phobic, anxious, and dissociated, was doing precisely that—making a proclamation? Can he have forgotten that humans make such proclamations/statements for a reason; that they have motives for saying what they do? In Mrs. Wever's case it quickly became clear that she feared her own potency and the weakness of men and her proclamation of illness served to protect her from that dreaded possibility.

One can only conclude that Gryfe listened to her literally and concretely because he did not want to know of her scorn and contempt for him and for men in general; that although he apparently did not recognize that side of Mrs. Wever at all, he also recognized it only too well. Why else would he recoil from it so totally? To listen psychologically means to listen for hidden motives, and Gryfe, like all of us, dreaded to know too much about the motives of his client. Or, more accurately, he dreaded to know that he knew her motives. Is there not a world of difference between knowing and knowing that we know? He was tempted not to listen to what she said to him and, at least in this instance, he listened to what his patient said as though it were concretely true.

It has, perhaps, occurred to the reader that speakers are, in the more usual mode of listening, thought to be perfect transcribers of their mental states, and therefore when a patient claims to be "falling apart," the therapist is liable to take him literally and to believe that his mind (his ego? his self?) is collapsing. By doing so she spares herself the troubling awareness that her patient knows himself less well than he believes, just as all of us know ourselves less well than we believe; that somewhere within all of us we are the perfect opposites of what we more comfortably believe; that Mrs. Wever is more angry, denouncing and vindictive than she ever dreamed; that to her, whatever else they are, women are she-bitches and men are cowards.

I continued to work with Mrs. Wever who, I suspected, was secretly annoyed at me because of my standoffish formality. But she soon became wonderfully charming. Her smile sparkled, her eyes flashed, and I, although professionally restrained, smiled and sparkled in return. My memory is that we were a witty psychotherapeutic partnership. Her whole life was a self-denying agreeableness, an agreeableness that led her to be repeatedly exploited. Although I ostensibly revealed nothing of myself to her, I realized, too, that I also revealed everything. Like every "good" patient she remained appropriately ignorant of who I am, apart from the tolerant professional neutrality that I presented to her. But, in addition, I assumed that, without realizing it, she actually knew everything about me that mattered. We shared a congeries of tastes, of biases, of snobberies. She, obviously, and I, secretly, delighted in our shared aesthetics. We were intimates.

Mrs. Wever, too, was a correspondent. For two years she had conducted a daily correspondence with Henry Bothwell, an internationally known musical performer whom she had once interviewed. A colleague had driven this musician back to his hotel and later, at lunch, told Mrs. Wever that Bothwell had been much enthralled by her. She had responded to her friend that she supposed that the musician was simply being courteous. Her friend went on, however, intimating that Bothwell had been very serious and very explicit and that his remarks could in no way have been construed as general courtesies. Mrs. Wever was curious and pressed her friend to say more and was amazed when he reported to her exactly what it was that Bothwell had said: "I would like to go down on her."

Mrs. Wever was rather proper and yet this information had excited her beyond what she herself would have expected. She found herself to be preoccupied by this idea and to be suddenly repelled by her then-current sex life with her husband. His persistent habit of premature ejaculation had long before led her to lose all sexual interest in him, and,

> for the past two years, she had simply lain passively while her husband masturbated and ejaculated upon her abdomen. She could no longer convince herself that such a sex life made sense.
>
> While in the city where Bothwell lived, she phoned and was able to arrange a meeting with him. As events transpired, that meeting became a sexual encounter. Mrs. Wever told this story coldly and cryptically: "He came in my mouth twice." That was all that she said. Since that time they had been daily correspondents.
>
> The letters that they wrote were filled with intellectual digressions but, in essence, were requests by Mrs. Wever that Bothwell should acknowledge whether or not he loved her and, on his part, evasive musings on the nature of love and reports on other loves that he had had. Henry spoke to her about the importance of visiting prostitutes and about "spiritual" and "intellectual" loves that he had, but, despite writing daily letters, acknowledged no love for her. His letters were clearly designed to torment her, and she was impelled to plead and suffer in perfect cooperation with his cruelty.
>
> Here is an event that happened during one of our appointments. One day her fingernail touched my wall and she recoiled with unexpected shock. "I was scared I would get nail polish on your wall." That would have been, as anyone can recognize, a catastrophe.

Note my use of irony. I refer to a trivial event as a "catastrophe" and treat it with mock horror. Is this an instance of psychotherapeutic skill or is it impolite and unkind? Had I spoken to my patient this way, would I thereby invite her to see ambiguity and complexity and by doing so, nudge her toward further illumination of her life? Or is such irony a reflection of my own cynicism—a bitter psychological position that can only lead to nihilism and despair?

Would you judge me as honest, courageous, and penetrating? Or as sour, undermining, and unfeeling? Why will some approve of my irony and others disapprove? In short, what are the respective psychologies of lovers and enemies of irony? Adherents of skepticism and of irony will find their disapproving counterparts to be naive and chicken-hearted; proponents of clarity and rationalism will find corrosiveness and darkness in their ironic colleagues.

I have no doubt about where I stand. Ironies abound—ironies that are sometimes dangerously close to sarcasm. My psychotherapeutic labor with Mrs. Wever prior to the nail polish event had seemed to me to be no labor at all, comprised, as it was, of smiles, sparkles, wit, and mutual coquetry. But there had been *some* labor after all. For example, I wondered with her why she, supposedly a depressed, lonely woman, never wept nor even complained of her lot in life?

> "For weeks and months you have brought to me wit and sparkle but never gloom, or pain, or tears. And today you are shocked that you might have stained my wall as though that too was to count as a radical forbidden."
>
> She had protested. "I should be more careful; your office is so tidy; it is impolite; women know better than to touch walls with painted nails; I didn't get any polish on the wall anyway, did I? Why do you make such a big point about it? Why should I come here and be a wet blanket?"
>
> "Methinks the lady doth protest too much."
>
> It reminds me of Freud's story of the woman who had been accused of making a hole in a pot that she had borrowed. She, too, had protested: "The pot was intact when I returned it to you; the hole was in the pot when you loaned it to me; I never borrowed the pot from you in the first place."
>
> I acted like a psychotherapist and listened silently, or should I use more provocative words and say that I listened patiently/stubbornly? Although the psychotherapist listens, she also says with her silence that she does not accept what has been said as being the whole story. Stubbornly, she indicates that there are worlds of ideas and meanings beyond what has been said so far.

Mrs. Wever responded with just such further worlds of ideas and meanings. "Did you ever notice," she asked, "that I never cough and never sneeze? You yourself have several times mentioned that I never weep. My stomach never gurgles either. I have learned to have a small meal two hours before I come here, which guarantees that my stomach will not gurgle from hunger, nor from the digestion of food. Whenever possible I go home and have a shower before coming because my hair is full of grease and I might get it on your cushion. I have often thought of bringing Kleenex for you—man-size—that would be bigger than yours because, even though you use a Kleenex, I am liable to get grease on your cushion. It's just that your Kleenex is too small."

She paused—did she screw up her courage? "One more thing. Before I come I always put in a Tampax—just in case—to make sure I don't stain you . . . uh . . . get a stain on your couch."

I thought to myself that her husband regularly stained her by spewing his semen onto her body. Thereupon I, too, paused, then said, "Ah, I see, you can bring to me only cleanliness, purity, smiles, sparkles, coquetry. I dare say you would never fart in my office?"

She looked pale and offended and I knew what she would think. Instantly I, not Mrs. Wever, had become the repository of filth and evil with my disgusting remark about a fart. A bit outrageous perhaps, and not in the grave manner some expect of a psychotherapist, but surely not disgusting. This was, to me, a comment made with wit, aimed at caricaturing what she so typically did. Had I made an ironic remark about the value of corks in preventing farts, a tender mockery of her solution-oriented style, would she have understood?

My notes state that we are enjoying the cleverness of these exchanges "too much". Despite my vulgarity (which was also, perhaps, wit) I was clearly aware of my private conviction that Mrs. Wever was indeed fortunate that she had come here; that

I would help her as no one else could; that this kind of work was thrilling. With such wit, courage, and audacity, what a rebuke I was to the weak thinkers whose theoretical detritus has accumulated since Freud's discovery of the repressed unconscious.

I hope that I also sat silently looking out of my window reflecting, thinking, worrying about this woman who treated herself as a container full of evil, filth, and demons. She was Pandora's box (pun intended) that must be kept tightly closed. Did she fear that she was, as in one version of the Pandora story, a female scourge that punishes and torments men? But what were those sounds intruding into my thoughts? Why was she lying there inflicting on me the unkindness of continuing and spirited talking, chattering? Good God, was she sparkling for me again? At times it was undoubtedly pleasant and the most typical manifestation of our affection for one another as well.

"Why, for once, does she not just keep still and let me think? This is a serious moment between us and she is damaging it with her yackety-yak. I don't want to listen to this crap, I want to digest what she has said, to labor over it, to play with it, and to savor it. I want to reverse it, complicate it, be horror-struck by it and to weep over it. And I want to enjoy the hilarity of it. Imagine Mrs. Wever farting in my office!"

The reader can, I hope, sense the manner in which the psychotherapist listens and thinks. From me, with many years of experience under my belt, such a therapeutic attitude is to be expected. It is heartening that, although they are not common, some precocious learners intuitively know how to do this. Certainly it was beyond me thirty years ago.

Her chatter irritated me a lot. That moment of ours was important to both of us and she wished to spoil it. I gradually realized that to be intimate with her she must, strangely, allow me to be a recluse. She must let me have repose. Would it help if I grunted like a pig, like an analyst, like an Indian? Should I make a joke about the reserve of Indians? "Reserve on the Reserve"?

Here, with my psychotherapeutic co-conspirator, I found duplicated the paradoxes of my wider life. I wrote letters to a woman who lived far away; closeness and enmeshment was an elemental part of relationships with patients with whom nothing would be consummated. In that sense my career is a reflection of very important things about my own psychology.

The psychotherapist must be alone in order to be deeply involved. She must lose herself in her private thinking place, her psychotherapist's place. Lost in her thoughts, she will, in a strange way, be more involved with her patient.

The therapist must always be "in between." She must half accept and yet, simultaneously, half reject what her patient says. She must half admire and half mock; be half fascinated and half indifferent; find her patients' stories half hilarious and half tragic. In other words, everything must, to the therapist, be transformed into a parody of itself. Only in this way can she achieve the chilling yet alluring objectivity required of her in her work. I wonder to myself how a person of passion can achieve the state of indifference that is required?

I was approvingly surprised by my realization that I needed to be alone in order to be truly intimate with Mrs. Wever. But why surprised? Many have taught that ambiguities are never transcended. I suppose that my surprise sprang from the explicitness of something that I had always understood implicitly.

A flood of my own ideas and memories come to me. A few weeks ago I showed a videotape of an interview to a group of students. One student, not really to my surprise, asked why I was so aloof and why I did not look the patient in the eye. Sure enough, there I was on the screen half turned away from my patient, forehead supported by one hand. I realized that I was endlessly various in how I listened. At certain moments my eyes gazed directly into his and at other moments my head sank and I looked gloomily downward. And at the moment that the student had taken note of, I was looking away and was alone. But this aloneness had a very special quality because by being alone I could lose myself in thought and, by thinking and dreaming, become sharply more intimate with the person with whom I spoke. In *Death in Venice* Thomas Mann wrote, "Solitude gives birth to the original in us, to beauty unfamiliar and perilous—

to poetry. But also, it gives birth to the opposite: to the perverse, the illicit, the absurd" (1936, p. 395).

A colleague once told me an anecdote that illustrates the thesis that, to be truly intimate, one must also be alone. My colleague was an applicant for psychoanalytic training in Great Britain and went for an interview with Donald Winnicott, an esteemed senior psychoanalyst. Winnicott greeted him warmly. "Do come in, Dr. Harrison; please have a seat." He paused briefly and then went on. "Dr. Harrison, would you be so good as to talk to me about yourself for a while?"

At that point, I was told, Winnicott sat half turned away from my colleague, put his forehead in his hand and closed his eyes. Was Winnicott imitating me or was I, on the videotape, imitating him? Was that Winnicott I was watching on the tape? In more conventional terms, were we doing the same thing? In other words, did he need to be alone in order to achieve that peculiar opposite to aloneness by way of which he could penetrate into Harrison's soul and mind?

Winnicott listened for forty-five minutes, looked up and gave Harrison a gentle and grateful smile. In his courteous English mode of speech, he said, "Thank you so much, Dr. Harrison, for coming and speaking to me today." There was a brief pause as both stood up. "Good-bye."

Is this an interview conducted by a ridiculous, if not bizarre, man, or is this a profoundly respectful and serious exchange? There was certainly no stupid chatter about the London weather! Another colleague once wrote a paper about Winnicott's personal supervision of some of his clinical work. This student, too, noted the astonishingly intimate listening powers of a man who simultaneously withdrew into aloneness. Perhaps this is why some psychotherapists sit out of sight behind their patients. And perhaps this is why a hermit or a recluse can so easily be imagined to be a counselor or wise man.

Flaubert is reputed to have explained his extrusion of a woman from his life by saying that "she wouldn't stay out of my study." Virginia Woolf, in a similar vein, wrote of "A Room of One's Own." Our youths abroad, busily trying to achieve existential despair, probably have the same idea in mind. Flit, flit—associate, associate. Winnicott himself wrote a scientific paper entitled "The Capacity to be Alone."

That peculiar reclusive attitude has also been written about by another of those evocative and provocative British psychotherapists—Wilfred Bion. When with a patient, he argued, one should suspend memory and desire—and even suspend understanding. If we approach a patient remembering our yesterdays or yesteryears with that patient, we introduce a bias that blinds us to that elusive unconscious message that we are meant to hear in the today. Desire and understanding serve the same blinding function. We should, he is saying, desire nothing for our patients and, furthermore, an understanding of them is to be shed and forever rediscovered—each time differently. The resultant therapeutic attitude he called "faith," which is a wonderfully provocative term to recommend to psychotherapeutic colleagues. Only a recluse can have such a contentless faith.

Freud's version of the therapeutic attitude had recommended that the practitioner put aside all feelings, even human sympathy, and to concentrate all her mental forces on the single aim of, like a surgeon, performing the operation as skillfully as possible. This element in the psychotherapist's attitude is her commitment to work. And the psychotherapist does, indeed, work. Patients are typically amazed at her single-minded puzzle-solving attitude—an attitude that radically excludes social interchanges apart from the bare minimum of required courtesies. Freud often conceived of psychotherapy using terms such as *dream work*, *analytic work*, *working through*, and the *work of mourning*. I could add to this Freud's war language, to wit, his use of terms such as *defense*, *resistance*, *psychic danger situations*, and *cathexis* (his word was *Besetzung*, that is to say, "occupation," as in the occupation of a country.)

To Freud, one of the greatest dangers faced by the psychotherapist was an attitude of therapeutic ambition—that obscuring desire that Bion has warned against. Therapeutic enthusiasm was, to Freud, an example of a naive Western (French and American) belief in progress. Freud shared Thomas Mann's embrace of the *bürgerliche* traditions of honest industry and of the inward rather than the outward look. The young student, it is hoped, will come to think in this way despite the handicaps of her youth, of her professional education, and of the progress-era in which she lives.

From time to time one meets a student who has made her own examination of Freud's work. She may already have begun this task during her earlier training and have instantly grasped the essential points. Somehow she may have managed not to be distracted by Freud's many intellectual discursions—discursions that have so often led his readers astray. It is utterly charming to hear such a student's excitement as she speaks of her awareness of Freud's great discoveries. One student seemed to believe, at times, that she had discovered psychological miracles in Freud and in her own patients that had never been discovered before.

Reclusiveness, shedding of memory and desire, single-minded analytic labor: what peculiar attitudes are being advocated here? Do psychotherapists do this? Should psychotherapists do this? Well, perhaps they should but certainly they do not actually do so. In evidence I offer my incorrigible love of irony and of mockery. Other psychotherapists, too, have their idiosyncrasies.

As a contrasting example, there is the utter technocrat—should I call her the Sober One?—totally dedicated to therapeutic praxis as technical expertise and sober interpretation. And then there is the Kind One—as incorrigible in her earnest kindness as am I in my (hopefully gentle and tender) mockery. What is essential is that mockers, technocrats, and kind ones know of their mocking, their technology, and their kindness.

For example, if I know of my endless tendency to indulge in mockery can I not then point out to my patients a terrible problem that they face with me? How can one be angry, they must realize, with a man who teases, plays with ideas, makes jokes? In my own defense I would mention that Freud, too, loved to make jokes and to see ironies, despite the fact that in his writing he tended to dismiss such attitudes. Pleasure and fun were, in contrast to work, seen by Freud as immature, neurotic, child-like, and feminine. The bias in favor of work is held more by those I have called the Sober Ones than by Freud himself. Because of my own contrasting bias, I eventually must wonder with all my patients whether they can see that my "mocking madness," although designed to promote insight, also has the secret aim of quieting them, warding them off, and seducing them into not hating me.

But it is not only the mockers who wish to dissuade patients from hating them. All psychotherapists attempt to do this. For example, who can hate the sober interpreter when she is so sincerely devoted to her work? Her great devotion to Freud's advocacy of therapeutic industry could not reasonably lead to any reaction in patients other than appreciation. Or could it? Could such a psychotherapist also be seen as uptight and as living in a psychological straitjacket? Can she, as most of her kindred spirits surely do, know of her own tendency to arid (as opposed to seductive) psychotherapeutic methods? If she does know, and if her patients know that she knows, then psychotherapeutic work/play will proceed willy-nilly.

And who can be angry at a kind person! She who is utterly kind fears challenge and outrage—most particularly in herself. And since one need only awaken each morning to know of the stupidity and evil in the world, the kind one must fear such things just as the sober one fears fun and the mocker fears seriousness. If she is blind to this, it seems highly unlikely that such a psychotherapist could ever help a patient introspectively to glimpse, let alone know fully, the depths of his own evil. But if she knows of her dread of evil, then the Kind One, too, can claim possession of the requisite therapeutic attitude.

Patients find a way to hate us, the psychotherapists, but not without great resistance on our part, a resistance paradoxically present even as we hope to be available as a target for everything. The psychotherapist will always attempt to adopt a psychotherapeutic attitude but, in attempting this, will do so in such a way as to satisfy her own madness, vanity, and fear. This eternal contamination of the psychotherapeutic attitude is, in fact, not merely a contamination. It is, psychologically speaking, more fundamental, more essential, and more subversive than the psychotherapist (and the reader) may think. The psychological theorist insists that this is not just a "taint" upon a fundamentally pristine therapeutic attitude because, what is fundamental is the therapist's own endless self-deception, a deception that will pour from her heart and soul even as she comes to recognize psychological truths.

One student, who argued this point with great skill, was a fine illustration of her own arguments. In her therapeutic work she constantly came upon the theme of disappointing mothers and of institutions that had failed her patients. If she and her patients could ally themselves with one another and together hate a mother who was elsewhere—was that not a cozy and blinding opportunity? "We are OK," they could conspiratorially decide, "and the locus of evil can be in that wicked other." Eventually, I assume, her patients had to ask themselves how to deal with a therapist who agreed with their denunciation of orthodoxy and of the corrupt mothers. Would they, for example, have come to see the cowardice in their therapist's posture, in her personal variant on the psychotherapeutic attitude?

> Mrs. Wever chattered on. Her face was glowing, her lashes fluttering, her teeth sparkling. I thought to myself that I ought to grant her the status of genius since only so grand a designation captured the magnificence of her sweetness, her coquetry, and her wit. I could detect no obvious urgency or obvious desperation as she performed her role. Intellectually, however, I knew that for her it was an issue of life and death that she should engage me, even if only momentarily, in the universe of smiles and flirting.
>
> Although it had always been known that chatter and fun kept us apart and although her urgency remained inapparent, I suddenly "knew in my bones" that I would finally be able to be alone despite her, and that I could, through aloneness, enter into her soul and spirit. Freud understood

that, to know someone, it is necessary to enter into their soul and their spirit and he therefore used the words *Seele* and *Geist*. But he did so for another reason as well: in the German language there are no other words for mind!

My annoyance with Mrs. Wever, I realized, was not merely annoyance: I was angry and I was furious; I was enraged and outraged. I suppose I hated her because she would not let me know her and she would not let me be the perfect psychotherapist that I thought I should be. I had struggled for countless hours to enter into her depths and, besides, she had hired me and paid me to enter into her depths.

But perhaps this hatred of Mrs. Wever did not matter because, by then, I was alone and could speak to her of how she would not let me be alone. In fact, I was offended by her and, simultaneously, in a state of wry amusement at the predicament we were in together. She, in turn, rebelled as I verbally played with our paradoxical love and hate, our mutual aloneness and intimacy. Once I said to her, "When I write my book, your chapter will be called 'The Patient Who Would Not Let Me Be Alone.'" She hated me for that remark. No flirting.

At that time I had a cold and Mrs. Wever brought me a plastic container of chicken soup. "For your cold," she said. The soup was unexpected because she usually practiced the typical orthodoxies of a psychotherapy patient. She came twice a week, said "Good morning," lay on the couch, and spoke her mind. She did so with marvelous good cheer and charm. Properly, she brought no gifts, discussed business matters after the time was up, rarely missed appointments. Yet on this day she spoke by way of a gift of soup. Fifteen minutes passed silently and I sensed that she was becoming tense.

"I want to take the soup back," she said, "I am feeling upset and frightened that there might be bones in the soup and that you might choke on them."

"That there might be a fart in the soup?" I wondered

irreverently. After all, body contents had clearly been of potential danger to me throughout the treatment.

"The thought that I am having," she went on, "is that I want to eat the soup for you." She wanted to eat the soup and the bones for me. Everything bad was to be in her. She was, of course, self-conceived as a container full of evil—stains, rude sounds, contaminating blood, and grease. If she could swallow it all, hold it in herself, then would I be safe? Did she swallow her rage? Is that why she specified about Henry Bothwell that she had swallowed his semen? And had she "swallowed" the weakness of the politician who had spoken foolishly? If she and I were two people merely flirting, was I then safe? But if I was able to think seriously about her and contemplate her would I enter her mind and be endangered? If we were involved, would she hate-hurt me and would I choke on bones when she put her soup into me . . . inside of me?

Another patient whose ancestry was German had told me that, during the Second World War, children bought War Savings Stamps once a week at school. At least, he said, the other children bought War Savings Stamps. Since his father was in an internment camp (under the auspices of a notorious war measures act) somewhere in the Canadian west, it was not to be expected that his mother would give him money for War Savings Stamps, especially since, as a German, she could not get a job.

In 1943, when he was 7 years old, he did a very clever thing. Shrewdly, he saved a bit of his allowance every week (where did money for an allowance come from?) and then, every three or four weeks, he bought a War Savings Stamp, thereby announcing that he was not disloyal and alien, but was a good Canadian, loyal to King and country and England, just like everyone else. (Stubbornly, he told me, he sang "God *shave* the king" every morning, as well as crossing as many fingers and toes as possible.) Shrewdly, on the way home from school, my patient ate the War Savings Stamp! He saved his father by eating the stamp. Mrs. Wever would eat the bones so that I would not choke. Was she imitating him or was he imitating her?

There was a continuing self-congratulatory quality to my reactions to Mrs. Wever. I endlessly relished the therapeutic work that we did together even though I knew that such a state of mind was, like every state of mind, just as hazardous as it was beneficial. I wondered repeatedly about the avoidance of the mundane and the unsavory.

Does Mrs. Wever ever touch me in my soul? Am I ever able to share her sick fear, the sick fear that must lie behind her cheerful masks? Can I ever feel the wretchedness and the nausea that she so successfully avoids by never gagging, retching, or spitting? What about revulsion and menstrual filth?

Another line of thought came to me. Mrs. Wever's fingernail would leave a smear on my wall, a smear that indicated that her nail polish was liquid. I also thought that in fact the polish would have been in flakes. Flakes and liquid reminded me that blood can be in clots or in fluid form. Women with severe menstrual bleeding may pass clots—large, soft, and glistening—as may women who are having a miscarriage. Would a menstruating woman in a tub of warm water also pass large, soft, glistening clots? Would a woman who had cut her wrists produce such clots? A suicidal woman who has cut her wrists—would she be in a bathtub full of blood? Would she weep? Would it then be a bathtub full of blood and tears? I feel the horror and revulsion now—the revulsion that I was just thinking about. Since she and I both know about it, should we be in one another's arms covered with blood and tears?

I, too, felt the revulsion and the horror. Would I faint in the office—faint like a woman? Had I not felt faint once watching a film in which a woman killed herself and sat in a bloody tub? This gush of bloodiness and femininity was unnerving and yet had a titillating effect as well. We were intimates, in one another's arms, covered with blood and tears. Am I presenting you, the reader, with my vulnerability in the same way that a wolf (a wimp?) offers its throat in surrender? Am I an effeminate male seducer presenting my buttocks to you? Am I tempting you to comment on my wit, to acknowledge what a clever smarty-pants I am?

> In our work together it became increasingly clear that Mrs. Wever was determined to create life in me at the expense of life in herself. She attempted to coerce that situation with all the skill and determination that she could muster. In the shadow of that attempt were the multiplicity of previous occasions upon which she had tried to die so that men might live—lovers, employers, and, most disturbingly to her, her father and her brother. Mrs. Wever's brother had been born with a congenital heart defect and she, throughout her childhood, had lived with the family's dread that the boy would die. I suppose that her brother spoke for the beliefs of the whole family when, as a boy, he said to his sister, "I guess when you were born I took one look at you and decided that it wasn't worth living."
>
> She had also been responsible, she thought, for her mother's stormy illness following Mrs. Wever's birth. Since she herself had always enjoyed robust good health, it was easy to assume that she was healthy at the expense of her thin and chronically blue-lipped brother. Her solution to these crimes—the thefts of life and health from others—was to eternally donate life to men. These acts of rescue eventually assumed dramatic proportions in her relationship with me.
>
> She had made increasing complaints that nothing was happening in the treatment, that she "can't do this anymore" and that she would never change. Furthermore, she told me, the treatment had been compromised because I, her therapist, had changed so dramatically and profoundly during the years that we had worked together. She had not changed but I had. She also became increasingly silent; she was now silent like a therapist. Once again she was me.
>
> Eventually she announced that she would be stopping the treatment in six months. She realized, she said, that her

> life and her treatment were futile and she had therefore decided that, upon completing treatment, she would wait two months and would then commit suicide. The two-month gap was intended to guarantee that I would not in any way be implicated in her death. It was important to her that the therapy continue as planned since otherwise, she feared, she would be unable to complete her plan.
>
> During our years of work together she had become convinced that if she decided to kill herself I would not interfere. I knew the intolerable degree to which she had suffered throughout her life; I respected the personal choices that patients make regarding themselves; I would not violate her trust. On a few occasions she briefly feared that I would interfere if she continued on her planned suicidal course. But, more often, she assumed that I would stand by her during these, her final "sensible" actions.

This kind of case places the psychotherapist in a terrible moral crisis. She believes it to be her duty to work psychologically with her patients no matter what happens, and to take no other action. As part of her therapeutic work with such patients, the psychotherapist continues to inspect her own behavior—to self-analyze—as rigorously as possible. I reluctantly confess some of my reactions to Mrs. Wever's potential suicide. Partly, I realized, I felt a cold excitement at the prospect of her death. Partly, I actually hoped that she would kill herself.

Is this the response of a monster to the plight of an unhappy patient? It is certainly not a reaction that is ordinarily made public. But the knowledge of such reactions is vital for the psychotherapist and, furthermore, is an expected reaction. It is expected because she is convinced that ungenerous and wicked sentiments are universal in human beings and that this should occasion no surprise. The key question for her is not whether she has such reactions, but rather the way in which she has such reactions. Mean-spiritedness is, to her, inevitable. What she does with her mean-spiritedness is what counts.

Some version of my reaction to Mrs. Wever was inevitable,

because that reaction was a direct response to her particular psychological coercions. It is also a peculiar version—or, at least, an "I-prefer-not-to-know-about-this" version—of psychotherapeutic neutrality. In this instance, therefore, I manifested the peculiar, disturbing, but requisite attitude of disinterest.

I can imagine the reader's uneasiness as I once again advocate disinterest as a requisite attitude of the psychotherapist. Would that uneasiness increase if I also came to advocate indifference, aloofness, coldness, and contempt? Can you know in yourself those same qualities of aloofness and contempt? Can any of us truly believe that we are made only of generosity and virtue? If we believe this of ourselves are we, then, fools or, worse, are we fiends?

4

The Transformation of Susan Wever into a Psychologist

> If you hate a person, you hate something in him that is part of yourself. What isn't part of ourselves, does not disturb us.
>
> —Herman Hesse

Mrs. Wever stopped treatment not long after these events took place. Suicide, however, did not seem to be a risk. She claimed that her improvement satisfied her and that life pressures were such that termination made good sense. But I was not so sure. Nevertheless, like a good psychotherapist, I did not promote nor did I impede her plans to finish. When the opportunity presented itself, I talked of the possible meanings of her plans, with regard to both her flight from further self-exploration and her reluctance to finalize her termination decision. What the therapist does is simply to analyze and interpret until the very end.

Two years later Mrs. Wever returned to resume the treatment. This time, however, instead of meeting twice weekly, our arrangement was to meet four times weekly. This decision, like all such decisions, was ostensibly a rational one, "rational" despite the psychotherapist's powerful philosophical opinion that the subject who knows—that is to say, knows rationally—does not exist.

This sober and unnerving position is, in a sense, the leitmotif of this book. The subject who knows final truths does not exist.

What other reasons might there have been for me to recommend to Mrs. Wever that she now should come four times weekly? Was there a grandiose determination in me that I would cure her come hell or high water; that I would not tolerate the lackluster "cure" that had been achieved two years before? So much for the desireless, neutral psychotherapist! But, in my confident rationality, I was a sure illustration of the subject who never really knows his motives.

Was Mrs. Wever sensible and rational in following my rational recommendation to come four times weekly? Or was she an unknowing puppet whose strings were manipulated by a madness—an unconscious—that demanded that she submit to the wise doctor? But, for better or for worse, we met four times each week.

The changes that eventuated were remarkable. As I will describe in a moment, in a period of one year she advanced light years beyond what she had achieved in the earlier four-year treatment. Was this due to the increase in the frequency of our meetings? To my sudden and none-too-soon awareness of my grandiose beliefs about my own powers? To a thousand other known and unknown elements that characterized the dialectic between me and Mrs. Wever? Since this discussion is about listening, could I say that she became different because I listened differently? Because *she* listened differently—to herself? To me?

Shortly after we resumed our work, Mrs. Wever arrived at an appointment accompanied by a close friend. I had often heard of Terri, an academic much admired and loved by my patient. Terri's social and intellectual powers led Mrs. Wever to feel privileged to have her as a friend. Terri, as I remembered hearing about her, was an intimate to whom all secrets were told, and who had a cheerful ability to offer tips and pointers on appropriate occasions. What a shock I got when she was brought to my office!

It was unorthodox that my patient brought another person along. After all, most patients assume that such things are forbidden, even though they also know that the therapist mandates few, if any, rules. Also, I was surprised to discover that Terri was not what she had been portrayed as being. In fact, she was ridiculous. In order to maintain a psychological stance and not to condemn Terri according to my own version of bourgeois values, I should say this with greater precision and with a more careful use of language. Terri portrayed herself with great skill and with great intensity as a superficial, cliché-ridden, bearer of a cornucopia of psychobabble, according to the prevailing judgment of the cultural community of which I am a part.

In a brisk and confident way she gushed and exclaimed over her friend, my patient, Mrs. Wever. "She just needs to express herself more . . . she's not in touch with herself . . . I keep telling her that she needs to do more body work . . . we all love her so much (this accompanied by enthusiastically administered hugs) . . . I'm going to get her to meet with Dr. X who will be in Toronto next week so that she can see how she communicates."

As a psychotherapist, it is incumbent on me to distinguish between my private tastes and attitudes and my psychotherapeutic determination that all ways of life are honorable. This meant that I did not say, for example, "How could you have as a friend such an asshole?" It is not that this is to be kept secret from Mrs. Wever but, rather, that she perfectly well knows my congeries of snobberies already. My job is not to convert her to my preferred universe of discourse but, with no implication that she ought to change, help her to see why she lives in the psychological universe that she does.

As events transpired, Mrs. Wever and I quickly came

to discuss an unexpected truth. She had always seen through Terri; she did not believe what she saw; she did not want to know what she saw; she was horrified that she would be judgmental about such a happy, successful "winner" as Terri. But she also (incomprehensibly, paradoxically, stubbornly) had never for a moment thought ill of her friend. Terri was good at everything; everything that she, Mrs. Wever, valued was embodied in her universally admired and universally beloved friend.

If, on occasion, I acknowledged to my patient that, yes, in my world Terri's values were odd and bourgeois (my patient knew very well that my cautious words really meant that I considered such values to be those of the know-nothings, of the intellectual "rabble"), Mrs. Wever was horrified. She was totally convinced that the life of her friend was commendable and desirable. In the next breath she anxiously shook her head at Terri's preposterous superficiality.

Quickly Mrs. Wever's complaints intensified. "I'm so judgmental" she announced over and over again. Just as quickly, her long-standing friendship with Terri began to falter. After many years of admiration and envy, she realized that her friend exploited and manipulated her. Traits once praised became insufferable and contemptible. In short, she saw through facades, and developed a Nietzschean scorn for the obvious and the conventional. She became . . . a psychologist? Or, to use the phrase that Mrs. Wever and I invented, she became a truth-speaker. Like Lear's fool and like all comedians and clowns, she had become a truth-speaker.

Why would I assign traits like scorn, contempt, and intolerance to she-who-is-a-psychologist? This is, indeed, a painful and awkward conundrum. It zeros in on the perilous line that the psychologist is eternally fated to walk. Even as she attempts to be neutral and evenhanded, the psychotherapist doubts and withholds approval from every psychological position. She claims that superficiality, for example, is as honorable a destiny as any other but, at the same time, doubts that superficiality has particular value or worth. Genius, too, is honored and dismissed.

Why should this be so? Surely genius is the place of honor and superficiality the place of disrepute? "Not necessarily," says the psychotherapist. "Ordinarily, of course, we psychotherapists privately share such value judgments. However, when we are clinicians and philosophers and thinkers, we judge differently. In that more analytic world we honor and dishonor simultaneously. And at a deep level of our being we scornfully dismiss every proposition and, again simultaneously, credulously, gullibly, and with great abandon, embrace and endorse what is commonly judged to be stupid."

"We are," she reminds us, "psychologists and not moralists."

> Mrs. Wever had become a psychologist. More accurately, she had always been a psychologist and now, to her horror, she knew that she was a psychologist and that she could see through the world. Like Adam, Eve, and Faust, she had the gift (the curse?) of knowledge. To her great sorrow, her friendship with Terri became a burden and a loss. Such an eventuality, as can be imagined, is also a worrisome burden for the psychotherapist. "I am not a destroyer of the precious, am I? The destroyer of friendships?" And worse: "Am I, on occasion, the destroyer of marriages?" The only comfort in such circumstances is that no one can pretend to know the answer to such questions.
>
> As these new recognitions came into being, Mrs. Wever lapsed into "whining." Her answer, when I asked about this, was that she was Jewish and that all Jews whine. Her mildly annoying tone accompanied her increasingly critical attitudes. As she spoke of Terri, her "whining" intonation indicated that she was disgusted with herself. Her words criticized Terri but her voice criticized and complained of her, Mrs. Wever. She was sure that when she spoke to her friend Terri, she was thought of as a silly crybaby. Terri, she said, put her down scornfully.

But as Mrs. Wever reported such conversations to me, I sensed that the whining, in fact, took place only with me. With Terri, she spoke forthrightly, if not bluntly. This, Mrs. Wever denied vehemently. Back and forth she went, vacillating between scorn for her friend, and the conviction that her friend was successful and worthy of her envy and respect. In effect she had begun to relinquish her position as the inferior of "the other"—except for me. With me she whined, and thereby announced that she was my inferior. The aggrandizement of the other was most obvious with me, that is to say, in the transference.

This was a most felicitous development, was it not? I have already said that I was to be her rescuer, her hero, her salvation. She confirmed this by bringing to me a Superman necktie. In such a gift one can see the quick "seeing through" of me. Now she saw me with clearer eyes, and could tease me about my vanity and my excessive belief in my therapeutic skills. God forgive us, the psychotherapists, for our vanity. That terrible vanity is inevitably to be found in those who set themselves up as the counselors, the confessors, the shamans. To make matters worse, our patients are in cahoots with us. All too often they are eager to revere us, whether we do our work well or not. And God forgive us for believing them.

Over a period of a few months, Mrs. Wever "saw through" an array of persons who had always been admired by her. In her words, and with a mixture of relief and horror, she "leveled" and "skewered" them. It may be that these were also my words but, in more technical language, we might rather say that she redescribed them.

In short order it came to pass that I, the therapist, was also redescribed. I had written a book and Mrs. Wever heard of its publication. She was deeply troubled by this turn of events. "I could tell from the way you kept quoting things that you were writing a book," she said, "but I never thought that you would publish it. I sort of thought that it was just a way of thinking and that you were playing with ideas."

Mrs. Wever bought the book but could not bring herself to read it. As long as she and I talked I was on safe ground because, in my clever-clever way, I would always be able to wriggle out of any conundrums that I got myself into. Now that I had committed my ideas to paper, I was no longer safe from her insightful eyes and from her scornful judgments, especially her scornful judgments about the weakness of men. With the expenditure of much effort, she forced herself to read brief passages from my book and, as she feared, she found problems. The book was, she said, full of vanity. I was all too often showing off.

The discovery of weakness—my sin of pride—had finally been brought into the situation with me. I didn't like it. It was not an intellectual knowledge that weakness is ubiquitous and that, like all persons, I had my faults. No, she had truly tweaked my nose or, more accurately, she had wounded me, and found my Achilles' heel.

If I say that her disappointment in men had entered the transference situation, would I be speaking with theoretical correctness? Of course. Would I be eluding the pain of her accusation and, despite my theoretical accuracy, would I be muting the more naked truths that Mrs. Wever was speaking?

Late in the treatment, my listening bore another small harvest. Mrs. Wever made one last stand in her campaign to convince me that she was flawed and damaged. "I've never told you before that I am dyslexic. I can't tell the difference between writing that is backward and writing that is forward. When I come to a glass door with "PUSH" printed on it, it sometimes turns out that the printing is on the other side of the door and I should really "PULL" on the door. I don't even notice that the printing is on the other side of the glass door because backward and forward looks the same to me and most of the time I can't tell the difference."

In the ordinary world of psychiatry, psychology, and education, Mrs. Wever's diagnosis of herself would be obviously true.

But the psychotherapist thinks otherwise. She is not so sure about dyslexia when she is thinking psychotherapeutically. In fact, she is unsure about dyslexia under any circumstances, unless it is the product of an objectively identifiable brain lesion. I reacted to Mrs. Wever's words with surprise because of her undoubted intelligence. I also remembered that she had told me that she had "mixed dominance." In other words, she wrote with one hand, threw with the other, and seemed equally proficient with both hands, both feet, and both eyes.

Quickly, I realized something else—realized it because I was listening like a psychotherapist. Mrs. Wever had not locked herself into a simple dominance pattern as do most of us. Her cognitive options and her perceptual options were fluid and, by ordinary standards, not consolidated. Did this, I wondered, give her an angle, or many angles on the world that most do not have? Was her "seeing through the world" talent the same thing as what she now wanted to call dyslexia? When a light went on for me and I saw that her dyslexia could be seen as a talent and as a gift, was I, for a moment, sharing in her ability to turn the world into a magical kaleidoscope of realities? And sharing her ability to see truths that frightened her, and me, and the world of the other?

What I mean by this is that reading from left to right is a convention that makes possible a shared world of written language but which also restricts us to the perception of conventional truths and conventional worlds. Could Mrs. Wever's perceptual problem also be an opportunity to know artistic and poetic truths that are usually denied to ordinary souls? Are most of us in the cave of Plato, and forever blinded to things that Mrs. Wever sees effortlessly and automatically, albeit at the cost of constantly being a nervous wreck?

Such thought experiments are the stuff of the psychotherapist's work life or, more specifically, are the yield of her special listening habits. I believe that such forms of listening and thinking are sorely needed in the disciplines that scientistically (not scientifically), simplistically and, worst of all, dogmatically, announce the "existence" of dyslexia. It is the same limiting form of thought that embraces notions of psychic deficits, or of "media disorders" such as fibromyalgia, and chronic fatigue syndrome (acceptable as long as it is called a syndrome, but a fatally flawed concept if pronounced to be biological).

The dyslexia flaw in Mrs. Wever was, in truth, her genius. Her genius was her neurotically feared sin—the sin of knowledge. The sin of knowledge is the sin of Adam and of Eve, and is the knowledge of what we are not to know. The world of convention teaches us the realities that we are permitted to know and teaches, as well, which darker and brighter Faustian realities are forbidden to us. If we embrace those latter realities we are, it seems, wicked or unwell. We have, the world will say, dyslexia, attention deficit disorder or worse. Could there be the beginning of a theory of psychosis in this line of thought?

One day I told Mrs. Wever the story of another truth-speaker. This truth-speaker was, or had been, another patient of mine. Such an exemplary telling is usually a mistake, although I expect that most of us cautiously try it out from time to time. Certainly, on this occasion, I was led into chagrin and embarrassment by having told a patient-story to Mrs. Wever. Before telling you the story, I will make one further disclaimer. The story is sexual and very intimate and, being a person as well as a psychotherapist, I am shy to reveal the intimacy that I told to Mrs. Wever. My excuse is that, to me, I was merely telling of a momentary stumble in a story of *Romeo and Juliet*.

A woman who had frequently sabotaged love relationships, gave an example of how she had "improved." Previously, she had hurt and angered her lovers by saying, during lovemaking, things such as "So-and so used to do such-and-such, and I liked it a lot." To her surprise, this had caused trouble because, to her beloved, this seemed a truth that was better kept quiet. She had made similar love blunders (except that for a long time they did not, to her, seem like blunders) with more than one person and, with her current beloved, had done the same.

One day this patient told of a love incident that, to her, was wonderfully intimate and infused with love. The previous night, while making love, her beloved had taken her hand and touched her fingers and his to their place of joining, and had then brought their fingers to their kissing lips. The words *place of joining* are my perhaps melodramatic words that at least try to capture the love and tenderness that apparently infused the love scene. But these were not the words that the patient used when telling of what had happened. She said that she and her beloved were "fucking" last night and then described, in rather unromantic language what, to her, had been of great romantic moment. She did with me what she had done elsewhere on many intimate occasions before.

This is the story that I told to Mrs. Wever. She was shocked that I had done so. To her, I was doing exactly what the other patient had so often done. I had revealed an intimacy that belonged only with that other patient and with me—just as that woman had coarsely said too much to her beloved. It was not, to her, a literary vehicle but, rather, an unwarranted intrusion of my personal (read "professional") life into my relationship with her. Moreover, she was fully aware of the various psychological implications of this, including the fact that I was acting as a "truth-speaker," that is to say, as one who tells truths better kept private.

I, she announced, was inflicting upon her a hurtful honesty—just like the "honesty" that I had so often laid open in her. All this she told me in such a way that I was exposed, defensive, and humiliated. More than that, I was confused. She is misunderstanding me, I thought, and that misunderstanding is hurtful and unfair. Why confusing? And why disorienting, and awkward? Like the male protagonist in David Mamet's *Oleanna*, I, the eternally conscientious psychotherapist, was revealed as prideful and vain. How hard we psychotherapists work to get our patients to expose our faults, rather than merely knowing them. And then, for better or for worse, how hurt and angered we are when they do so. With not a little bitter irony I recalled that Mrs. Wever had once said that she knew my faults. I had mused aloud to her about whether, in addition to knowing my faults, she could expose my faults. Well, she could—and did. Only at a distance in time can we come to chuckle at such events.

But from time to time, Mrs. Wever reminded me that I was different from other psychotherapists. I had a kind of non-blaming integrity that was a source of amazement to her. She had friends who were in therapy and, as she listened to the stories told about those therapies, she was reminded of her good fortune in seeing me. I was a tough determined bugger, she said, but I never judged her or her behavior and, although it took a long time before she really believed it, I declined to judge any behavior as "sick" or "pathological."

All too often, I assume, I responded with ironic comments like this: "Well said, Mrs. Wever! I might have said that myself. Now you have insight and now you are psychologically minded!"

I hope that, once in a while, I reminded her of what she already knew—that, over the years, I had slyly demanded of her that she "join my club." Agreeably, she had come around and, with me, was convinced that we were a splendid intellectual pair. The hypocrisy, the mediocrity, and the selfishness of the world were transparent to us, the enlightened ones. Like all psychotherapists, all groups, all nations, we determined that we were better than the other guy.

Herein lies a great psychotherapeutic truth. *The most difficult and well-nigh impossible task faced by the psychotherapist is for her to know and be exposed in her own vanity.* Having been cast by destiny, by herself, or by her culture into the shamanic role, she will be forever persuaded of her own magnificence. No humility or determination will permit her to escape from the sin of pride—the first and fiercest of the seven deadly sins.

After about a year Mrs. Wever stopped therapy. To me she was transformed in a way not achieved in the first period of our work together. Was she better? Most would say she was. The psychotherapist has a fear of saying this too enthusiastically and prefers to note only that she had come to understand her world differently or, better, to note that she had come to know fresh and previously unsuspected worlds. She, the therapist, understands about "feeling better" and "getting better," but places little emphasis on this. In her odd way, she wants only to carry on with her listening.

5

How the Psychotherapist Becomes Who She Is

Become who you are.

—Nietzsche, *Zarathustra* (1884, IV, 1)

There are those who suppose that they are natural born psychotherapists. Almost always they are mistaken. To believe such a thing requires that she-who-thus-appoints-herself must be a believer, and be convinced that she has an eternal message to give to those who suffer. My counsel is never to believe what is said by a believer. There is a terrible and disturbing audacity in believing that one has the inside track on how to live a life. Such self-appointed ones typically have recourse to the idea that what they proclaim is "obvious." I say in reply that "raw feel" is the argument of every tyrant.

Instead, it is wiser to assume that psychotherapists of promise approach their new careers wary of conviction and with a sense of their own ignorance. For all who aim to occupy that role, this means a period of preparation, and, for most, that preparation never ends. The various training programs that are available range from the intense preparation given by psychoanalytic institutes, to the partial, but (usually) still adequate training given to young psychiatrists, psychologists, and social workers.

This chapter discusses the sources of knowledge that ought to be tapped by the student of psychotherapy. As will be seen, these sources may be unexpected and, to the dismay of the scientifically inclined, less related to science than to art and literature.

There is no substitute for reading. To start, the student must read the works of her shamanic ancestors such as Freud, Jung, and Janet. But reading them will be futile if the student has not read the greatest psychologists of our Western tradition, namely, our poets, playwrights, and novelists. They, more than any other source, will have taught the prospective psychotherapist the attitude with which she will eventually have to approach her work with patients. From literature, she will learn the "once-removed" position of neutrality, disinterest, and objectivity.

Logan Pearsall Smith (1931) said "People say that life is the thing . . . but I prefer reading." This means that, for the soul of many, reading is an escape, a solace from the woes of work, family, marriage. As a psychological ironist I might ask whether this preference for reading is as effective with regard to sex as it is for work, family, and marriage. The point here is that the psychotherapist's work and, indeed, her healing powers, are inextricably linked with the once-removed world of reading. As a preparatory and continuing education, nothing can beat it.

Having achieved that anticipatory education, the student is ready to read especially Freud, but also Mesmer, Charcot, Janet, Jung, and Adler. Unless she is enrolled in a professional school, she will be under pressure to read authors and theories that are trumpeted as "modern," and therefore, automatically better. Weak logic, but promoted ubiquitously. Much of the modern fades after a few years, especially in the field of psychotherapy. Some among the modern will endure and, from time to time, I will refer to those who have principally impressed me.

Some may wonder why I particularly name Mesmer, Charcot, and Janet. Others may even wonder why I name Jung and Adler. What makes them attractive to me is the fact that, first, they embody a strong tradition of scholarly thought that takes note of amazing and uncanny characteristics of human behavior, a noting that is denied serious attention in much of modern psychiatry. Even the psychiatric call for a phenomenological approach is usually a misunderstanding of the phenomenology for which they are calling. I fear that few have studied the ideas of Edmund Husserl well enough to understand the radical nature of the phenomenological stance that they are proclaiming. The amazing and the uncanny are the constituents of the ubiquitous unconscious, so deftly ignored by the world of behavioral engineers. The historical figures to whom I am referring the student take psychic phenomena seriously and offer no glib answers, glib answers embraced by the bulk of modern "evangelists" who, I assume, will none-too-soon fade away.

Before she makes her foray into psychological theory, especially into the theories of Freud, the student psychotherapist ought to know the theoretical strategy that is safest and most fruitful. I have already given a sample of this strategy in Chapter 1 as I struggled to portray the psychotherapist by way of a barrage of metaphors. In the original German, it is easier to see what Freud is up to, because in Strachey's English translation the multiple nature of reality is unacknowledged. Where Freud takes upon himself a shower of models or metaphors, Strachey always tries to unify and to reduce. It seems to me that he has missed the point of what Freud intended, probably because he had a (physics-based) model of his own.

Freud was sometimes inclined to do this himself, but just as often eluded being pinned down to a single model. I propose now to examine several of Freud's metapsychological points of view with the aim of showing how diligently he avoided getting himself cornered into committing himself to any single theoretical belief system. In other words, he was at great pains not to fall prey to any Romanticism, be it poetic or scientific. I will take a certain poetic license: I will speak for Freud as though he were always clear about the rhetorical path that I claim he was following.

David Rapaport and Merton Gill (1959) argue that every psychological phenomenon, be it feeling, thinking, or behavior, is to be examined and registered by the psychotherapist in five different ways: three points of view that they attribute to Freud—structural, dynamic, and economic—and two more that they believed to be implicit in Freud—adaptive and genetic. The underlying idea is that reality cannot be captured by adopting only one vantage point. They could be read to be saying that psychological matters can be exhaustively rendered by way of their five points of view but, to me, a stronger reading would be that there are an infinite number of "takes" on reality.

The structural theory, in its essence, is simple. The person's mind, it says, can be modeled on a physical object. Like a bridge, a house, or a motor, it can be understood to have material parts that interact in certain ways. The remarkable extensions of this model are not pertinent here since I aim only to illustrate the theoretical style.

This is only the first of the models under examination. Rapaport and Gill propose it as a straightforward mechanical assumption of Freud's. Oh how simple things would have been had they been right. Unfortunately for them, Freud had many words for the structural notion. Sometimes, for example, he talked of an apparatus, but, as has been carefully documented by Darius Ornston (1985), he was just as liable to use the phrase *psychical contraption*. The irony and mockery in such a phrase was intended. Freud as a writer had a highly literary style. He was determined not to write in a way that would limit the number of metaphors that he could use for the complex mind that he was trying to evoke. Unfortunately for the English reader, the translations fail to convey the degree to which he did not want even the structural theory to be, in any sense, foundational.

A crucial translation of Freud's own words clinch this noncentrality of the idea of structure: "I think we may give our suppositions a free run, as long as we keep our cool perspective [*Urteil*] and do not take our own scaffolding for the building [*das Gerüst nicht für den Bau halten*]" (Ornston 1985, p. 391).

The three major structures that are put forward as part of Freud's tentative scheme—the ego, the id, and the superego—can all be divided into many substructures. The id, for example, is an overarching conception that includes the economic and even, in a sense, the dynamic point of view. The structural model is also the place in formal theory where the superego, the moral sense, is located. To me, Freud the moralist is the Freud to whom we must pay the most attention. Like all great writers, he finds the state of moral dilemma to be the essential starting point for any great psychology. Although I count this as fundamental to a psychological theory, I also insist that the student, no matter how heartily she agrees with this position, draw back from full conviction. Patients are, for example, also victims, albeit victims who suffer because of their moral revulsion at their moral dilemma about what has befallen them.

The analysis of the superego yields detailed, polychromatic complexity fraught with dilemma, confusion, and richness. Moral decision, as it turns out, is as complex as any prudential decision. Among other things, such an analysis results in the awareness that all self-reflection is a form of self-critique. In some patients this is stunningly clear. Every observation that they make about themselves is a subtle self-insult. And, all too often, there is no subtlety at all. For example, one patient proclaimed, "When I do that it shows that I'm a borderline."

The same complexity pertains for the other metapsychological points of view. For example, when we talk of dynamics, we mean mental forces, as in mechanical forces in physics. True enough, introspection and the sympathetic appreciation of others quickly reveals that all persons are enmeshed in a web of contradictory moral forces. To this, to that, and to everything, persons assign value and moral order. You, for example, may want to work some more, but at the same time may want to watch the televised hockey game. I want to punch the guy next door on the nose, but I also want civility to prevail in the neighborhood.

But are such things really drives as Freud suggested? Or are they desires? Are they wishes, libido, aggression, the life instinct, or the death instinct? If one attends carefully to each of the available terms, one can detect a subtle but crucial difference in meaning in each term. Most blatant is the difference between a drive and a desire. A drive is a blind force that impinges on me; a desire is me in all my lustiness and with my heart in it. The point is not whether one of these terms is better than the other; it is that a host of terms is required. A simplifying attempt is bound to make us lose theoretical ground.

The same thing goes for the economic point of view. That stance asks us to think quantitatively. For example, now the patient is more defensive and later he is less defensive. Or is he? I think that all persons, patients included, are full blast defensive at all times. This is so because the word *defensive* has two meanings in psychological theory. When used in its ordinary sense, it simply describes behavior; when used as a theoretical term it refers to just that—theory. That which is theoretical cannot be seen and is to be denied concrete existence.

If my patient is cooperative, insightful, and motivated, the theoretical word *defensive* still applies because, by being cooperative, the patient is squelching—repressing—every lazy, cranky, unworthy element in himself. He is just as defensive (theoretical term) when he is cooperating (descriptive term) as when he is telling the psychotherapist to go to hell (descriptive defensiveness).

The same convoluted thinking is to be applied to a word like *resistance*, which is almost a synonym for the word defensive. The word *anxiety*, too, is used both as a description of overt behavior and, on other occasions, as a theoretical term. The cooperative patient cited in the last paragraph is only anxious theoretically, which means that an unconscious motive leads him to produce an anxiety signal. He does not feel anxious nor, indeed, does he feel anything other than what he says he feels. This is because when we speak this way, we are referring only to the theoretical term, and not to a state of mind or a feeling state. All the poor psychotherapist gets to see is cooperative behavior. Serious theorizing is never simple.

Rapaport and Gill's (1959) adaptive point of view just means that, if I have a nervous breakdown, it is a type of adjustment to a variety of inner and outer circumstances. It is as "adaptive" as winning the Nobel prize. The scare quotes are intended to emphasize that, once again, theoretical and descriptive terms are to be distinguished. In ordinary language, adaptation means adapting according to the standards accepted by society at large. Theoretically, adaptation means that persons find some sort of psychic balance that may or may not be judged as worthwhile.

The genetic point of view means that, among other things, a full understanding of any behavior requires thought about its history—about its genesis in the past.

One metapsychological assumption not mentioned by Rapaport and Gill is the topographical point of view. The work performed by this theoretical term is not adequately carried out by the five figures to which they draw attention. The topographical model draws our attention to the fact that every psychological act takes place in many locales or on many stages. For example, if a patient says of his wife, "She just doesn't get it," the psychotherapist assumes that he has this belief about many people. By watching closely, the psychotherapist will find that there are many performances of this idea on many stages.

The patient that I have in mind mentioned many other women who "didn't get it," most notably when he told his therapist that Kim Campbell (past prime minister of Canada) "just didn't get it." Later still he daydreamed that, when his therapist would finally bring him to his knees, and when she regretfully kissed him—too late, of course—she still wouldn't "get it," just as Salomé "didn't get it." The same scene on many stages. It would be almost banal to mention that, yes, his mother had also not gotten it.

In reading about psychotherapy, the student is well advised to pay particular attention to case histories. Theories come and go but real life, the real life of patients, endures. Freud's favorite patient was himself. He studied his own psychology endlessly, sometimes explicitly acknowledging that he was doing so, for example, in his famous analysis of the dream of Irma's injection. Students who attend too forcefully to theoretical readings are, regrettably, led into deadening intellectualizations and nonsense jargon such as "narcissistic fixations," "oedipal preoccupations," and "primitive object relations."

Since Freud gave us the clue that we can look inward upon ourselves to learn about psychological matters, I recommend that prospective psychotherapists join in. They should also scrutinize their friends, their families, and their colleagues as well as their patients. These sources of psychological knowledge, indispensable though they are, have their drawbacks. The biggest problem is time. Students are young and lack the experience of life that older practitioners have.

This is where reading comes in. To read *The Brothers Karamazov* is to read and to learn fast about an extraordinary family. The characters are complex, mad, bizarre, and "human, all-too-human." Dostoyevski plies us with their secrets, and with their sex, shame, and triumphs. The novel, like all good literature, is a cornucopia of psychological insights. Not only that but the student will find all the Karamazov characters in her office at one time or another. If she is smart and brave, she will also find them in herself. Also crowding into her office will be Hamlet, Lady Macbeth, and Orpheus. I pray that she will recognize them when they arrive because their presence, and her recognition of them, will be the salvation of her patients and the greatest fruition of her psychotherapeutic skills.

In *Hamlet*, Shakespeare demonstrates "thick description" for the student of psychotherapy. I can, for example, identify in the play five theories of psychosis—of madness. Polonius believes that Hamlet's madness is due to thwarted love. He is also greatly impressed by the wisdom that is to be found in the speeches of the mad. Rosencrantz and Guildenstern think that

Hamlet has become crazy because of thwarted ambition. Hamlet's mother, Gertrude, is sure that her son has become mad because of his father's death and her own overhasty marriage. Ophelia considers Hamlet's condition to be simple lunacy, whatever that might mean! Her explanation by labeling illustrates the thought-ending consequences of many of our usual labels for deviant mental behavior. Claudius, with the shrewdness of the pursued, recognizes that Hamlet is feigning madness in order to deceive him.

Hamlet himself unleashes upon us countless psychological bon mots:

> But I have within which passeth show;
> These but the trappings and the suits of woe. [I, ii, 85]

> There are more things in heaven and earth, Horatio,
> Than are dreamed of in your philosophy. [I, v, 166]

> There is nothing either good or bad, but thinking makes
> it so. [II, ii, 259]

> Thus conscience does make cowards of us all. [III, i, 56]

If she pays attention, the student will learn from the story of Macbeth and Lady Macbeth the vicissitudes of guilt. In Macbeth, she will find hesitation and doubt in anticipation of the crime of patricide, and in Lady Macbeth, self-revulsion following the crime of patricide.

King Lear forfeits his kingly dignity and then, by way of madness, finds himself—and his dignity—again. What follows is the story of a professor of English speaking of Lear's shame. What he thinks is that he is teaching English. I claim that he is a teacher of psychology. In turn, he would probably claim that I am teaching English.

> Gloucester says, "O, let me kiss that hand," and Lear replies, "let me wipe it first; it smells of mortality." . . .

> "Lear feels shame. Shame is one of the biggest emotions." He paused for a second, and then glared at some of the men in the class. Now he was almost shouting: "You're breaking out with pimples; your girlfriend comes upon you when you're masturbating. It's shame! . . . Look, in the beginning of the play, Lear wants to be loved. Lear says, 'Which of you shall we say doth love us most?' But what won't he give? In order to receive love, you have to be seen through, and not just seen. You have to let people see your murderous impulses as well as your benevolent ones.
>
> Thou rascal beadle, hold thy bloody hand!
> Why dost thou lash that whore? Strip thy own back.
> Thou hotly lusts to use her in that kind
> For which thou whip'st her. The usurer hangs the cozener.
> Through tattered clothes small vices do appear;
> Robes and furred gowns hide all. [IV, vi, 157]
>
> "See?" Taylor [the English professor] said. "Lear has truly recognized himself. You recognize something in yourself and you punish someone else for it. You want to fuck that whore, but instead of doing that you punish her. This is a play about shame and love and recognition." [Denby 1994, p. 96]

Anna Karenina, Madame Bovary (the same character, in many ways), and every other literary figure teach us—fast—about our patients, which is also to say that they teach us about ourselves. I pity the poor student who is assigned lists of journal articles to read and who, thereby, is robbed of the time needed to read novelists like Margaret Atwood, Joseph Conrad, Thomas Mann, and short-story writer Alice Munro.

In Chapter 1, I mentioned Lucifer as a possible metaphor for the psychotherapist. That possibility has not been lost to great writers of the Western canon, all of whom recognize the importance of the disrupters and the crisis makers. I will begin with the appearance of the devil in *The Brothers Karamazov*. The point that he, the devil, makes is that God is the enemy. If all was good, and all was love, and if everything were rational and the way it should be, there would be no events. Nothing would happen. The devil is necessary for there to be life, variety, and spice. Freud (1911) put it this way: "It is the fate of psychoanalysis to disturb the peace of the world" (pp. 32–33).

Nietzsche, perhaps taking a page from Dostoyevski, makes the same announcement. Be it the Übermensch, Zarathustra, or the "Blonde Beast," they are all assigned the same mission. They are evil, the disrupters of convention and of the status quo, who challenge mediocrity and vulgarity. Thereby they become the new good. Like all new scientific theory, they destroy what went before. To Nietzsche and to Dostoyevski's devil, the conventional is a position of intolerance—dangerously moralistic. The psychotherapist may privately agree but, in her practice, she only half agrees. In her professionalism she is conventional in the extreme; in her psychologizing she is subversive.

I wonder, too, whether the study of the lives of public figures, or of culture heroes and antiheroes, would help the student of psychotherapy. Luther, Gandhi, Hitler, and pianist Glenn Gould come to mind. I suppose, for that matter, that many have benefited from the study of the life of Freud.

I will mention only one example. To the psychotherapist, accustomed as she is to the self-defeating "chronic suicide" that she finds in all people, the consistent winning behavior of a world-class athlete is a wonder. It is not that she considers such a person to be an exception to what is usual. It is simply that such consistent triumphs are rare, and the ordinary stupidities of personal life seem so remarkably absent or so radically excluded from their professional world.

This is to be found in all highly accomplished persons. I recall speaking to an actor about her understudy. "Do you not," I asked "feel bad for your understudy, who never, it seems, gets to play the role?" This splendidly talented performer, gentle and generous to a fault, answered "It's my show. She will never get to play the part if I can help it. In fact, it's my job to see to it that she never plays the role." The fascination and the learning springs from the fact that the human tendency to injure ourselves and to lose—due to ubiquitous human guilt—is usually more visible.

Schönberg's opera *Moses und Aron*, difficult, provocative, but nevertheless instructive, is an indispensable study for every hopeful psychotherapist. Those uninitiated to Schönberg may be in for a bout of incomprehension or, worse, a bout of rage. If the twelve-tone music is not for everyone, perhaps it is not for anyone at all. By being impossible and incomprehensible, it raises the very challenge that it wishes to teach.

Let me begin with the name of God. Yahweh is not to be named or, at least, his name is not to be said. From personal experience I can report how hurt an Orthodox Jew can be if the name of Yahweh is uttered. Why should this be? The answer is remarkably modern and, furthermore, remarkably pertinent to the thought of the psychotherapist. If I name God, I limit Him. He is concretized and thereby delimited, circumscribed, and delineated. This fate is not to be imposed on an infinite God. Yahweh is incomprehensible and not to be rendered less by being named.

The psychotherapist could not agree more. Every statement, every narrative, every word spoken by the patient locks him into a particular linguistic world. Only in silence can he spare himself that limiting fate. This is precisely why the psychotherapist is a quiet solitary. She must reside in her aloneness in order to achieve the crucial once-removed attitude that is demanded of her. That noninvolved stance is, as I have mentioned before, a characteristic of Shakespeare's nonmoralizing disinterest. Far more than the uninitiated reader will have imagined, the psychotherapist is silent.

In the Bible and in Schönberg's opera, Moses stands for inarticulate silence, and Aron stands for speech and the definition of the world and of God. Moses comes down from the mountain and, to his horror, finds that Aron and the Israelites have fallen to worshiping the Golden Calf. They have articulated God, and incarnated Him. In the opera, Moses and Aron struggle with a terrible problem. Aron's position is that mortals must incarnate God in some way. Could Moses really believe that mere mortals can worship a God who takes no shape and who has no presence? Moses's position is that the naming or representation of God ruins His infinite nature and the difficulty created by such a problem must simply be borne. To make matters worse for Moses, he himself must have a "Word" for God to give to his people, but no word can ever do. Like Faust, he does not know what to do with the "Logos."

From such an examination of music and of the Bible, the student finds herself faced with the gravest of psychological dilemmas. How can she emancipate her patients from their wordy prisons without replacing those words with other, equally imprisoning, words? She must, she will learn, undo her patient's words, her patient's new words and, most difficult of all, her own words, if she is to stand firm for the multiple nature of reality. And, in achieving this small but crucial psychological task, she will come to understand something of Schönberg's *Moses und Aron* (Steiner 1958).

What else must the aspirant do to become a psychotherapist? In traditional training, she is expected to attend reading seminars, to treat patients under supervision, and (usually) to have personal treatment of her own. For most students, such requirements are indispensable. I doubt that I could have felt myself to be a genuine psychotherapist without the various degrees and documents that certify my status.

But all the training in the world does not make a psychotherapist. Some come to training with great psychological sophistication whereas others, despite years of training and personal treatment, never seem to "get it." I think that my proposals for aspiring psychotherapists will only work for those who already have a knack for it.

I want only to add a few more odd angles to what a self-designed training program might look like. Students typically meet with senior colleagues to discuss their cases. They must meet with someone who is experienced and who is in the business. At first they will need concrete guidance about the mechanics of how to proceed, how to give a bill, how to set up an office. But I wonder if, after a while, they could not do something more imaginative. Could they, for example, buy consultation time from other psychological experts—perhaps novelists Margaret Atwood and Robertson Davies, or journalist Janet Malcolm? How about Saul Bellow or John Updike or Alice Munro? If she were alive, would one not want to discuss cases with Emily Dickinson?

Who knows the answer to such questions? But unfortunately official curricula always become sterile, hypertrophied, and bureaucratized. These eventualities are the end of psychology.

6

The Self-Education of Jan Schweitzer

All theory, dear friend, is grey,
But the golden tree of actual life springs ever green.

—Goethe

This is the story of a student of mine who, acutely aware of matters psychological, profited from a stay in a remote Indian community. He discovered there that psychology—the golden tree of actual life—springs green wherever there are people to display it. Three ideas pertinent to psychotherapy unexpectedly come together in the adventures of this odd but perceptive young man. First, as every student should, he learns psychological ideas and psychotherapeutic stances from all of his observations of human behavior.

In particular, he recognizes in the cool, quiet attitudes of the aboriginal natives, a variant on the psychotherapist's "analytic attitude." Finally, and in anticipation of my discussion of culture in Chapter 9, he realizes that, despite superficial appearances and our typical glib assumptions, the native culture is resilient and enduring.

At the time of these events he was a medical student; later he became a psychiatric resident who I supervised in his psychotherapy assignment; and later still, just before its completion, he abruptly ended his psychiatric training. For a period of time he privately continued with his supervision with me because, although he was disillusioned with organized psychiatry, he was determined to be a psychotherapist.

What first struck me about Schweitzer was an idea that he regularly wanted to discuss with me during his supervision. He was ever preoccupied by a particular and preferred psychological position that he often referred to as the "attitude of repose." (He got the word *repose* from F. Scott Fitzgerald's *Tender is the Night*). This was his personal version of what Freud called *neutrality*, a term that, if not qualified, may be weaker than one would like. He was most fascinated by it when he found it in unexpected places.

While a medical student, Schweitzer worked for two summers in a regional hospital in northern Ontario. The Sioux Lookout Zone Hospital is located in a remote part of northern Ontario, fifteen hundred miles from Toronto, well beyond Thunder Bay. It is accessible by highway, railroad, or private plane. As well as serving as a hospital, the Sioux Lookout center sends medical personnel to the interior of the zone to serve the medical needs of numerous small satellite communities. These small Indian settlements are accessible only by air and none of them has an air strip. Takeoffs and landings are therefore made on pontoons in summer and on skis in winter. The villages, each with its own nursing station, are located one to three hours by light aircraft away from Sioux Lookout.

Medical needs in that remote region were such that, even though Schweitzer was still a student, he was permitted to work as a physician. Apart from the fact that all of the patients were Cree and Ojibway Indians, he found that the practice of medicine was remarkably similar to what he had known in Toronto. There was a high incidence of alcoholism and its consequences, but such problems were already well known to Schweitzer. The incidence of tuberculosis, in contrast, was a surprise. He had naively assumed that tuberculosis was a rarity in Ontario. When dealing with many supposedly familiar disorders, he quickly demanded of himself a high index of suspicion that tuberculosis might be involved.

Schweitzer already had an interest in psychiatric disorders. In fact, during the first summer in the zone, he spent his spare time reading. First he read a textbook on clinical psychiatry, and then, armed with that overview of modern psychiatry, he tackled Karl Jasper's awesome *General Psychopathology*. When he could, Schweitzer told me, he continued his examination of Freud's work and already then began to suspect that the riches of Freud were concentrated in his early psychoanalytic writings. For Schweitzer to have reached such a conclusion (with which I am in cautious agreement) at so young an age is remarkable. In any case his interest in psychiatry was not lost on his Sioux Lookout colleagues. Their medically typical lack of interest in that field made Schweitzer's presence welcome to them since psychiatric cases could be steered in his direction. Schweitzer, as might be expected, had no objection.

Schweitzer's major assignment was to the general wards of the Sioux Lookout Hospital. Because of his interest in psychiatry he was occasionally able to visit the closest mental hospital, which was located in Asileton, a few miles away. The most exciting assignment was when Schweitzer, like the qualified doctors who visited the zone hospital, was sent to the interior. According to his reports, such trips were high adventure.

Lansdowne House was the particular settlement to which Schweitzer was assigned. Although he periodically visited other communities, the hope was that he and the inhabitants of his assigned community would come to know and trust one another. He looked forward to seeing "his" village. He became excited as they flew northward and as he looked at the map. What, he wondered, might be found in places like Winisk, Lac Seul, Savant Lake, or Cat Lake?

Soon he arrived in his own settlement, Lansdowne House. As the plane taxied across the lake Schweitzer could see that the arrival of the plane was an important event and that many of the inhabitants were gathering at the dock. As soon as he stepped out of the plane he was approached by a man who pressed upon him forms and a pencil. He had by then become familiar with the remarkably noncommittal manner of Indians but was particularly impressed by it on that occasion. The man, without speaking a word, was requesting that Schweitzer help him to fill out a welfare form. But when Schweitzer responded with puzzlement and asked what was wanted, the man's reluctant verbalization of his request was oddly made.

"Fill it out . . . ?"

Curt, gravelly voice, almost inaudible. When Schweitzer tried to clarify what was being requested, the response was no different.

"Fill it out for me . . . ?"

Although Schweitzer momentarily experienced the typical revulsion of whites confronted by such a situation, he also felt puzzled. This Indian man was clearly not a "noble savage," nor did the word *dignified* seem to apply. Yet Schweitzer claimed that he found the Indian's manner attractive. He had, Schweitzer said, a reserve and a reclusiveness that he would not relinquish in the service of adopting the more chatty conventions of white society. This reclusiveness—repose, Schweitzer called it—intrigued him because ultimately, as part of his personal interrogation of the psychotherapeutic attitude, he came to advocate a very similar stance to the listening psychotherapist.

Not only are the Indian and the therapist reclusive, but they are noncommittal. And not only are such psychological kinsmen noncommittal, they are, he insisted, peculiarly obstinate. In later years Schweitzer wondered whether the therapist should, Indian-like, also be monosyllabic. Or, he wondered, should a psychotherapist emit noncommittal grunts?

The pilot explained. "Indians don't work, or at least most of them don't work, because there are no jobs. They live on welfare. The wives don't cook. They give money to the kids who just go to the 'Bay'—the tiny Hudson's Bay store located in most towns—and buy cokes, chips, and chocolate bars. That's all they eat. Sometimes they buy canned food to eat. Half the time the husbands buy booze with the welfare money."

Schweitzer realized that the plight of Indians in their home communities was far worse than he had expected. He looked around at the many children at dockside. Most were dirty and had pussy crusts of impetigo on their faces. Even pubertal children seemed to be so infected. He soon learned that large amounts of antibiotic ointments were prescribed to combat the epidemic impetigo.

But how could this be, he wondered? Could Indian hygiene be that bad? Could elementary cultural practices, the grooming and cleaning of children, be damaged and destroyed? Have we destroyed their culture irreparably? Did they let us destroy their culture?

A pretty white girl in jeans pressed forward. "I'm Susan, the nurse. How do you do?"

Schweitzer was a medical student and Susan was a nurse. They were to live in the same tiny community of three hundred for the next week. I believe that on that first trip to Lansdowne House he slept and ate in the nursing station where Susan lived. It had not occurred to Schweitzer that the nurse might be young and attractive, nor could he have imagined that she would suggest that later that day they might water ski. The idea was bizarre but, sure enough, the nursing station had the necessary equipment and soon Schweitzer was skiing across the lake, totally isolated from civilization. Susan drove the boat. *Time*, *Newsweek*, and Madison Avenue had come to the zone before Schweitzer. So much for northern repose.

"She had on a bikini swimsuit, of course."

Schweitzer had the peculiar feeling that he was enacting a script. What he meant by this was that there was a complex set of conventions that dictated how he and the young nurse should behave. He did not mean to say that the conventions were absolutely fixed but that there was an array of conventional behaviors in which they might indulge. In fact he sensed there was no possible interaction between them that was not prescripted and hence familiar. Even if he desired her—which he did—that desire appeared only in one familiar guise or another. It would be some variant of soap opera. For Schweitzer, the preferred story line was a romantic one. As he observed his participation in events, he recognized the irony of excitedly living out real events that were also lockstep enactments of personal and cultural scripts.

After supper Susan suggested that they should visit her friends in another part of the town. Schweitzer was disappointed to find that the friends were whites: the Hudson's Bay factor (the factor runs the fur-trading post), two young men who operated a local weather station, and a schoolteacher. The disappointment was heightened when he realized that Susan and one of the young men had eyes for one another. So much for the natural pairing of medical student and nurse. A script modification had occurred and Schweitzer had obeyed the convention by being privately hurt and publicly lighthearted. The ecstasy of life, said Schweitzer, resides in the awareness that paradoxically we savor all our little tragedies.

Things became worse. It was soon clear that Schweitzer was viewed by the little group of whites as an intruder, as a "southerner," as a rich snob from the big city. They considered him a phony do-gooder and said so directly. Schweitzer was amazed at the crudity and unanimity with which he was attacked. Although Susan was also a city slicker from Toronto, she made no move to protect him. Most of all, she seemed curious to see how he would withstand the mistreatment. Schweitzer defended himself and even fought back.

Ultimately he was disappointed in his efforts, especially since he considered all of them to be his intellectual inferiors. He was at some pains to draw to my attention his adroitness in establishing his own state of disappointment. Like any ordinary mortal, Schweitzer said, he was hurt that Susan was so obviously attached to the young man that Schweitzer judged to be the most uncouth member of the group. He said it was one of the weather station employees. "As convention dictates that I should, I'll tell you that he was a beer-swilling boor."

Thus Schweitzer, therapist-in-the-making.

Settlements such as Lansdowne House were far away from the urban world in which Schweitzer had always lived. The only link to the Sioux Lookout Zone was by shortwave radio and that link was dependent on proper weather conditions. Apart from radio contact there were twice-weekly stopdowns by small aircraft.

Despite the isolated location of Lansdowne House, they had water-skied and, although Indians fished for food, whites occasionally fished as recreation. Because of the remoteness of the settlement, it was rare to see persons from outside of the community. Nevertheless, a group of fisherman docked at Lansdowne one day and came into town. They had been flown to a nearby lake and were to be picked up a few days later. Schweitzer managed to be invited to accompany them on an overnight excursion. Schweitzer and the fishermen reached their campsite late the first night and, having built a fire, prepared to cook their plentiful supply of freshly caught pickerel. In such isolated lakes the fish were bigger and fatter than any Schweitzer had seen before. In addition to the fish, one member of the group had captured a duck, which he assumed would be added to that evening's menu.

But as they sat around the campfire, Schweitzer demurred. "We have plenty of fish. Why don't we just let the duck go?"

A debate ensued. Most thought that Schweitzer was making a ridiculous suggestion. He, however, debated the issue well. His point was that the duck was alive and deserved not to be treated as a creature of inferior status. Here in the wilderness, he argued, all were on an equal footing. These arguments anticipated Schweitzer's later skepticism about our common hierarchical assumptions, that is to say, our assumptions that certain persons, certain races, certain genders, certain psychological positions, are inferior or superior.

A compromise was eventually reached. Rather than arguing further, they would take a vote. Schweitzer opposed that suggestion. Nevertheless it was decided that a vote would be taken.

"As a matter of civility and courtesy," argued Schweitzer, "couldn't the duck be afforded the privilege of being able to influence its own fate? Opinion within the group is divided, which suggests that killing the duck or sparing the duck are each positions that can be supported. And if it is to be afforded a position of dignity, shouldn't the duck, too, be given a vote? In fact, since the duck is the only member of its species present at this meeting, I would prefer that the duck have as many votes as do we humans. But if we will not agree to the duck's being given six votes (I assume that we all agree on how the duck will vote), I recommend as a compromise that the duck be given one vote."

Schweitzer's eloquence won the day and the duck's dilemma was put to a vote. The duck was included as a voter. Ballots were counted but unfortunately the group decided that, despite Schweitzer, the duck, and one or two others, the duck would become part of the dinner. Schweitzer's only satisfaction from that turn of events sprang from the fact that the duck's flesh was tough and bad tasting.

This incident eventually led Schweitzer to rethink his position with regard to fishing. He told me that once, when he came upon a group of fishermen, he threw rocks into the water and shouted, "Don't kill the fucking fish." Perhaps he did, but it may be that he was confusing himself with pianist Glenn Gould, who, it is said, did the same thing when his father fished.

Yet another story followed. He recalled a teaching demonstration that he had once attended. Five people were brought to the stage, were presented with a hypothetical problem situation, and given fifteen minutes in which to come to a conclusion.

"Here is the problem they were given. They were to pretend that the five of them had been shipwrecked and were in a lifeboat. They were to imagine that one of them had a 3-week-old baby with her, and another had with him a famed police dog. The boat was overloaded. For the safety of all it had been determined that either the baby or the dog must be thrown overboard. The group was to debate whether the baby or the dog should be sacrificed. They had fifteen minutes to solve this problem.

"The participants in this exercise varied in their responses. There was a nervous giggle or two, some perplexed shrugging of shoulders, and an awkward silence. Finally someone suggested that obviously the dog should be thrown overboard. The others agreed. They still had ten minutes left and the organizers made no move to bring the demonstration to a close. Annoyance and boredom prevailed on the stage and in the audience. A few more nervous giggles.

"When the time was up, the organizers of the program dismissed the participants and called to the stage five more volunteers. To the amazement of both participants and audience they were given the identical task. You could see that the audience was getting pissed off at the stupidity of it all.

"To everyone's further amazement, those on the stage behaved differently. One of the participants argued that the baby should be sacrificed rather than the dog. At first his fellow group members thought he was joking but once his seriousness became clear, the debate became heated. He was an interesting bugger and made surprisingly good debating points. He cited the established service record of the police dog. It had contributed to the solution of unwelcome social problems and had saved lives. It could be anticipated that, if it was spared, the dog would save more human lives. The baby, on the other hand, had no record of performance at all. Besides, he said, it was highly questionable whether or not the child was a person. Although it was undoubtedly a member of the human species, it was highly unlikely that it qualified for personhood. He could imagine that certain nonhumans might be persons, for example a Martian, but not a 3-week-old infant whose mental and moral powers were nonexistent.

"The other imaginary occupants of the lifeboat broke into a storm of protest. Animated replies evoked equally animated answers from the dissident group members. Psychological name calling eventually was replaced by pointed intellectual debate. All too soon the instructors announced that the discussion time was up.

"The end of the teaching demonstration was devoted to explicating the point that the instructors were trying to make. The man who had argued to save the dog had been a plant and his unexpected position had been predetermined by the instructors. Dissent is valuable, they argued. If all agree, a discussion bears little fruit. When a difference of opinion exists, the participants in any group process are provoked into producing powerful, interesting, and novel arguments. This is what they wanted to illustrate. The final implication of what they aimed to teach was that, although the dissenter's views were obviously ridiculous, his dissent was valuable.

"This supposedly reasonable conclusion," Schweitzer said, "is a point of great uneasiness to me. Why is it 'obvious' that the dog is inferior to a human or, for that matter, inferior to a person? Why am I better than a dog or a duck or a fish? Or to a tree or to a landscape? If I announce my superiority to a patient, am I not in a state of unattractive vanity? Or worse, far worse?"

The nature of his adopted Indian community quickly became known to Schweitzer. The surface impression was of a dilapidated, impoverished, backwoods version of the rest of the North American world. People had illnesses and he, the doctor, was consulted. Treatments were administered just as they were in the south. Psychiatric problems—usually identified by the nurse rather than by the afflicted person—were typically construed to be family problems and it was expected that Schweitzer would visit the family in their home.

Some lived in tarpaper and corrugated iron shacks, insulated with newspaper. Often such shacks were fitted into a depression in the ground or against a hillside. The surroundings were always littered with garbage. Others lived in government-built row housing. These dirty, pastel colored homes were similar to the least expensive urban house that one could imagine. They were small and few had furniture. Often they were incomplete or, if they had been completed, vital parts—such as sinks—had disappeared. The only furnishing that Schweitzer consistently noticed were assorted mattresses and bedding.

All in all, it struck him as a pathetic version of Toronto poverty. Perhaps more accurately, it appeared to be a northern incarnation of a hostel for derelicts. The majority of psychiatric problems fitted the setting. Most commonly Schweitzer was asked to visit families with problems of drunkenness, delinquency, and glue sniffing.

As the community came to know him, other issues were brought to his attention. One day, when he passed her crossing a small field, Florence Yes-No asked to speak with him.

"I'm jealous of my husband. He runs around with women," she said.

Schweitzer assumed she wished to talk of jealousy, of her anger, her sadness, and of what she might do about the situation. To his considerable puzzlement, Schweitzer and Mrs. Yes-No seemed to find themselves in a situation of mutual awkwardness. Schweitzer had difficulty sensing what she wanted, especially since she said very little. She, in turn, seemed to assume that he understood something above and beyond his initial "southern" expectations. She was waiting for him to respond.

"Neither of us seemed to know what the script was," said Schweitzer. "More accurately, we both skillfully followed a script that indicated that we were creatures of alien cultures and both of us made polite acknowledgment of our good intentions, of our confusion, and of our cautious contempt for the stupidity of the other and his race.

"I ran into Mrs. Yes-No again a day or two later. She told me that she regularly attended the films shown on Wednesday nights at the church hall. Such statements seemed to be her way of feeding me bits of information that she expected would clarify for me her dilemma. The movies were, she emphasized, white people's movies. White women get jealous when their men go out with other women. Upon inquiry she asserted that Indian women do not get jealous since all Indian men run around with women.

"Frankly, I doubt that it is true that all Indian men run around, or that Indian women are not jealous, but when we first spoke I took her words at face value. Later I wondered whether she really meant that Indian women did not *react* when their men ran around. In other words they were Indians: noncommittal, reclusive, and obstinate. Nowadays I would add 'like a psychotherapist.' Mrs. Yes-No's difference from the other women was not in the fact of her jealousy, I concluded, but in her lack of repose. But this elaboration still did not explain what was going on.

"Eventually she gave me the key piece of information. One of her grandparents was white. Therefore, like a white woman, she was jealous. In my modification of her complaint, it could be said that, like a white woman, she did not have repose. And like a white woman, she consulted a psychiatrist. She was quite right about the latter conclusion since, in the many months I spent in the zone, no other Indian consulted me independently.

"I think that eventually she had a tiny crush on me and I reciprocated. Transference and countertransference existed even before I knew what they were.

"I don't know what I said to her. But if I had it to do again I would say to her that, as a white woman, she was fated to be eternally jealous of her husband. And like a white woman, I would add, she could never hope to attain the reserve and dignity of an Indian woman."

Schweitzer sensed that the destroyed Indian culture was only a manifestly destroyed Indian culture. Subtle signs of intact cultural modalities (inapparent even to the Indians?) could be seen if only one had eyes to see.

Schweitzer was informed that a man with cancer was dying. He walked to the man's home. A crowd had gathered outside but, although Schweitzer was a bit uneasy, he maneuvered his way into the house. It was full of people. The old man lay on a pile of bedding on the floor. He was partially propped up by his wife and his sister. Schweitzer realized that the man was on the verge of death as evidenced by his obvious agonal breathing. Both his wife and his sister were intensely busy wiping the perspiration from his forehead and chest, cleansing his mouth and tongue, and making sure that his eyes were gently closed. Someone stood above him—the old man was on the floor—and cooled him with a fan. At the side of the room an Indian lay brother read aloud from the Bible. Children and adults filled the one room house and stood silently watching. Several tikinagens with babies in them stood against the wall.

Schweitzer was the "doctor" in the town and his presence was demanded by the white medical tradition. The Indians ignored him. Although accustomed to death he was very frightened. In this setting he was, he thought, an obscene outsider. He had the disturbing thought that the crowd of people, all of whom belonged in the room, might turn and attack or devour him. No one invited him to "take over" as would have happened in a white community. Here, everyone knew exactly what to do and his presence, although tolerated, was entirely unnecessary. When the man died, Schweitzer approached the widow and said he was sorry. She made minimal acknowledgment of his words and carried on with her work, which now was concerned with attending to her husband's body.

Early the next morning the dead man was taken by canoe to be buried on an island a few miles downstream from the village.

It seemed stupid to think that a white man could be a psychiatrist for the Indians who lived in the zone. Nevertheless, proper psychiatrists—Schweitzer was still a medical student—visited and claimed that they had a role to play. Schweitzer disagreed. He believed that locally recognized shamans must exist. Such figures were not publicly known, at least not publicly known to the white community. Yet one heard about witch doctors, medicine men, and shamans.

The nurse in one community had heard that the school janitor was a witch doctor. Schweitzer spoke to the man on several occasions but found no way of getting beyond vague references to traditional healing practices.

In another settlement, the nurse asked Schweitzer to visit a girl who had suffered several major convulsive seizures. When they visited the home, the family announced that the seizure problem was solved. A traditional healer—a witch doctor—had visited the community a few days before and had given to them the information needed to prevent further seizures. The young woman was never again to eat sturgeon and this would ensure that no further fits would come upon her. Not only that, but her sisters, who were virgins, were also to avoid sturgeon. Schweitzer expected that such a prescription might well be effective since the description of the seizures strongly suggested to him that they were hysterical in nature. The vulgar words of an adolescent ditty suddenly reveal a crude psychological perceptiveness.

> Caviar comes from the virgin sturgeon.
> The virgin sturgeon's a very fine fish.
> Since very few virgins need much urgin'
> That's why caviar is my dish.

Schweitzer was surprised to learn that the visiting witch doctor had charged the family a twenty dollar fee, which was, in the late 1960s, as much as a qualified psychiatrist would have charged. He also learned that there had been no sturgeon caught in that community for many years.

At times Schweitzer wondered whether the local leaders, the chiefs, were not the logically appropriate agents of "psychiatric" care. Eventually he became repelled by his own patronizing assumption that he had worthwhile opinions on this topic.

"Instead of knowing what to do about problems, I settled for a personal depression. Depression has never been my style but, robbed of my personal conviction that I could always cure or help people, I lived through some of the blackest months of my life. I had thought the Indian culture to be damaged, if not destroyed. This I attributed to a cultural vulnerability uncharacteristic of more advanced cultures. Instead I found the Indian culture to be impervious to my attempts at white man penetrations."

One night during Schweitzer's first visit to Lansdowne, he attended a film in the Catholic church hall. Young teenagers made mischief and, to his great surprise, he suddenly realized that sheets of newspaper had been set afire and stuffed under his chair. Repose. The adult moviegoers (apart from Schweitzer) demonstrated universal repose. Without apparent urgency and seemingly bored, they got pails of water and doused the flames. A man, Jimmy Pequin, said to Schweitzer that he was tired of the misbehavior of the young people and that he planned soon to gather his possessions and with his wife, to set off into the woods to find a better place to settle in.

They talked further and Schweitzer learned that Jimmy was a carver. The next day Schweitzer visited his shack and purchased several items. There was a particular carved object that Schweitzer wished to obtain—I believe it was a sled with a hunter and dogs—and it was arranged that Jimmy would have it ready for Schweitzer when he returned to Lansdowne House in six weeks. On his next trip Schweitzer found Jimmy to be drunk every day—so drunk (or so reclusive?) that he could not speak. Even drunk he was reserved, impassive, noncommittal. He betrayed no drunken hilarity, drunken boisterousness, or drunken bad temper.

Schweitzer watched these drunken scenes with the expected revulsion but, to his own great surprise, he was also fascinated. He remembered his many encounters with silent and monosyllabic Indians. Ostensibly, he informed me, this was evidence that they were members of a destroyed culture but he himself could not quite believe this.

"What I realized was that they have 'backbone.' Every Indian has a rigid back, a poker spine, Marie-Strümpell disease. What I mean is that they are stubborn. They have a position in the world that they stick to, even when drunk.

"But they did pay attention to me. It isn't that they changed the subject or lightened the mood. They sort of looked at me poker faced, or else looked away from me, but still attended to me with a sort of gloomy quietness. They live in a universe that they aren't going to give up and they won't adopt a new idea without giving it a lot of thought. There is a luscious consistency to their reclusiveness. My shenanigans (and everybody else's too) must have been very vivid to them since they didn't join in with my ways at the expense of their own centeredness. My attempts to get a conversation going and to joke around had no impact whatsoever. Nor did they give in to their own emotions or even to their own drunkenness. I have the idea that they are undistracted by anything and that therefore they can catch the full detail and richness of everything that goes on around them."

"Am I God? I see so clearly!" [Goethe, *Faust*]

What fascinated Schweitzer was an attitude that he later came to advocate as an element in the attitude of the psychotherapist. I have already discussed Shakespeare's disinterest, its contribution to his greatness as a psychologist, and I point now to its resemblance to the reserve of the Indians.

Schweitzer himself, one of those wonderful young psychotherapists who disappear from sight once their training is completed, was destined to exemplify this since he, too, turned out to be a man with an inflexible spine. He had a theoretical rigidity, that is to say, he rigidly maintained the position of a man without rigidity. He was, so to speak, a man of disinterest, and without belief. When he became a student of psychotherapy, this posture allowed him to evaluate detail with exquisite thoroughness. It may be of interest that his personal life was quite different. He was emotionally and behaviorally profligate, although, as far as I could tell, this rarely impinged on his way of working.

Schweitzer learned from Jimmy's wife that Sandy, his daughter from a previous marriage, had recently been placed in the mental hospital in Asileton close to Sioux Lookout, several hundred miles away. Asileton and Sioux Lookout were, to Jimmy Pequin, part of the mistrusted and alien white world. Schweitzer had developed a curiosity about the drunken artist and, since he was returning to Sioux Lookout at the end of the week, he promised the Pequins that he would visit Sandy in Asileton.

She had just turned 14 and was tied to her chair in a seclusion room. Both her wrists were heavily bandaged. On the previous day she had attacked several hospital staff members and when attempts were made to restrain her, Sandy had punched both fists through a window and made back and forth sawing motions with her wrists against the jagged glass.

She lived in Sioux Lookout with her white mother—Sandy herself did not look Indian—and a few weeks before had been baby-sitting for a neighbor's child. The child's father walked her home and, in a clump of bushes, had seduced or raped her. A few days later Sandy had become wildly psychotic—hallucinating and delusional—and was sent to the regional mental hospital in Asileton. She was destined to spend most of the next five years in that hospital.

"I read Sandy's chart and, being excessively enamored of intelligence, was thunderstruck by the report of psychological tests that indicated that her IQ was 150. I also admit that she was a pretty girl and I quickly (but secretly) resolved that I would be her psychotherapist. Things were pretty loose in the hospital and no objections were made. During that first week I saw her for a couple of hours each day and thereafter I saw her for one hour each day. This went on for three months during my first summer in Sioux Lookout and for over three months the second. The only times we did not meet were when I traveled to the interior of the zone.

"She was very crazy at times. During one period of several weeks she was catatonic and did not move, did not eat, and did not speak. She was fed by nasogastric tube. I knew that she loved Sweet Marie chocolate bars and I brought her one every time I came, although I do not know whether, during her catatonic period, she ate them.

"I had no idea what I was doing but I already had the stubborn conviction that sense could be made out of her craziness. I was determined that there was a purpose behind her psychotic behavior. Sometimes I was scared shitless, especially when she wanted to sit on my knee—can you believe that I allowed it?—or when she attempted to hug or kiss me. I remember walking down the corridor one day with a tray full of hypodermic needles and syringes. I guess I was drawing blood from a bunch of patients for Wassermann tests or something. Suddenly Sandy jumped at me and grabbed my crotch shouting, 'You promised me, you promised me a feel of your cock!' The old-fashioned glass syringes went flying.

"On another occasion (psychotherapists don't ordinarily have to do this) I was required to nasally insert into Sandy's stomach a feeding tube. Her terrified shrieks on that occasion are also burned into my brain. 'Take it off my nose!' she cried. 'Stop doing bad things to my nose!'

"By the end of the second summer Sandy showed no more signs of psychosis. But she was angry, wild and impulsive. Our contacts thereafter were by mail. One thing that upset me was that a few years later she had a baby. The child was black and she had no idea who the father could have been since there are rarely blacks in Sioux Lookout."

That is all that I know of Dr. Schweitzer's story. A few months after he had interrupted his psychiatric training, he also ended his psychotherapy supervision with me. I heard that he had gone to a faraway exotic country, took on a new artistic career, and that he would never return. Later still, I heard that he had returned to Toronto and was experimenting with very personal and unusual forms of psychotherapy. I'm sure that this was all very idealistic but, nevertheless, I disapproved. Had he become one of the blamers? Had he become a blamer despite his wide-ranging observational powers, his discovery of the analytic attitude in a foreign culture, and his shrewd awareness that the aboriginal culture, just beneath the westernized exterior, was vital and enduring?

7

Description and Redescription

> There is *only* perspective seeing, only a perspective "knowing"; and the *more* affects we allow to speak about one thing, the *more* eyes, different eyes, we can use to observe one thing, the more complete will our "concept" of this thing, our "objectivity" be.
>
> —Nietzsche

There is a conceit in psychology that we are scientists and that, like all scientists, we are making progress toward concrete truths about human nature. Would that it were true! More honestly, we should thank God that it is not true. Instead, I suggest that our job is to speak truths that are known in all cultures, albeit using languages not easily transferable across borders and across time. Although these truths are known to us by way of myth, sacred texts, and art, the psychotherapist's attempts to promote her ideas are forever under siege by purveyors of the trivial, the arbitrary, and of every current enthusiasm.

It is hard for me to understand why the title "scientist" is so crucial to the self-respect of so many psychotherapists. To be truthful, I am convinced that, insofar as she is a radical doubter, she is in the best scientific tradition. However, if someone affirms that she is not a scientist, I am content to accept that and to say that, instead, she occupies another honorable estate, that of rhetorician. Like all lovers of rhetoric, I like to use catchy quotes, especially quotes about literature, that bolster my arguments:

> Science progresses all the time, literature never. How should it "improve" over the centuries when its very subject is the enigma, the inaccessibility, of the human condition? [Kazin 1994, p. 73]

When we try to make our "science" progress, we ask the question why. With that question we announce our intention of reducing the patient's behavior to a form that we can comprehend, which usually means to reframe it in terms of our reality. For example, when we ask someone from another culture why they do something, we have great difficulty unless they explain it in terms of our culture.

Dr. Schweitzer (Chapter 6) spoke to a native who told him that, during the last winter, Jake Pembina had backed his snowmobile out of the shed and had killed a neighbor. They had taken the snowmobile out onto the lake, cut a hole in the ice, and dumped the snowmobile into the hole. When asked why this had been done, he said that the snowmobile had killed the neighbor. Dr. Schweitzer, dissatisfied with that culturally alien answer, persisted in his questioning. Jake Pembina, along with his friends, was nonplussed, and persisted in this type of answer.

Schweitzer then took another tack. In southern Canada, he explained, if someone is killed in a car accident, the driver is held responsible, and may well have to stand trial for a crime. Pembina and his friends found this to be preposterous and laughed uproariously. Further talk led to no meeting of the minds. Schweitzer was clever enough to realize that to him, explanation was only acceptable if framed in *his* terms of understanding. The natives suffered from the same cultural blindness. Although the natives agreed that the accident was caused, to them the agent of causation was different. In a more radical state of dissonance, one could imagine cultures in which even causes might not be invoked.

All of us are radically self-centered and expect that adequate knowledge requires explanations in terms of causes and in terms of particular causal agents. Other modes of knowledge are considered to be primitive, or just plain stupid. The recognition of this egocentricity is the centerpiece of the psychotherapist's thinking and is the reason why she is hesitant about explanatory systems. To be as accurate as possible, she aims to describe. By *describe* she does not mean mere description, as some would have it; *her* description, if done thoroughly and conscientiously, has a potency that, to the uninitiated, is not immediately obvious.

There is a second reason why the psychologist is keener on description than on explanation. Every explanation requires reduction of behavior to another sphere of existence. When psychotherapists try to explain, they all too often have recourse to things like drives, structures, concretized selves, and other metapsychological fictions. Such absolutes are anathema to the true psychologist who, although interested in such foundational explanations, is unwilling to grant them anything but temporary and metaphoric status.

To succumb to such explanations is, to the psychotherapist, to be distracted from the enigmatic and the problematic—puzzlers that she holds to be vital to any psychology that is worth its salt. Having been defined by me as a worry wart, she is also fretting about whether or not her descriptive effort will be so thin that it will turn out to be the feared mere description.

The greatest danger of thin description springs from misguided attempts at objectivism, a stance eminently suitable for mechanics and Newtonian physics, but useless for the psychologist and the anthropologist. At its worst, it is a purely phenomenalistic (as opposed to phenomenological) act that treats people like physical objects with the qualities of mass, dimension, color, taste, and smell. Such a description is carried out in a manner no different from the description of a desk or a sirloin steak. Such a flat portrait has absolutely nothing to do with psychology, but it is certainly objective! The psychologist, faced with such a description, will cry out, "What about *le plaisir*, *le désir*, and *la demande*? And what about *la demande impossible?*"

Objectivity sometimes works just fine for describing persons, for example, in the orthopedic clinic. Fixing bones, stanching the flow of blood, and correcting an imbalance of insulin require objectivity. The doctor would be ill-advised to spend time dreaming up novel metaphors for broken bones.

To be objective in this way in psychology is a kind of barbaric incomprehension of what persons are about. When teachers ask students of psychotherapy to be objective, they surely do not mean what they say. Nor is this what is meant when it is said that "she treats him like an object." In this latter instance it usually means that she is definitely treating him like a person but, without more information, we cannot know what category of person it is that she is turning him into. Although this is not really a matter of treating him as an object, we do sense that there is some sort of unkind treatment implied, which means that "treating him as an object" is a metaphor for mistreatment. Unfortunately, this metaphor is what has been called a dead metaphor since it is used as though it refers to a concrete truth.

To know what the speaker means, we need more facts or metaphors for what that speaker has in mind. Perhaps she means that he is being treated as an inferior (although he is not necessarily spatially below her)? Or perhaps he is being treated as a handy dildo (although he is not an elongated cylinder)? Does the speaker mean that he is being treated as an attractive decoration or as a ready source of cash? Decoration and cash are two more metaphors, since in psychology we are stuck (blessed?) with metaphors as our daily bread and butter (another metaphor). And in human affairs, you and I are helpless without them. Every statement I make, including this one, only adds to the storm of metaphors that you are plied with.

For another, and more detailed example of exhaustive—exhaustive and, hence, psychologically acceptable—description, my portrait of the genre "psychotherapist" in Chapter 1, may be of help. Another appearance of the thinking that I have in mind took place in my office, where I have a collection of horses made of wood, metal, straw, and ivory. A patient looked at them wistfully and said, "Those horses come in all shapes and sizes, but nobody ever says that any of them has a personality disorder." The patient was being a psychologist and decried the judgmental labeling of patients that is all too common. Since "borderline" is currently the commonest form of name-calling in use, the remark might have been even more telling had that epithet been used.

Many metaphors make for "thick description" and make for good psychology. And many model horses make for a good survey of the imago *horse*. Being locked into one metaphor is "thin description" and is the end of psychology. That is why psychotherapists are not traditional scientists but, instead, recognize science more thoroughly and more deeply than do many hard scientists.

I am always amazed when I read in the newspaper that it has been discovered that the universe is X billion years younger than was previously thought, or that the universe is expanding at such and such a rate. It seems to me that the universe is also being found out to be older than previously thought, and that it is shrinking fast. Don't these reporters know that they are talking about theories, that is to say, about metaphors for comprehending the universe? And do they not know that certain theories are valuable for this purpose and that others are valuable for that? That if one approaches the data one way, the universe looks like this, and that if one approaches the data another way, the universe looks like that? And do they not know that there will never be a "final" picture of the universe?

And, turning now to psychology, do we not all know that if we look at people this way, they are angels, and if we look at them that way, they are clearly devils? It is easy to see that children are lovable, and it is just as easy to see that they are cruelty incarnate. For those who have trouble with the latter point, and many of us do, Margaret Atwood's *Cat's Eye* provides a reminder of our childhood experiences.

Steiner (1958), in a discussion of the English translation of the Bible, illustrates my point exactly, that the Bible is the repository of a multiplicity of styles, metaphors, and language sources.

> It is with Tyndale that the English Bible attains the rather paradoxical glory of being more eloquent than some of the Hebrew and most of the Greek original. Where translation diminishes a text, it traduces; where it surmounts the original while yet being loyal to it, it transfigures. [p. 190]

All this multidimensionality is necessary because of the kaleidoscopic nature of persons. We cannot anticipate the long-time loner turning into the impulsive killer; the heterosexual friend becoming homosexual; the banker going to work in a winery. That versatility and unpredictability is both infuriating and wonderful. Psychologists love this about people; many others find it discomfiting.

In the 1960s I worked on a unit for very disturbed children, some of whom were autistic. It was well known to the staff that these autistic children only watched commercials on television. Like the rest of the human world, the action on television was unpredictable—except for the commercials. In their day-to-day life, these children liked light switches, telephone dials, and doorknobs, because, like television commercials, they were predictable. But something strange began to happen. We noticed that the autistic children began getting upset by the commercials and began avoiding them. We were initially puzzled but, suddenly, a staff member figured out what was going on.

The television programmers, it turned out, had changed the commercials. For a few weeks, the advertising was shown following a certain format and then, once the public had been educated to them, the commercials were run in an abbreviated form. The trained audience only needed a reminder in order to get their advertising fix and, since a short reminder was cheaper to produce, the commercials had been shortened. But the change gave the autistic children nervous fits. They became upset or avoided the commercials completely.

Psychology is, therefore, to be understood as the antifoundational science. In her clinical thinking, the psychotherapist declines to plant her feet anywhere except in the world of psychological dilemma. Her professional or business stance—her work setup—is quite different. As a practitioner, although prudent and humane, she acts in a highly businesslike way. But as a thinker, a psychologist, analyst, or philosopher, she disavows any ultimate truths, including any "business" truths. She believes as little in a fundamental human nature as she does in metapsychological and material facts. "Facts is precisely what there is not" (Nietzsche 1888, p. 481).

Her disavowal of facts, however, is impossible. But this is not because there is, after all, a world of facts that ultimately defeat her; it is just that she is repeatedly rendered "foundational" (metaphysical, metapsychological) by language. The very grammar of language guarantees that we will think of causes, that is to say, in terms of explanation.

> "And when the Lord saw that Leah was hated he opened her womb, but Rachel was barren." Just for that reason. It is an attempt at explanation, as good as another, a hypothesis, for we have no direct and authentic utterance of El Shaddai as to the meaning of this decree and doubtless one never existed. It would be proper, however, to reject the interpretation if I knew a better one; but since I do not, I prefer to consider this one as essentially correct. [Thomas Mann, 1934, p. 209]

It is hard to stay on the safer and more scientific ground of description because all statements are framed in causal form. For example, when we say "It is raining," what is the "it"? It ("it" again) is, obviously, merely a grammatical convention that pervades all language. When we say, "Why is he crying?", we expect a concrete causal answer. Like Descartes, we constantly say *cogito ergo sum*: there is thinking, therefore there is something that thinks. I suppose that God, if his poetic and multifarious nature is neglected, can become another simplistic "cause" of the universe.

A more fruitful question is the one typically asked by the psychotherapist: "Tell me more about the crying—and more and more, and furthermore, by way of my silence, I insist that there is always more that you can say about this crying." A proper answer, too, requires legions of metaphors—even though in ordinary life this may be impractical and unconventional. But for the psychotherapist, that impractical and unconventional approach is what is called for.

Why should language have come to take on this explanatory and causal form? A linguist might give a thoroughgoing answer to the question. I, only a psychotherapist, can assay only that causal thinking is very practical for building bridges, rocket ships, and sand castles. It is also fast and economical. But it is useless for understanding human psychology, for healing the soul, and for the artistic and poetic revitalization of the spirit. The Bushmen and we, the European barbarians (can anyone contest that we are barbarians after the events of this century?), alike, have urgent recourse to art and ritual.

As a consequence of all this dry but necessary intellectual worrying, there is a great sacrifice to be made by the psychotherapist. She must give up two of her most precious theoretical possessions. If we are to be describers only, and since motives and the unconscious are invisible and silent, the theory of motivation and of the unconscious must go. Even though this is my argument, I am going to be a very hard sell on this score. The notion of the unconscious is central, and the idea of motives is inextricably entwined with the unconscious. This means that a hundred years of psychoanalytic persuasion could be lost if this argument is not delicately made. Any sweeping injury to the notion of the unconscious and of motives can only be destructive to the difficult psychology that it is our fate to wield.

The *unconscious* and *motives*, as nouns, are members of the class of causes that I have disqualified from the psychological brotherhood. If reified—and they constantly are so reified—they become dead metaphors that stifle openness and imaginative thought. "Ah," says the naive commentator, "he is crying because he is mourning the end of his psychotherapy." Such a motive—mourning—is never explanatory. It is only illuminating. And, being additive and illuminating, it is never exhaustive. To reify a motive is to risk closing off the descriptive metaphors that will render an even deeper comprehension of what is going on. Does he weep in order to prompt the psychotherapist to tenderness? Does he weep to announce that, no, he does not want to clobber the therapist for having accomplished only a modest cure? Does he weep to re-create, and to bring back to life in himself, his emotionally honest father, now dead? To be just as emotionally false as his tragic mother? And so on.

The unconscious, although violently kept in abeyance, is understood otherwise as well. In every act, thought, and feeling, the unconscious, although subtle and disguised, is there to be seen. For example, the man who is exclusively good eventually gets on one's nerves. After a while, we begin to say of him that "he is so saccharine!" The therapist who is always understanding and whose comments consist of some version of "I know how you must feel" and "It must be terrible for you that . . . " soon comes to be experienced as false.

In addition to the dishonesty of portraying herself as purely virtuous, that is to say, as someone who cannot possibly exist, such a psychotherapist, with her perpetual pretense of kindness, imposes on her patient a guilt-inducing demand for reciprocal "goodness." How can he then show his unattractive side or, to be more straightforward about it, allow his evil, cowardice, and pride to be seen?

This reminds me of the proper answer to be made when a store clerk says, "Have a nice day." The response to such a sugary cliché is as follows: "No thanks, I have other plans." In other words, these ostensibly kind people display a patronizing, infantilizing, and condescending unkindness—even as they themselves think they are being good.

Their kindness is not caused by an unconscious hostile motive. Their kindness is, instead, to be understood as being a definitive fragment of meanness, although also kind and, most of all, claimed to be kindness. It is unconscious, but only in a descriptive sense. As long as motivational words and unconsciousness words are used descriptively, they pass muster because other metaphors are still allowed access to the field. But since motive and unconscious are nouns, they will be misused and abused forever. These are the eternal problems of language.

When we analyze a patient's symptoms or narratives, we are really only doing thorough, exhaustive, "thick" description. We are redescribing from another angle, usually by way of another vocabulary. Since prejudgment is inevitable, the psychotherapist must tend to her own bias, lest she unwittingly try to convert the patient to her universe rather than simply illuminating what her patient is displaying. That prejudgment is such that the injunction that I have just laid down is always doomed to failure. The psychotherapist must always work on the assumption that she will never do it right, and that she must be eternally skeptical of her own intentions.

The psychotherapist wants to get it right. She wants to describe the patient in terms as clear and as enlightening to him as she can manage. She wants to get at the unconscious, too. But she is in no hurry. The patient's story—and, to the psychotherapist, symptoms are stories—is primary. It must be known in exquisite detail, both by the patient and by the therapist. Often, the patient does not know the very story that he himself lives in. He has, it seems, never paid attention to it.

The psychotherapist's assignment (in addition to maintaining her psychotherapist's attitude of disinterest or once-removedness) is to interpret what the patient says. Interpretation is a difficult notion. It is a philosophical concept that spoils our usual innocence about truth and reality. We can never know the world as it truly is, says the psychological theorist. When we describe, we can do so only through our personal distorting lenses or our truth-creating lenses. Even when we do the recommended "thick description," we can never achieve an "I-am-a-camera" picture of a thing or of what a patient says to us. We can only give our personal interpretation.

Such knowledge is easily lost, particularly when we deal with precious words that we need but that can lead us into misunderstanding. One such word is *self*. Because it is a noun, it can distract us from our psychological assignment. For example, it is of the essence of the self—not that it is cohesive or fragmented—but that it stands in some reflective relation to itself. Thus, a statement of, say, self-fragmentation, is a way of reflecting upon oneself. Also, it is of the essence of the self that it deceives itself. Every thought position excludes all other thought positions. If we treat self descriptions otherwise, that is to say, as direct observations of an existential self, we are in danger of losing our psychological wit.

Both the patient's story and the psychotherapist's interpretation of the story are fundamentally framed by him and by her and, if the story at stake is the patient's claim that he is fragmented, the psychotherapist recognizes only that this is his way of thinking about himself. She would never fall into the trap of believing the patient to be transparent—to be a perfect transcriber of what he is made of.

The psychotherapist must feed back to the patient what he has initially reported to us. But, in view of our confinement to the world of interpretation, we are destined never to achieve this. No matter how carefully and accurately we feed back to our patient what he has told us, we will have changed things. When I commit to memory "Three Blind Mice," I will have changed it according to my own mode of capturing the world. It is wonderful to be in full possession of this emotionally loaded fragment of childhood. When we sing "Three Blind Mice" as a round, we are changing things explicitly. At that moment, we savor difference rather than sameness. That focus on difference is what happens later in the treatment when we redescribe—interpret—in surprising and altered terms. The important point is that, early on, feeding back to the patient something similar to what he has told us is vital. It's his story, after all. And do not underestimate the importance of repetition, even if we can never get it perfect. We never tire of what we have learned by heart.

> What's in a name? that which we call a rose
> By any other name would smell as sweet.

> Four score and seven years ago, our forefathers brought forth on this continent a new nation, conceived in liberty, and dedicated to the proposition that all men are created equal.

Thick description, redescription, and interpretation are the same thing. Despite any effort toward pure repetition that she may put into it, the psychotherapist is always redescribing. Eventually, she is trying to display the unconscious by interpreting what the patient says in terms that are surprising and contradictory to what was consciously intended. This deeper (but not better) form of interpretation, which is examined in depth in the next chapter, is easier said than done. If, for example, the tyrant behind the posture of victimhood is to be brought into the open, God help the psychotherapist who attempts to do so without a high level of skill. Victims are tyrannical in their revenge when one's timing or tact is not exquisite. The same thing goes for the resolutely tough and self-reliant patient. It is no mean feat to help him see his secret vulnerability and longing for tenderness. The contradictory repressed is the enemy of the patient and, since the psychotherapist is allied with the contradictory repressed, she is the enemy, too.

8

Interpretation

Proofs weary the truth.

—Georges Braque

The thick description that I have emphasized in the last chapter has, as its defining characteristics, an emphasis on thoroughness. Most commonly, thoroughness is achieved by way of a democratic abundance of metaphors. There is, however, a danger that description will be understood as a neglect of the theoretical. It would thereby place value only on surface and on the manifest, with a concomitant neglect of depth and the unconscious.

If I deny this, it is possible that the opposite will happen. It is all too easy to dismiss obvious behavior as superficial and as merely a screen for the more important latent unconscious. This means that in contradistinction to my cautionary words, the interpretation of the unconscious—non-reproductive interpretation—is often considered to be central, crucial, and revelatory in a much more profound way than is the interpretation of that which is more obvious. And, since the forgetful neglect of the unconscious is an ever present danger, those who worry about this may be quite right to do so.

To nail down the centrality of the interpretation of the unconscious, some like to call it "interpretation proper" or "Freudian interpretation," as opposed to interpretation of the manifest, which they would prefer to call "preparatory" or "preliminary" interpretation. I agree with these commentators without wanting to suggest that reproductive or "surface" interpretation is a lesser breed, or that one ought to get it over with in order to get on with what really counts.

Reproductive interpretation is relatively easy. It expands consciousness and illuminates what the patient already knows. It adds nuances, illustrates patterns, and awakens the patient to the self-reflective method. Indeed, it is the central maneuver in many forms of psychotherapy. To display the array of angles, aspects, and details—in short, the metaphors—of a life, encounters little resistance. It is interesting to patients and sometimes even fun to realize just how unique and complex they are.

But to display what is unconscious is quite another matter. That deeper aspect of our patient is repressed; it is violently expelled from the patient's world of knowledge. Much of the time, its illumination is heavy intellectual labor; sometimes its display is an interesting exercise in shrewd detective work; and at still other times it is the product of unexpected hunches. In contrast to reproductive interpretation, the interpretation of the unconscious is sporadic, piecemeal, and forever eluding us.

Once we have grasped a piece of it, it is just as likely that it will slip out of our minds again. The contents of the unconscious are fascinating and repellent. They are both the desired topic and what is feared. Consciously, both the patient and the psychotherapist want to know about the unconscious motives that lie behind the symptoms and the suffering but, willy-nilly, both flee from it ubiquitously.

> If the book we are reading does not wake us, as with a fist hammering in our skull, why then do we read it? So that it shall make us happy? Good God, we would also be happy if

> we had no books, and such books as make us happy we could, if need be, write ourselves. But what we must have are those books which come upon us like ill-fortune, and distress us deeply, like the death of one we love better than ourselves, like suicide. A book must be an ice-axe to break the sea frozen inside us. [Kafka, quoted by Steiner 1958, p. 67]

Stefani Clark, a young impoverished artist, spoke despairingly of her unsatisfactory life. She longed for a life in which all her time could be devoted to her art or, better, to pursue her art in a remote locale, populated by "the simple people." A remote native community seemed inspiringly appealing. How, she wondered, could she quench her longing? Despite the psychotherapist's words of cautious skepticism, the patient was convinced that her utopian longings made good sense. The simple and happy people really did exist, because she had seen them and visited with them.

One day she spoke with great emotion about her love of the artist Modigliani. The ethereal and wholesome faces of the painted subjects filled her with happiness. She disliked intensely the prints of Egon Schiele that she had seen in her therapist's office. They troubled and repelled her, she said. The therapist's comment—her hunch—noted just what the differences were between Modigliani and Schiele. Modigliani's portraits were sweet and pure; Schiele's were raw and almost profane.

The therapist remembered, too, that Ms. Clark's pots were uncanny portrayals of vulvas, at least to the insider's eye. Did Modigliani paint vulvas that were pure and sweet, the psychotherapist wondered? And did Schiele paint explicit and dangerous-looking vulvas? It is, indeed, true that Schiele's portraits of women often show glimpses of disturbingly dangerous, yet vulnerable, vulvas.

A few days later, Ms. Clark brought to the therapist a copy of a magazine with reports of a major survey of American sexual habits. Like many people in the survey, she said, she had been very sexually naive. At the age of 18 she had not known that she had a "hole." She was shocked when a friend told her this news. She realized now that Modigliani's women have no holes and that Schiele's women have enormous, wound-like holes.

What the patient's words illustrate is the universal ambivalence in our culture (in all cultures?) about the female genitals. Such ambivalences are very widespread and we humans are of two minds about everything. But, in the case of sex, the double registration is troublesome and capricious. And, in the case of the female genitals, that ambivalence is prominent and conscious. Why that should be so, I do not pretend to know.

This is how the phenomenon typically manifests itself: Both men and women have a conception of the woman's genitals as unattractive, as having a smell, as disgusting, unsightly, and repellent. At the very same time, the female genitals are found to be tender, appealing, luscious, wonderfully succulent, and excitingly aromatic. These contradictory imaginings are variously represented in different persons. To some, the former truths predominate or are exclusive; to others, the opposite is true. To still others, different times, different circumstances, and different moods evoke different responses.

Ms. Clark, for example, was determined that she was sexually repellent and that the desired state of sexual attractiveness existed only in the other—in Modigliani, in her world of art, and with "the simple people." This, despite the fact that it was clear to her therapist that she had been a beloved, adorable child. More than that, her therapist said, in the patient's mind, she had been a sexually formidable youngster and easily outshone both her mother and her maiden aunt. In other words, her psychological status as the "unfulfilled one" served to relieve a terrible fear, namely, the fear that she was loved beyond propriety, and so loved at great expense to the happiness of the other women in the family home.

Her solution to this moral unfairness was a semipermanent perception of herself in which she was the possessor only of a "hole" or "crack" (take note of her choice of unappealing language), and not of a wondrous sexual treasure. The debased genitals were a defensive vision that contradicted her triumphant femininity.

At about this time in the treatment, Ms. Clark began seeing her young man again, having ended things with him a few months before. Now, however, their sexual moments together were, according to Ms. Clark's reports, a world of wonder. What had previously been "the hole" (the crack, the gash) had unexpectedly been transformed into the delicious and the glorious. In her past life, including her past married life, the world of sexuality had ranged from disappointing to frankly oppressive. She wondered of her therapist how such a change could have come to pass. To her, it was akin to a miracle. That miracle, she implied, was a product of their psychotherapeutic work together. Could that, indeed, be true? Can a shift in the moral attitude to sex occur as a result of merely talking? The young psychotherapist wondered to herself whether such a moral shift could possibly endure. Does the change depend on the continuing presence of the benign conscience/therapist, she wondered, and will the "cure" disappear when the patient is on her own?

This fragment of a case history exemplifies the interpretation of an important part of the unconscious. Even when the psychotherapist wants to stay very much on the surface, she will inevitably change and redescribe what the patient has told her. In this case, the therapist has done more than this and has created a radically new interpretation of what was going on in a patient.

What she did was to interpret and bring into consciousness a fragment of what, on some moral grounds, has been warded off by the patient. The patient's devalued genitals came to be understood in new terms. Now it was a proud and precious aspect of the patient's desire. In other words, what had been unconscious was reappropriated to consciousness.

Without intending to be too definitive about this, one could say that the therapist has performed the classical interpretive act. But no single interpretive understanding of the matter at hand is permitted. Whatever is interpreted can be reinterpreted. In fact, everything must and should be reinterpreted. No interpretation is definitive.

What is interpretation? In the previous chapter, I suggested that what is called for is "thick description." Now I say that the psychotherapist's crucial therapeutic act is interpretation. Every descriptive act is, if one thinks about it, the therapist's interpretation of what she sees. Description and interpretation are the same thing, but the psychotherapist strongly prefers the word *interpretation*. *Description* has a subtle implication that something can be accurately observed, and hence accurately described, but the psychotherapist balks at this suggestion. *Interpretation* specifies that the observed is variable, depending on circumstances, mental set, and who is doing the observing.

Whether a dancer is judged to be a piece of vulgar trash, or, contrariwise, to be a woman wittily enjoying her youthful body, is a matter of interpretation. Is a balanced budget a capitalistic rip-off or the salvation of our economy? Is thinking about psychology as I do the ultimate in intellectual sophistication or is it intellectual phony-baloney? Or is it an exercise in nihilistic solipsism? Urgently important? Irrelevant? Depressing? Inspiring? It depends on how my psychological thinking is interpreted.

Even though interpretation is all that we humans have—everything is an interpretation, after all—in a strangely paradoxical way, "all that we have" is a secondary phenomenon. Interpretations are always secondary, are things "made," and are, therefore, fictions. It is not that they are false but only that they are "as-if" or metaphoric. The paradox comes in because, although interpretations are always secondary, they are also all that we have. There is nothing else. The real, to the psychotherapist, is unknowable. Our psychic realities, our interpretations, are it. Just as patients live exclusively in their personal psychological worlds, so do we, their therapists.

Are there no truths that we can agree on? I suppose that we could all agree that the earth beneath our feet is solid, but such truths are banalities, platitudes, and clichés. Such truths are never controversial and in no way define who one is. Truths that everyone believes in are relatively uninteresting. But truths that matter, that are of interest, are those that must be sustained against opposition, often severe or violent opposition. For psychological purposes, all precious truths and disturbing truths are interpretations. Even obvious and banal truths are interpretations, but I am not philosopher enough to make the argument to my own satisfaction.

I hope that by now I have made clear my point about the importance of repetition. The psychotherapist must awaken the patient to his manifest stance on life, to his patterns of behavior, and his way of constructing and construing the world. Now I wish to turn more explicitly to the discovery of the unconscious.

Psychotherapy focuses on unmeasureables, with a certain intriguing irrationality (or a strange rationality) that never disappears. Nor should it ever disappear. Ambiguities, contradictions, and peculiarities are, to the psychotherapist, of the essence. People are fated to forever live as creatures divided within themselves. The first imaginable logical operation has to be a binary opposition. No psychological universe is possible without two opposing terms. For example, a universe can exist if the world is divided into the edible and the inedible. Anything can be categorized in these terms and therefore located in such a universe. Although boring, it constitutes a complete universe.

There are many other simple binary oppositions, such as self-other, good-bad, love-hate, male-female, and phallic-castrated. These neat distinctions would be wonderful for the psychotherapist if only we strange humans were as consistent (boring?) as this. For better or worse, this is not how we do it. Our oppositions get all tangled up. In our language we are never finished confounding things. *Cleave* means that things adhere together and, contrariwise, means that things split apart. *Secret* means to hide but also means to give off. *Siccus* means dry, but *succus* means juicy. This reversibility of meaning reflects something fundamental about how we humans think.

There is a reverberatory quality, a back-and-forth quality, to our thinking that is central to our notions of conscious and unconscious. But it is also very obvious in our conscious day-to-day life. Isn't dancing a back-and-forth act? Doesn't lovemaking share the same characteristics? Even a good orator and her audience communicate back and forth, as do the psychotherapist and her patient. Every sadomasochistic pairing counts on a similar dialectic as does every occasion of hysterical contagion in a rock concert audience.

Theoretical words for these phenomena abound in the psychotherapeutic literature. Identification, fusion and flux, projection and introjection, and mirroring—all are words that struggle to capture the strange reverberatory thinking of all persons. It is seen very dramatically in the psychotherapist's daily work. Such binary oppositions are seen most remarkably in persons with eating disorders. These patients, in the unique dialogue that constitutes psychotherapy, talk, for example, of dead or living persons who they protect or contain by carrying them within themselves; of internal penises that they can donate to depleted others in order to revive or save them; of bodily contents that can be robbed. There is a madness in such thinking but, in another example of opposites, it can also be seen as the source of artistry, creativity, and genius. These various unusual forms of thinking cannot be measured. They all turn into their opposites. Such is the psychodynamic mode of thought, recognizing, as does quantum physics, a multiplicity of mutually contradictory universes.

There is a wonderful madness in all of this. What we are tempted to call madness is—in another exemplification of opposites—also what is most vital, most creative, and most human. In his theory of relativity, Einstein has taught us that if speed is considered to be an absolute, then space and time are relative. The corollary is if space and time are absolutes, then speed is relative.

If I apply the same logic to certain human affairs, I end up with peculiar ideas like this: if you are pricked by a pin, you will feel a pain. The pin causes the pain. But can one turn the logic around and say the pain causes the pin? After all, the pain was felt first, led one to search for and find the pin. But surely this is madness. And yet it is precisely the mode of thinking that Einstein used. Space and time are absolutes and speed is relative—correct? No, said Einstein, speed is absolute and space and time are relative. These various unusual forms of thinking cannot be measured. This is the mode of thought that the psychotherapist wants to enter into, because it recognizes a multiplicity of mutually contradictory universes. It makes possible the infinite contradictoriness that cultures bequeath to us.

Many writers have emphasized the developmental aspects of such processes, arguing that they represent early and "primitive" stages of development. The psychotherapist, in her pure state, would emphasize that such processes are ubiquitous, normal, and necessary. In addressing you, the reader, she would say that she cannot do so effectively without putting herself inside of you, that is, identifying with you and imagining how you will receive her words. She must speak for herself and, if she wishes to communicate effectively, she must anticipate what you will hear.

As the psychotherapist displays to herself and to her patient the "repetitive"—as she reproduces the patient's world interpretively—she comes to be in possession of a series of stories. Such stories are the important material upon which the therapist depends as she does her work, often referred to by other, more technical, terms: the patient's *narrative*, the *manifest*, or the *manifest content*. All of the manifest is considered to be motivated behavior. All manifest stories are a response to the problem of hubris. Ms. Clark, who had the hubris to believe that she could outshine mother and aunt, achieved in her manifest life a fitting response: she was a sexual dud. The punishment fits the crime or, as the psychotherapist says when she wishes to be technical, the solution devised by the patient is in accordance with the *lex talionis*. In the modern vernacular, one would say that "what goes around comes around."

In all things, thought the Greeks, there is a balance and harmony that is not to be disturbed. And therefore, if such a sense of proportion is expected in all things, then every psychotherapeutic venture should participate in this universe of good sense, of *bürgerliche* (not bourgeoise) values. No matter what explosiveness characterizes the therapeutic adventure, overall it is anchored in a code of propriety within which the temptations of hell can be examined. For those who commit the sin of Pride—the first of the Seven Deadly Sins—the Greek world offered death. The Fates, who spin out the thread of human life, cut that thread of life when the time has come to die. And for those who trespass beyond the bounds of human propriety, the solution is premature death. W. H. Auden's two Fates speak this way:

> Wiser not to ask just what has occurred
> To them who disobeyed our word;
>   To those
> We were the whirlpool, we were the reef,
> We were the formal nightmare, grief
>   Or the unlucky rose . . .
>
> The sky is darkening like a stain;
> Something is going to fall like rain,
>   And it won't be flowers . . .
>
> We've been watching you over the garden wall
>   For hours:
> The sky is darkening like a stain;
> Something is going to fall like rain,
>   And it won't be flowers.
>
> [Auden 1927–1932, p. 63]

Hubris has to do with the fulfillment of one's potential. The usual social requirement is that we should limit ourselves to the expected, to the norm, and to the cliché. If a man will not fulfill the expectations of his father, he violates the family law, the cultural law, the oedipal law. It is hubris to believe that one is exempt, and that one can do other than what is expected. This is the sin of pride and the penalty is hell or, even worse, psychological hell. Hell is for the pure of heart. Only he who believes in goodness can suffer. After all, one can only sin against one's own purity. "Thus it is arranged," Thomas Mann (1934) teaches us, "and hell is quite certainly inhabited only by the better sort; which is not just—but then, what is our justice?" (p. 1023).

Freud was right to avoid reading Nietzsche. Had he done so, he would have found an uncanny closeness to his own thinking. The danger of knowing one's own depths is the key to the psychotherapist's work and no one described those dangers better than Nietzsche (1886):

> Anyone who has looked deeply into the world may guess how much wisdom lies in the superficiality of men. The instinct that preserves them teaches them to be flighty, light, and false. . . . whoever stands . . . in need of the cult of surfaces must at some time have reached *beneath* them with disastrous results. [p. 261]

The patients who I have discussed have achieved for themselves a similar punishment-fits-the-crime solution. The word *solution* indicates that what the patient calls his problem, the psychotherapist calls the solution. The problematic symptoms and way of life of the patient are the response-solution to a hidden problem, a hidden conflict that is only revealed by analytic labor. Such labor has much in common with detective work. To a Sherlock Holmes, there is a crime, and the perpetrator is to be found. Then a judgment and penalty will be imposed. In the case of the psychotherapist, what she comes upon is the judgment of wrongdoing and the penalty. The criminal—the patient—is known but the psychological crime must be found out.

Socrates did the same sort of thing. Although he was a cheerleader for the "logos"—for logic and rationality—he spent his time demonstrating its fallibility. Like any psychotherapist, Socrates was an underminer of belief, especially of the glib and the conventional.

And all of this is familiar. If the Messiah comes, he must die and be lost to us. Whether it is concretely true or not, we live with the notion that the artist, in proportion to his talent, succumbs to his TB, his AIDS, or his drug habit. Thomas Mann, throughout his writings, was preoccupied by the price paid by the artist for his hubris, that is to say, his seizure and display of knowledge forbidden to ordinary mortals. Similarly, the triumph of Oedipus must end with his self-defeat. Never mind the grand triumphs of history. The empires eventually fade and recede.

The psychotherapist's patients are forever developing new stories, new narratives, to quell their disquietude. These narratives, these defenses, are their positions of healing. Their fears and torments are appeased, cured, and solved by way of symptoms, their style of life (also a symptom), and by their dreams, parapraxes, and achievements. Behind those manifest worlds lie the unconscious crimes. The ostensible struggle to improve, to progress, to find a better way of life, are all, says the stubbornly skeptical psychotherapist, self-deceptions. He who strives simply announces to the world and to himself that he is in the wrong place. The idea is not to do better tomorrow—the idea is that he is in the wrong place now. The striving only underlines his unhappy psychological place of residence.

Here is another typical scenario. A depressed, sick, frightened, and self-defeating woman turns out to have the unconscious conviction that she has a profound sexual effect on men. This, she is sure, is why her young brother died. "Obviously," says she, pointing to her unhappy current life, "these sexual powers cannot possibly exist in me. I am stupid, histrionic, and 'brain-damaged' and have resolutely made sure that no other idea about me can exist. I am much reassured by this because, relative to me, men are strong, and certainly none could find interest in a pathetic sicko like me. Just the same, to make absolutely sure that I am never misread to be sexually potent,

I am utterly devastated when men speak to me. That's how I can continue my reassurance to the world that I am not hurtful, competitive, and overwhelmingly seductive."

In her pursuit of the interpreted unconscious, the psychotherapist encounters many a headache. When she reads the professional literature or hears her colleagues talking, she is uneasily aware that there are strong opinions about what she should do in the clinical situation. She is liable to hear comments such as:

> What is the best or correct thing for the psychotherapist to do?
>
> How does she decide how to intervene?
>
> What is the correct interpretation to make?

The questions are badly posed. They imply that the technique of psychotherapeutic work can be prescribed. In a weak sense, I suppose that it can be. But, in a much stronger sense, the psychotherapist is inclined to think these questions postscriptively rather than prescriptively.

> Why did I speak of this? And why at this time?
>
> Why did I say this so emphatically? With such cunning cleverness? So charmingly? So cautiously?

The psychotherapist's approach is post hoc in principle and never in the service of "doing it the right way." Apart from the professional and business arrangements, doing it the right way is a product of questioning the reasons for her every psychotherapeutic move. Should she ever succumb to the belief that she "knows," she would, in her own eyes, no longer be a psychotherapist. Her psychological and philosophical commitment is to never be committed, to never be one of the thought tyrants who "know."

One of the innocent-sounding injunctions that is regularly foisted upon the psychotherapist is that she should work toward and encourage the development of a therapeutic alliance. The therapist craves cooperation from her patient, but this does not mean that she believes that this should be striven for. After all, such an attempt to develop a therapeutic alliance can only mean that she wishes to censor certain states of mind in her patient.

My critics will probably say that I am misrepresenting them. Actually, they will argue, they want to know of the same unsavory elements in the patient that I do. But "elements" are not unsavory states of mind. The latter are elemental rather than being "elements" in a more extensive and perhaps more palatable whole. What they wish is that the patient should be in a state of mind in which, although the unsavory can appear, he can at the same time appreciate what is appearing on the psychotherapeutic stage. What is unsavory, they will imply, is an aspect of his person. The sensible, background person, the core of the patient, with his fragile but salvageable awareness, will, in the context of the therapeutic alliance, keep things in perspective. From that vantage point he will be in a position to integrate knowledge and to disengage from madness.

In contrast, I believe that, under such circumstances, the patient will not know and be possessed by the unconscious in its full, mad, reality. My hope for the patient is that he will be radically aware of the great affront to himself that will be revealed if only he (and I) are brave enough. Even though this is what the psychotherapist wants, she succeeds only partially, intermittently, and reluctantly. She, like her patient, is reluctant about the very thing that she wants. To keep a sensible perspective on things can only render insights even more pallid and more intellectualized.

Here is a remark that the psychotherapist might make to a very cooperative, good patient. Note that there is no congratulatory attitude afforded to what some might call a "good therapeutic alliance":

> Why is it that our work together is so typically agreeable?

And here is the same question/interpretation stated more boldly:

> Why is there so often a flirtatious element in the way in which we deal with one another?

These comments by the psychotherapist are not yet interpretations. They are an introduction to the idea of curiosity about conscious and unconscious behavior. Then the psychotherapist begins to address what is unconscious.

> Could we thereby be guaranteeing that nothing ungainly or unpleasant will go on between us?

Or, instead, she could say:

> One can see that both of us are determined that nothing negative or hurtful should happen here.

I doubt very much that anyone would find fault with this kind of psychotherapeutic commentary. But the psychotherapist is determined that everything is open to reinterpretation. Even if a cohort of psychotherapists could reach a consensus that these are proper interpretations, another therapist might offer a minority opinion: "Why is this therapist so busy looking for the negative unconscious?" she might say. "Is she fleeing from the dangers of affection, of love, eroticism and sexuality?"

Two contradictory interpretations. How disturbing for the ardent rationalist and yet, how wonderful. Is that disturbance and wonder a reflection of the disturbing genius of the human mind? The psychotherapist embraces the fact that both interpretations are correct. As far as traditional science is concerned, I can only say that consensus is not at all scientific when it comes to matters psychological. Is there, perhaps, consensus that the variability and ambiguity of psychotherapeutic activity illuminates, and that, when there is consensus on one interpretation to the exclusion of others, the consenters are psychologically missing the point?

Looking for the "correct" interpretation is a prescription. It is a little like a prescription for composing a symphony or writing a poem. Interpretation and psychotherapeutic practice is, by definition, postscriptive rather than prescriptive.

Even when we are enjoined to be empathic, our enjoiners are barking up the wrong tree. No matter how hard she tries, the psychotherapist could never follow this injunction. The best she could manage would be a false kindness. Here is how the psychotherapist makes her point against what is, after all, simply another prescription:

1. Empathy is an intuitive ability possessed by all people and the psychotherapist will therefore be empathic willy-nilly. For those who doubt this, I refer them to the definition of empathy in Dilthey (1894) and Husserl (1929).
2. The confidence man, not at all helpful, has empathy for his victims, which he uses for purposes of deceiving. Should we use our empathic abilities in this way?
3. Psychotherapists would be wise to claim that, in principle, empathy must always be accurate *and* mistaken—just as is true of the earlier proposed interpretations. This is so because, as in every human act, there are always unconscious motives inextricably entwined with every act of empathic understanding. Even the confidence man, supposedly out to profit from his actions, has other, usually self-defeating motives in play as well.

When we hear the prescriptive admonition "psychotherapists should be empathic," we should translate the injunction into something like this: "Psychotherapists are empathic like all other persons but, having thought carefully about psychological matters, have become acutely aware that unconscious motives eternally corrupt our empathic understanding." The latter formulation is self-reflective rather than prescriptive.

Unending interpretation, even though I am promoting it, is a prescription for trouble. First, it is experienced by some as a kind of diver's intoxication, a "rapture of the deep." To others, it is a plunge into Satanic chaos. Intoxication, they fear, leads to a blissful wallowing in the interpretive work and, contrariwise, "chaos fear" is liable to lead to psychotherapeutic retreat. If the psychotherapist can avoid the retreat from that uncanny unknown, she is still faced with the second question posed by infinite interpretive possibilities. How, she must ask herself, can one come to a psychotherapeutic ending? Does one analyze forever?

The relief of symptoms does not seem to be a reliable guide, because symptoms disappear quickly. The psychotherapist's shamanic exercise seems to require more than symptom relief. At this juncture, the scientific practitioner could find herself to be in big trouble. What comes to her rescue are the practicalities of the psychotherapeutic situation. For whatever the reasons, the psychotherapist finds that termination comes along just about when it is expected.

Time and money play a role. The payoff no longer seems to be worth the effort. The cultural tradition urges that the time to stop has come. With students of psychoanalysis, the treatment, with great regularity, goes on for five years. Persons from backgrounds of limited education stop much sooner. The psychotherapist must be very careful not to fall into the potential judgmental trap that looms when one ponders such a differential. This is a matter of cultural expectation; what counts as valuable, good, and proper for psychoanalytic students versus what counts as valuable, good, and proper for those with limited education.

Unfortunately for those who crave a clear statement of how to do it, psychotherapy is about contradictoriness, the awful, and the unpredictable, or as Freud called it, the "plague."

I have tried to demonstrate that interpretation has to do with, first, the reproduction of what the patient tells us and, second, the unearthing of hidden, unconscious meanings. There is a third important element in the psychotherapist's interpretive actions. As she looks for a reproducible pattern, and for unconscious motives, she discovers important causes. Let us suppose that she has been able to display the patient's personal way of negotiating the oedipal dilemma. Even if she is inclined to allow that there are, indeed, causes for the patient's state of mind, these causes are forbidden any explanatory status that is final, reductionistically complete, or exhaustive. And even when she does, tentatively and experimentally, allow a cause to stand, she quickly discovers something else.

To her great interest, just as it was of great interest to Freud, she finds that the cause now is in existence between her and her patient. In other words, the oedipal dilemma is now alive and urgent in the therapeutic situation. What she had been prepared to cautiously acknowledge as a cause now has become a dialectical program between two people. As the psychotherapist does her archeological excavation, that pursuit becomes a transference-countertransference dialogue.

The love life of Ms. Clark, who was described at the beginning of this chapter, eventually blossomed. But that blossoming, not unexpectedly, prompted new anxieties. Soon, the (female) therapist came to be an object of worry. Ms. Clark worried that the psychotherapist had no ring on her finger, looked drawn rather than glowing (Ms. Clark, of course, was glowing), and seemed increasingly to be down in the dumps. Ergo, the cause of the patient's woes is suddenly an "in-your-face" manifest event. At the same time, it has become an event caused by what?

This dialectical reality is the transference. It is not, as the previous paragraph might suggest, a turn of events that comes along by and by. The transference format of the psychotherapeutic situation is there from the very beginning. As the treatment continues, the transference narrative unfolds unpredictably. Furthermore, in keeping with the psychotherapist's theoretical position, transferences are always talked about in two registers: there are always conscious and unconscious transference stories.

Transference refers to the model interpersonal configurations by way of which people structure and understand the social world, and to the concrete and vivid social realities characteristic of a particular individual. These transference realities are defined by psychotherapists as making up both the conscious truth world of the patient and, simultaneously, his warded off and unconscious truth world. Transference is ubiquitous and eternal and, rather than being static, is narrative and progressive in nature. There is, for every person, an array of typical narratives, each of which is constituted of previous life narratives, and each of which is vividly populated by psychological reincarnations of important persons from the past. The vividness of these reincarnations is facilitated by the permissiveness of the treatment situation, and the presence of the unobtrusive and neutral therapist.

The psychotherapist has no thought that the transference is a problem or that the patient should be cured of his transference. To think that would only be a misunderstanding of what is going on. As a result of the psychotherapy, the nature of the transference may change. The therapist, however, has no agenda of change in mind as she watches the transference story unfold. She just sticks to the business of making interpretations about what is going on. Her goal is never explicit change, but only to help the patient to know himself better.

The transference is an instrument of understanding. Every relationship is fundamentally structured by its past history, and that structuring is indelible. If a patient changes, this only means that the relationship with the psychotherapist has been added to the past repertoire. Future relationships will be different, but the past, in principle, is the same. This is not to deny the fact that the past is re-created, revised, and reinvented; a new past—the past with the psychotherapist—has been added.

Transference has nothing to do with being "normal" or "neurotic" (the psychotherapist does not distinguish), or with whether or not the person is a patient. Transference is a universal characteristic of persons. It is never resolved in the sense of "going away." Instead, it is re-solved, solved again—and again.

Patients get angry—"transference anger"—at their therapists, sometimes overtly and sometimes subtly and unwittingly. Young psychotherapists commonly say to the patient that he is angry. Such a statement is banal, boring, and unhelpful, because everyone is angry. The only helpful thing the psychotherapist can do is to promote insight into her patient's personal way of being angry, what the angry narrative is that is being enacted, and what is being denied and masked by being angry in this way, at this time, under these circumstances. The most striking and common circumstance is when anger is the patient's way of guaranteeing that friendliness, tenderness, and eroticism toward the psychotherapist will not appear. Similarly, the erotic is a wonderful way of not knowing about hatred and scorn.

The odd psychotherapist that I am inventing is also the "perfect" therapist. She is an impossible character because no mortal can truly achieve such psychological equanimity. In her perfect equanimity she has to infuriate. What else could one do with such a conscientious, diligent, and fair-minded creature? She is bound to induce guilt in her patients.

Although not perfect by any means, many highly trained psychotherapists work hard, think hard, and don't judge. Unfortunately, most believe that they work hard, think hard, and don't judge. Since psychotherapists are sinners, weaklings, and cowards—just like everybody else—that belief is dangerous. It is inclined to be virtue-claiming belief. The guilt-inducing act of the virtuous sheds fault and relocates it in the other. This illustrates that the transference is just as alive in the therapist as it is in the patient. In psychotherapists it is called the countertransference.

The blame-shedding psychotherapist is only another example of how we can relocate pieces of ourselves in someone else. This psychological trick is common in the depressed who, in contrast to the usual shedding of blame, are liable to do the opposite. *Their* typical maneuver is to donate virtue outside of themselves. They claim the unattractive for themselves and expend much energy announcing how worthless, hurtful, and downright stupid they are. In fact, the essence and the core of depression is this resolute self-vilification.

Hand in hand with their self-abuse, the depressed are donors of virtue. Others are good and deserving. They are undeserving of the hurtful presence of the depressed virtue-donor. Anna Karenina, Madame Bovary, and Hamlet's Ophelia, are all marvels of self-reduction and the elevation of the other. These women are particular experts at the elevation of men. This is the classical case of penis envy, that is, the skillful exercise of a pathetic falsehood—that men are better endowed than women. Despite the histrionics of the know-nothings, Freud was correct about our paternalistic culture's invitation to women that they should aggrandize men. When Freud declared this to be a final interpretation of the psychology of women, he was in error. No final truth is to be accepted.

The wonderful opposites of Ophelia and her psychological sisters are three other women, Lady Macbeth, Salomé, and Electra, claimers of proud potency. They are wonderful nondepressives, although, in their own ways, wonderfully self-injurious. The psychotherapist is ever alert to the patient's relocation of aspects of himself. Some are net donors; others are net claimers. Some relocate evil, some relocate the good. All have their various reasons for doing so.

In the case of one male patient, what was disavowed was softness and vulnerability. He had difficulty achieving orgasm, partly, he thought, because he was convinced that his girlfriend had been sexually loose before he had met her. Through a series of mental associations, he came to equate Saabs (the automobile), sobs, weakness, and looseness. To have an orgasm meant that he had to let go, to be passive, and, to coin a phrase, be "loose." Surely he was not loose! And not a passive sissy. "Loose" was her, his girlfriend. Sexuality, vulnerability, and orgasms were in her and not in him.

A woman had a similar problem. She always managed to pick a fight with her husband just prior to lovemaking, although for a long time she was unaware of this. One day her therapist, having forgotten a detail from the previous appointment, asked her to remind him and confessed that he had forgotten. The psychotherapeutic moment was one of warmth, so the psychotherapist was taken aback when the patient said, "You're always such a dork on that topic." She wanted no mutuality with the therapist either. In other words, she picked a fight so that she and the therapist could not "have orgasms" together. Nor, some months later, could she have an agreeable, "orgasmic" relationship with her new employer.

As the psychotherapist's mind flits from scene to scene, from narrative to narrative, new psychological angles come to her attention. Most commonly, the patient tells of the specific and the concrete. Sometimes unwittingly, and sometimes intentionally, the therapist's mind will drift to the opposite. When the patient is concretely ruthless, the therapist thinks of her patient as a reincarnation of the general, the mythological, and the historical. Harold Macmillan's "night of the long knives" comes to her mind, as does the story of Alexander cutting the Gordian knot, and of Tamar's determination to bear the seed of Israel. The patient's specific leads to the typical (or archetypical), the caricature, the stereotype, and the general.

When the patient is intellectual, abstract, and theoretical, the therapist thinks in the opposite way. Now she is inclined to nail down what the patient is doing at the moment, especially in the transference. "Why," she asks "do you speak vaguely of 'people,' and not name anyone? Why the terribly boring word *anger* when you really mean that you want to humiliate your employer, rape your wife, expose your father? What, after all, could you possibly mean when you say, 'I should have expressed my feelings?' Do you mean that you should have yelled and screamed; had a tantrum; fallen to the ground in a fit?"

She reverses her field when patients insist on defining themselves nonspecifically, for example, as creatures of history and mythology. "I guess that I am just another siren who likes to turn men on." Is she just a siren? This, after breaking up a marriage? The therapist cautiously, cautiously, pushes for the concrete. "Is it possible that part of you got a kick out your powers—that you were glad that his wife suffered?" And, on other occasions, she might be able to say, "That time you put the dagger in her heart, and twisted it."

More commonly, the psychotherapist avoids directly specifying that the unattractive is in the patient. Instead, she focuses on the defensive elements involved in the abstract and the mythological. "If it is a siren that has broken up this marriage, then you were not the agent of these events." Or, "The power of the mythological created this turn of events. You have been a spectator on these untoward happenings."

Archetypes are alive and well in all of us. To be an interpreter, the psychotherapist need not fulfill all the requirements of the archetypal shamanic priest. She needs no incense, ritual sacrifice, or holy water; nor does she need to froth at the mouth or roll her eyes. Plain interpretive talk will do. But that does not mean that she is not an incarnation of Merlin or of Zarathustra for, more powerfully than she may imagine, she is one of them. The overtones of the general, the typical, and the archetypal inhabit every psychotherapist, just as archetypes inhabit the mad, the artist, and the priest. More powerfully than any of us imagine, we are enactors of archetypal scripts. There is an eternal oscillation between the specific and the general that informs every psychotherapeutic interpretation. Indeed, it must inform every psychotherapeutic and every human behavioral moment.

There is a fourth characteristic of interpretation: it is a reading and interpretation of messages or, better, a reading of signifiers. All that the psychotherapist ever knows is the words and signs conveyed to her by the patient. The topic of language, signs, and signifiers must, however, await the next chapter.

9

Culture and Irony

Morality is the herd-instinct in the individual.

—Nietzsche, *Die Fröhliche Wissenschaft*

In an earlier chapter, in the company of my student, Jan Schweitzer, I made a cultural excursion into a remote aboriginal community. There I hinted that, for the psychotherapist, culture is not to be understood as referring only to the concrete behaviors of people but, rather, as having to do with complex belief systems and community-wide psychological attitudes. Partly tongue in cheek, I further suggested that the Ojibway and Cree of the Sioux Lookout Zone, like the psychotherapist, have an attitude of "repose." They displayed a peculiar, quietly observational stance not usual with us, the chatterbox "southerners."

Culture refers to the sets of rules, plans, and instructions about what is to count as good and bad (right and wrong, valuable and useless) and that is believed in by the community in question. These rules and instructions constitute a "cultural law," which, in psychotherapeutic circles, is usually referred to as the "oedipal law." Freud (1913, 1930), the original describer of the oedipal law, postulated powerful links existing between the oedipal and the cultural laws.

Freud (1913, 1930) argues that culture consists of rules that ultimately become part of every individual's personal heritage. The rules that he particularly focuses on are the laws against patricide and against incest. There are two ideas that he puts forward with which I disagree. First, he assumes that cultural laws become part of human biology by way of Lamarkian inheritance. In other words, ideas (including the ideas in which laws are embedded) acquired during the course of life are passed on genetically. The inheritance of acquired characteristics is long abandoned as a theory, and today we attribute personal knowledge of cultural rules to learning.

The second disagreement that I have with Freud's claim, is that the cultural—oedipal—laws are in conflict with human biology. To him, the immediate inclinations of biology are necessarily sacrificed in the service of long-term cultural and biological survival. The consequence of this is, he says, that man is thereby forever fated to be in a state of conflict. I agree that man is forever fated to be in a state of conflict. But for me that conflict has a completely different origin. Culture offers us a contradictory agenda, not necessarily in conflict with biology. This contradictoriness is of great survival value.

Contradictory cultural injunctions guarantee that people will never have clear-cut guidelines for how they should behave. A corollary of this is that our species is not locked into rigid patterns of thought and behavior; hence, it is flexible in its approach to the world. In short, *cultural ambiguity forces us to think*. Conflict is of enormous human value since it creates the circumstance in which thinking is inevitable.

It is a dubious theorizing that pits against one another forces from different theoretical domains—the forces of civilization against forces of biology. It would be logically permissible to say that a person's idea of the cultural law is in conflict with that person's idea of his biology. This would simply be saying that psychological forces are in conflict. It would also be permissible to say that materialistic or physical forces are in conflict with biological forces. But mixing realms of theoretical discourse can only make more unwieldy and confusing theoretical efforts that are already of great complexity.

The culture asks us to contend with various contradictory injunctions. All of this matters intensely to the psychotherapist because the suffering that she sees is understood by her in a particular cultural way. To her, psychological suffering is due to perceived violations of the cultural law—she likes to call it the "oedipal law"—and the guilt consequences of such violations. Cultures are peculiarly two-faced since the values and morals that they enjoin us to follow are never straightforward and simple. Double messages are the order of the day for every non-trivial matter, thus guaranteeing that guilt and conflict are ubiquitous.

This theoretical position is not the only contender for explanatory priority. Indeed there are scores of theoretical positions on this subject. In Chapter 1 we saw that, because theorists are short on concrete facts, the proliferation of theories can never be limited or harnessed by recourse to solid data. The psychotherapist does not bemoan the shortage of data but, instead, takes the position that the pursuit of psychological "facts" is futile. More than that, she says, the pursuit of data distracts from the psychological truths that she is after.

The psychotherapist is not as tolerant as this may sound. She is annoyed when colleagues and theoretical rivals voice their ideas and does her best to refute them. But at her wisest, she knows that rival theories can be neither proved nor disproved, which only means that competitive theories are in the same position as is hers. For better or for worse, she is a rhetorician through and through. When her physics envy does not get the better of her, she finds rhetoric to be the ultimate scientific stance. Science is at great pains to forever doubt, challenge, and to change its own theories. The psychotherapist finds that her preference for rhetoric is shared not only by science, but also by censors and by tyrants. Therefore, she hastens to assert that worthy rhetoric is embedded in a world that permits equal time to her theoretical enemies.

If a theory offers practical and "desirable" consequences, the psychological theorist only acknowledges momentary or tentative conviction. Unlike physicists, whose equally tentative theories may, nevertheless, permit the building of a bomb or of a rocket ship, the psychologist's theories, when they seem solid and illuminating, make only weak behavioral suggestions—suggestions that are always to be treated with irony and doubt. In principle (if not in practice) the very same thing ought to hold for the theoretical physicist. She, too, can claim no ultimate truth status for what she postulates. And, like the psychotherapist, the physicist agonizes over the consequences of her theories, for fear that they will lead to univalent (e.g., "bomb the hell out of them") thinking.

Theorists are at perfect liberty to embrace learning, trauma, social oppression, destiny, the Divine, or bad parents as explanatory strategies. The psychologist that I speak of does this too, but tries to grant only tentative explanatory privilege to any of these or to any other explanatory enthusiasm. Her mandate, she says, is to describe. When she does so, she is predisposed to see guilt—guilt over violations of the cultural law—wherever she looks. Is this a bias that blinds her? Yes and no. Since most psychotherapists are, in their very bones, psychologists of a certain kind, they typically have that bias to start with. And, like every bias, it blinds her and puts the spotlight on things she might otherwise miss.

But there are two other reasons why she looks at people with an eye on guilt and its self-penalizing consequences. First, it puts her in the company of the novelists, philosophers, and poets who, in her view, are the great psychologists of our culture. She *likes* the way Shakespeare, Dostoyevski, and Proust think. They are cultural icons, and she identifies with them. The cultural law, in one of its subsections, *demands* that she identify with them. If she does not, she is stricken with guilt and, like every other mortal, suffers the pangs of conscience.

The second reason why this is the psychotherapist's preferred theory (if "description" can be called a theory) is because it is the view of mankind that yields the richest harvest. People become complex, ridiculous, inspiring, enigmatic, polyphonic, and baroque. In other words, she makes the description of guilt central to her theory on aesthetic grounds.

Some animals are hard-wired to behave in certain ways, for example the parasitic egg-laying habits of cowbirds and cuckoos. Since they grow up in the nests of other birds, and have therefore never met their parents, their future laying of eggs in alien nests is unquestionably innate. Other species, especially primates and humans, must learn much of their behavioral repertoire through social observation.

The need for such a culture is most striking in humans but, even in primates, the need for a culture is crucially important. Monkeys raised without parents are irreversibly handicapped by that eventuality (Harlow 1958, McKinney 1989). To an even more extreme degree, humans deprived of parenting are similarly handicapped (Spitz 1946a,b). Clearly, the nervous system demands and needs a culture with which it can negotiate the world. Without it, the offspring are mindless monstrosities or are dead.

Writings on this topic refer to these traumatizing events as being due to the absence of the mother. This is, at best, a partial truth and the work does not give us any knowledge of how such infants—human or primate—would have fared without a mother but in an otherwise intact culture, that is, with a father and family. It is the *culture* that these infants are deprived of and the absence of the mother is only a particular instance of an absent culture.

But there is no doubting the horror of the absent mother that infuses the infant observation literature. That horror is, in cultural terms, another cultural mandate. Mothers are to be revered and considered indispensable, and their centrality in the infant's life is never to be questioned. By putting into words these ideas I am guilty of doubting what it is obligatory to not doubt. The contradictoriness of culture being what it is, I am also behaving in accord with my cultural destiny as a scientifically inclined writer—I am struggling with ideas, especially with ideas that are not called into question.

The facts may well be otherwise. If I am right, and that what a child requires is to live in a culture that includes many elements, including the element "Mother," then the actual role played by the mother is different. The memory of a dead mother and the stories about her may contribute to a child's residence in a culture—a culture that thereby includes a mother. An intermittently available grandmother, an aunt, a sister, and teachers may also supply cultural equivalents. What about the universal knowledge of the genre "Mother," in other words the gloriously ambivalent archetype of Mother?

Man is the creature most in need of a culture. Without an extragenetic, outside-the-skin, set of culturally mediated guidelines, we humans are nonviable. Biologically, we are potentially many things, but are only loosely mandated to live our lives in any particular way. Mostly, we live in and adopt only one culture but, under certain circumstances, humans may well have occasion to adopt more than one culture during the course of a lifetime.

The law of evolution applies not only to animals but also to cultures. A particular culture will flourish in a geographic, political, or climatic situation, whereas another culture will die. These same geographic, political, and climatic circumstances may be lethal or, by the selection of viable cultural elements, may lead to cultural evolution. Just as a biological species may evolve, so may a culture.

As a consequence, we are dependent on having a culture for our survival. It is not that we humans have the ability to make use of a culture; it is that we need a culture. Cultural evolution has come to be independent of biology and, once our culture became the instrument of our survival, we could no longer live without it. In a state of nature, we die.

Part of our modern cultural mandate is to be nonjudgmental. Thus, I will not say that a "good" culture will survive, and that a "weak" culture will die. But different cultures have, under various circumstances, more or less survival power. Note that, in citing our modern culture, I say only that part of the culture demands that we be non-judgmental.

But at the same time, cultures (and the oedipal law) are as judgmental as hell. In an era of sexual liberation there is a concomitant insistence on "zero tolerance" for certain all-too-human sexual frailties. This is not surprising because cultures do not have consistent rules. Nor should we expect them to. It is said that parents should be consistent but I am not so sure. It is good if trains are consistent, but a consistent person would be insufferable. The same goes for cultures.

Cultures are more rugged than we sometimes think. An obvious example is the Jewish culture which, after millennia of dispersion, is alive and well. Not only that, but elements of the Jewish culture that have been isolated from one another for a small eternity are still clearly recognizable even to an outsider. Sometimes we think of the Jewish culture as exceptional in this respect. That culture has evolved in such a way that it can successfully adapt to various surrounds.

It can be argued, for example, that the Jewish culture has survived because it has embodied power in the "Word." This has made it a culture without external props, hence more portable than are most cultures. An invisible, not-even-named (and not-even-allowed-to-be-named) God is also portable.

But let us not too quickly conclude that other cultures are weaker or disappear and die. Take, for example, the aboriginal culture that was discussed in Chapter 5. Upon close scrutiny one can see the survival of a culture that, to the superficial observer, seems irrevocably damaged or destroyed. Since the time of those observations, the cultural practices have been somewhat revived, albeit evolved into a new shape.

The American black culture, too, is alive and well. If one visits Europe, Asiatic Russia, or Africa, the music created by African-Americans is to be heard everywhere. The power of the culture is of extravagant proportions. Any talk of a damaged or weak black culture is peculiarly witless. That black IQs are, on average, lower than those of whites and Asians is a cultural phenomenon and is not to be judged as good or bad.

Those professors who invented IQ tests, have missed the boat. Their tests measure what is valued by white professors of psychology. Who is to say that their value system is to count as intelligence? The psychotherapist, for example, knows that for many of her patients, less concern about time, progress, and getting better—perhaps characteristics more common in the black culture—may well be a good thing. The administrator of the IQ test doesn't measure this variable. The psychotherapist also knows that the talents required to achieve a high score on an IQ test are wonderfully adaptive talents for certain ends and, at the same time, are preposterous, cheap values that can exploit the weak and exploit the environment.

Think now of the dramatic fashion influence that African-Americans have given to the world. Think of hair styles, of the vernacular language, of recreational and postural habits that all of us are adopting. Some think this is a corruption of our culture but, in fact, it is not. It is just a cultural evolution that people like me hate. I don't hate it because it is bad, but because it's not my way and I don't want to learn it at my age. The grammar appalls me, but it ain't bad grammar. It's just different. As any linguist can illustrate, the bebop language that I consider to be "bad grammar" follows rules that are as strict as are my rather Britishy rules of grammar.

The paradox that opposing cultural values are promoted by our society is wonderfully illustrated by the ironic position that white Gentiles find themselves to be in. On the one hand, they envy Jews who they stereotype as being more successful than they are in achieving middle-class goals; for example, more of their children go to medical school. At the same time, they envy African-Americans for being relaxed and less driven, "cool" and "laid back." This, I assume, is the unenviable fate of the WASP.

As far as disturbing social behavior of African-Americans is concerned, a sociologist can make wiser comments than can I. My point is a psychological one. Cultures evolve in one direction or another. They are powerful and enduring far beyond what we usually think. The demands placed upon us by our culture are very great. It is not at all easy for me, for example, to happily embrace cultures even modestly alien to my own, so ingrained in me is my own. I am probably a good illustrative example because, despite a career that is devoted to "neutrality," I am not at all neutral about these matters.

As biological specimens, we are equipped to be sexual. But the equipment is useless without a culture. Even a chimpanzee cannot copulate without the benefit of imitative learning. For a person to make love, he or she must have mastered an enormous array of rules about what constitutes lovemaking. Not only does a person know this, he also knows what is good or proper lovemaking. He also knows what constitutes bad or improper lovemaking. If he does not, he has not lived in a viable culture.

To make matters worse, cultures are ambiguous or even two-faced about what the rules are. The culture says that sex outside of marriage is forbidden. Never mind the naive assertion that the rules have changed. When a child comes home from college with her boyfriend, they don't usually sleep in the same room of the parent's home. And if they do, the family is gossiped about by those who know.

Similarly, divorced parents don't usually bring home their lovers for the night if there are children at home. The rules are of extraordinary complexity, and, of great importance to the psychotherapist in her work, the rules contradict one another. All persons are destined to be in conflict over every nontrivial matter. Here are more examples. Men are to be tender, complex, and artistic lovers, and men are to be macho conquerors of women, and men are to rescue maidens in distress, and men are to treat women as equals. Women are to be nurturing supporters of the masculine heroic image, and they are to be full partners, and they are to be arousingly feminine, and they are to be prettily naive in the boudoir.

No one is to be interested in vulgar "screwing," and yet, for better or for worse, the ideal of "screwing" with many people is alive and well in our culture. Although vulgar, and although traditional romantic lovemaking is also publicly promoted, there is, as well, scorn (another resolute value position) for romanticism, the traditional, and the "missionary position." The usual response to this point is to say that these contradictions are due to the changes taking place in our culture or, in contrast, to the fact that our culture is going through a period of temporary degeneracy.

The argument is weak. The rules have always been inconsistent, fortunately. One need only read "The Miller's Tale" in Chaucer's *Canterbury Tales* to see the joy in naughtiness—a joy only possible if naughtiness is promoted (promotion is a sort of rule). Only then can the misbehavior be pitted against the conventional rules of marital fidelity. The antics of the biblical characters of the Old Testament, and of the Gods of Olympus, are further cases in point. The moral lesson is that life governed by uniform rules would be insufferably boring, if not impossible. It would not be life. Attempts to promote zero tolerance of, say, racial intermarriage, or of love and sex between people who work together, are naive in the extreme.

In addition to the identifiable demands of human culture, there is also an ambiguity in language. This ambiguity is due in part to the human tendency to speak, and therefore to think, in binary opposites. Examples are self–other, good–bad, love–hate, and male–female. When working psychotherapeutically with patients, we discover that they hold to peculiar stereotypes (binary oppositions) about people such as phallic–castrated, weakling–rapist, and virgin–witch. These polarizations tend, psychologically, to alternate within the oppositional pair, an ambiguity that language institutionalizes.

Such reversibilities of meanings reflect something very important in human interpersonal relationships, a kind of reverberatory quality that makes human interaction the rich, gratifying (depleted, frustrating) thing that it is. Take, as an example, dancing, which depends on reciprocity, alternation, and responsiveness. Desirable forms of lovemaking, too, must contain this reverberatory element. Reciprocity and alternation are indispensable to any fine conversation, including every psychotherapeutic conversation. The reverberatory practices that psychotherapists are so interested in are, at times, referred to as *introjection* and *projection*, often with the implication that they represent early and "primitive" stages of development. But such processes are ubiquitous, normal, and necessary. In addressing you, the reader, I cannot do so effectively without putting myself inside of you, that is, identifying with you and imagining how you will receive my words. I must speak for myself and, in an anticipatory way, listen on your behalf if I hope to communicate effectively.

The greatest difficulty posed by a theory such as mine is to explain the urgency and the potency of desire. How can a set of cultural laws possess us with the passion of love and sex as all of us have known it? The psychotherapist that I am constructing stands her ground and will not yield to reductionistic biology. No drives and instincts for her, nor will she acknowledge blind forces that impel and impulses that overwhelm. Instead she has theoretical recourse only to the power of the cultural law and its embeddedness in language or in linguistic signifiers. The signifying chains, the threads and strands of meaning, are better explanations by far, she says, than are the theoretically ungainly drives, instincts, and impulses.

But how, many will protest, can the power, the intensity, and the "demand" of desire be located in signifiers or in language? The answer is that the signifiers are carriers of the cultural law and that law is of life-and-death importance. Without a culture that demands from us a coherent standard of behavior, all would be lost. In the case of desire, the urgent obedience to the cultural law looks something like this. The case in point is a man in passionate commerce with his beloved:

> This dramatically confirms that, as is my obligation, I am a man. That I am, at times, a sissy or a fool is, by virtue of what I am doing right now, irrelevant.
>
> That I am energetically sexual, and heterosexually so, confirms that the cultural law is intact. In the anticipation, the enactment, and the recall of my desire, I am suffused with

> satisfaction that I fulfill my demanding and precious cultural destiny.
>
> My beloved is Woman, as she should and must be, lest the meaning of life and of love be forever lost. Our lovemaking affirms and reaffirms that great truth, a truth that I know to be a cultural mandate but, in accordance with that very law, I prefer to speak of in romantic and poetic ways.
>
> My penis, the Phallus, is wonderful, and gives and receives pleasure as is mandated by God, the poets, and the muses.
>
> The vagina, even though not symbolically named as is the Phallus, is the essence of Woman, and stands for safety, warmth, comfort, absorption, nurture, and fecundity. I know, too, that the vagina can be frightening and repellent but, in my moment of love, I am absorbed in my passionate state of possession by the desire that the culture has bequeathed to me.

That the penis seems to occupy center stage in my fictional example should come as no surprise. We live in a phallocentric culture, after all. The symbolic potential of the penis is nicely enunciated by Malcolm Bowie (1991):

> What of the every day uncertainties that beset the male member? If we remind ourselves of these, a promising "Lacanian" scenario may begin to emerge. The penis may be rigid or flaccid, and either condition may arise opportunely or not. Its discharge may be premature or indefinitely delayed. It may be short and wished longer, or long and wished shorter. It may be proudly displayed, or apologetically concealed. It may be the instrument of will or seem to possess will of its own; an object of fear, disgust, admiration, envy. . . . This capacity for variation within pre-ordained limits seems to make it into a dialectician *par excellence*, a nexus of signifying opportunities, a fine example, in all its modes, of the Freudian *fort/da*. And the fact that these are features of a mere organ does not disqualify that organ from entering the Symbolic. For the word *penis* is no less a signifier than the word *phallus*, and its relative lack of cultural dignity

> cannot be of consequence in the rigorously non-élitist world of the signifying chain. [p. 125]

Erik Erikson (1963) has produced the most sophisticated theory of culture available to the psychotherapist. He makes explicit the centrality of conflict in human psychology. To him, the culture offers "modalities" by way of which humans can enact their lives and, if the reader is not careful, one might assume that he is a behavioral advocate. In part, this is true, and I propose to complain about that at length. Like Freud, his clinical writings are impeccably psychological, but, in the pursuit of a rational (rather than an "ironic") theory, he is liable to wax positivistic.

Those things that are to be found in humans and that need to be enacted, says Erikson, are "modes." The innate modes are activated according to the modalities offered by the culture. The problem in Erikson's work is that he gives us leeway to assume that the modalities available in a culture are uniform and consistent. For example, he argues not only that trust is a valuable cultural modality that is available, but also that the attainment of basic trust is a necessary sociocultural health achievement.

Erikson is referring to a very special kind of trust that he dubbed "basic trust." But the topic of trust in general is a worthwhile example of what I am trying to argue. Trust, I would say, is a role available to any member of our culture. But, even though it is often advocated as a behavioral obligation or as a "healthy" attribute, as a unitary attitude trust would be fatal. If I trust everybody, many will take advantage of me and I will repeatedly be in trouble. The culture is clearly aware of this and therefore says to children "don't trust strangers," and to everyone "don't trust salesmen, Jewish lawyers, women, men, the paternalistic culture" and so on. It also is liable to say to us that we should trust the very same people, including our doctor, our parents, and our politicians.

The culture wisely presents to us an array of opposing opinions about trust. Contradictory advice forces us to think. By virtue of the culture's contradictoriness, we find ourselves in the unique situation of being neither biologically hard-wired nor culturally compelled to behave in particular ways.

The moral is that if the psychotherapist says "trust me" to patients, she is to be dismissed as a legitimate contender for acceptance as a proper psychotherapist. She is to be dismissed because if she indulges in such sloganeering, and univocally encourages trust, it means that she has not thought about these matters as thoroughly as she should. Erikson has helped us to grasp the centrality of cultural rules, but his promotion of specific cultural modalities is clearly misplaced.

The culture promotes its rules with extraordinary urgency. The arts extol and encourage the paternalistic culture. Who of us has not been brought to tears by a great poem or by a corny love story. The culture has convinced us. The culture also cautiously promotes a little protest against the paternalistic culture, against the notion of hero and maiden-in-distress. But not too much.

The psychotherapist sometimes thinks of herself as being in the "against" camp. But when she does so, she errs. Although she fights tooth and nail against enslavement by the cultural law—against superego incited self-abuse—she also stands for prudence. Instead of subjugation, she proposes prudence. Her patients are, from her observational point of view, creatures of conflict. That conflict has been extracted by them from the culture in which they live and adapted to their own grotesque self-injurious ends.

Some readers will protest that biology is being neglected. If I say that marital infidelity is a specimen of the cultural law that certain persons use for certain purposes, I am liable to be shouted down. The most popular refrain that I have heard on this score is that people are by nature polygamous. That's why marital infidelity occurs! A variant on this is that males are by nature polygamous—that's why men are unfaithful. But if men are the usual culprits, who are they unfaithful with? How, without culture, could they be maritally unfaithful, since the very idea of unfaithfulness depends on the existence of a cultural standard? Without a culture, these unfaithful ones would all be dead, not having survived infancy. What is "natural" for humans is damnably hard to pin down.

Freud insists that all persons are destined to be forever in a state of conflict. For him, the conflicting forces that are to be taken into account are different from the factionalist forces that I have insisted on. Freud's argument is that biological desires—the id—are pitted against societal demands that have been internalized by the individual. His point of view is that, tragically, and by virtue of living in culture, every person must always struggle within himself.

Much is at stake here for Freud. He is betting that the psychological theory of choice is one that focuses on the borderline between biology and the mind. He feared a purely psychological theory on the grounds that it would not be scientific. More specifically, his fear was that, if biology was left out, it would no longer be an Aristotelian or Newtonian theory. He was right about this, except that his exaggerated fear of a pure psychology was misplaced. Had he opted for a non-Newtonian theory, he would have had to put up with theoretical styles like mine, forever laced with a love of metaphor, irony, and the poetic.

What I have argued is quite different from Freud's drive-oriented id—his wordless, nature infested, unconscious. My contrasting examination of conflict finds culture to be conflictually structured in its very essence, and so structured for good and necessary reasons. The mind, in identification with these cultural modalities, is an analogous hotbed of conflictual, wordy demands, construed without recourse to biology or any other blind forces. A unitary, logical, Aristotelian set of cultural rules would fate us to be in yet another tragic position: we would be robots. The contradictory cultural rules force us to think, allows for changes and experimentation in cultural practice, and thereby creates a system that allows for mutations perfectly analogous to genetic mutations. The remarkable survival power of our species is witness to this.

Some will argue that the variety that characterizes cultural injunctions is experimental and thereby promotes cultural evolution. This is undoubtedly true, but variety serves another adaptive function that more directly pertains to psychology. Thinking, the natural consequence of unclear and conflicting behavioral guidelines, is psychologically pivotal.

The opposing injunctions of which I speak are not balanced, nor can they be. Were this the case, half of us would follow rule A and half of us would follow rule B. The culture always inclines us in a particular direction so that there is, indeed, a coherent culture. The culture must have a typical and expected set of demands that it places on us. Otherwise we would have no families, no laws, no civilities and courtesies, and no standards of beauty and truth. Marriage, for example, is enjoined more vigorously than is, say, being a bachelor—although being a bachelor is (moderately) lauded by the culture. Bachelors, it is said, have access to freedom and to adventure. Nevertheless, the overall tendency of the culture is to privilege marriage.

On the other hand, to be a spinster or an "old maid" seems to not be promoted at all. The phrase itself carries connotations of "don't do it," "avoid," "you are non-sexy," and "if you choose that, be ashamed." Women, the phrase suggests, ought all to marry. In keeping with the changes that take place in cultural injunctions, the current era avoids the term *old maid* and attempts to create new, less-unattractive models for a woman's unmarried state. That cultural flux, I might say, is less substantial than the rhetoric that it has generated.

Does this mean that the culture prefers that all women should have children? Is that why the "old maid" was invented? Is a male bachelor acceptable as long as childbearing females do their job? Was female infanticide as a means of population control responsible for an excess of unmarried males, and was there a need for a culturally acceptable role for these extra men?

A weaker apprehension of conflict is to be found in common discussions of trauma. Writers on this topic often have the idea that parental neglect (often conceptualized as a "failure of empathy") or wounding life events lead to fragmentation of the ego or self. Apart from the problematic existential status of the ego and self, one can only be puzzled that ordinary, day-to-day language practices should be so literally adopted by a theoretician. We might say, "I was shattered by what she said to me," or, "I was broken to pieces after my husband left me." But it is quite another matter to concretize interesting metaphors so that they become reductionistic banalities.

Theoretical pronouncements about fragmented egos or about fragmented selves are precisely the reductionistic banalities that we must always fear and avoid. In addition, the fragmented debris of these injured structures, fragments supposedly in conflict with one another, have no theoretical imperative to be in conflict. The great virtue of Freud's theory—and of mine—is that vital and urgent conflict is inescapable.

Is anything natural, you might ask? Well, we know from the testimony of "naughty masturbating nannies" that 6-month-old infants are capable of having a complex, apparently innate, sexual response. Nannies have apparently used their knowledge of this to pacify fussy babies. If masturbated, infants become aroused, breathe heavily and perspire, make pelvic thrusting movements, and apparently achieve orgasmic climax. Then, serving the purpose of the nanny, they tend to go to sleep. Such a response is innate, all right, but still requires a viable, culturally resident infant.

Also, biologically intact infants smile in response to a moving, smiling, face—be it the face of a person or a crude drawing of a face. If I open my mouth or blink my eyes for a baby, it will tend to imitate me, a response which is innate. But it has little to do with the complex lives that persons live. Every person eats, but this is one of those trivial truths that the psychotherapist has little interest in. It is transparent and is merely what we see on the surface. What she is fascinated by is the *way* a person eats, the *way he gags and vomits*, and the *way a garage door comes down in his throat when he thinks of a penis*, which is, pure and simple, a fascination with atavistically seized-upon cultural roles.

Every biologically intact person is sexual, but the way he acts sexually, and the ways in which he cannot be sexual, are culturally mediated. He just doesn't know how to do it without a culture. And cultures being inconsistent, the psychotherapist will forever be in business, especially since our patients pit cultural modalities against one another with unremitting fury.

Even something as individual as aloneness is culture-bound. Every solitary has his role model. Be it Nietzsche, the genre "hermit," or the lonesome cowboy, there is a model. That model, although offered as a possibility by the culture, serves different purposes for each person who adopts it. It is a persona that skillfully solves an array of painful conflicts. The same holds true for those persons labeled schizophrenic who, with consummate skill, are also enacting a role—the role of madness. Depression, victimhood, and proud independence are painful games (I wish there were a better word than "game" but, like Wittgenstein, I cannot find a better one) that can be performed for psychological purposes.

The syndrome of childhood autism remains for me a puzzler. Without exposure to the autistic model, how could this be the enactment of a cultural role—even though I am inclined to think that it is such an enactment? Are there in the culture enough fragmentary samples of autistic behavior that a particular child can identify with in such a massive way? The particular case of autism is not pertinent to the psychotherapist's central concerns. Nevertheless, I hope that glib and foundationless biological explanations of autism—and weak complaints like mine—will not be allowed to stand uncontemplated.

Psychotherapists protest against a nonpsychological explanation because, just as is the case with schizophrenic persons, all the signs and symptoms are psychological. This has not prevented a storm of opinion on the biological cause of schizophrenia. I have heard, "We are on the verge of discovering the cause of schizophrenia" for forty years. What biology are they referring to, I might ask? Nor has it stopped a less common, but equally ardent rhetoric about the "myth of mental illness." If schizophrenia is the adoption of a cultural role, that adoption is done unconsciously. Purposeful imitation is a pallid aping of a role; identification possesses us, drives us helplessly before it, and has a mind of its own. Purposeful imitation is like tickling oneself—it is silly beyond imagining. To be psychotic or autistic is to be possessed by flamboyantly demonic cultural roles.

The psychotherapist cautiously wants to deny her patient access to the role of illness. The psychotherapist knows that her patients suffer and, having opted to practice her profession, she has a concern about unwellness and the woes of life. Since this is in her very nature, she must be ever alert to the problems of the "illness" role.

Are pimples and dandruff illnesses? Is baldness an illness? They certainly cause suffering, and people go to doctors about these problems. If patient and doctor agree, then any of these matters can count as sickness. But what if a government health insurance plan pays for these medical transactions? Then a social decision has been made that pimples, dandruff, and baldness are illnesses.

Following this line of argument, neurosis is an illness and should be covered by medical insurance. Psychotherapy patients suffer, not only symptoms, but find their very way of life to be at stake in the treatment. People don't go to a psychotherapist frivolously. However, there are grave and immanent dangers in any easy belief in the idea that our patients are sick.

The problem is that psychological illness, for purposes of psychotherapy, is self-designed and self-created by the patient, although not created in the usual sense of conscious intent. In addition to his role in the establishment of his own madness, the sufferer has a stake in holding on to it. The psychotherapist conceptualizes all psychological symptoms as highly complex ways of living a life, ways that are skillful, albeit painful, solutions to a myriad of psychological dilemmas.

What the patient calls his "problem"—his illness—is apprehended by the psychotherapist as his "solution." This flies in the face of the usual understanding of psychological disorders, an understanding that is another cultural demand system. We are supposed to think of our patients as having problems.

There is a psychological state that is a particularly vexacious head scratcher for the psychological theorist: the person who suffers from the painful consequences of a traumatic event. Surely this has the quality of an affliction, as something that befalls someone in the same way as does a traditional illness like pneumonia or cancer.

The answer is that only a *person* can have a traumatic reaction to an assault or to a catastrophic family event. Let me offer the analogy of an automobile in which the fuel pump has been damaged by a vandal. The cause and explanation of the automobile's dysfunction is exhaustively explained by the vandalism, correct? Well, actually not. It is explained, but it is certainly not exhaustively explained. I can also say something quite different: the car does not operate because it has a damaged fuel pump—a crucial distinction. To get the car running again, I must repair the fuel pump.

This is the reasoning of the psychotherapist. An assault may occur, but the solution is to deal with what is in the patient. The patient's unique psychological adaptation to the event is the only target the psychotherapist has interest in and can do anything about. As a fellow human being, she is likely to be outraged at a world that is hurtful and neglectful. But as a psychotherapist, she loses her therapeutic poise, leverage, and footing if she becomes a social advocate. She may be one in her private life or in another part of her professional life, but as a psychotherapist she abstains from all forms of activism.

Occasionally there are situations in which she must abandon her role as psychotherapist and take some form of direct action. When doing so, she must know that she is jeopardizing the psychotherapy, an action that is not to be undertaken lightly. Furthermore, she must be acutely aware that such an act may be an unwelcome, usually therapeutically undermining, countertransference reaction. Because there is an intact social network that she has underestimated, she has fallen into the trap of believing that only she can salvage the situation. Only she has enough concern and enough knowledge of the situation to take the proper rescuing action.

Most of the time, there is a helpful world around, even though the patient has tried to convince the psychotherapist that the world is not helpful, and that she, the therapist, must intervene. Only the therapist is wonderful enough to save him, the traumatized victim. The transference, the damn idealizing transference, is never finished sabotaging the psychotherapist and convincing her that when she is praised, the patient is making a statement about a true state of affairs.

If he succeeds, the patient will have deflected the therapist from the psychology of the situation and to the person of the traumatizer. Usually there is little that can be done because the trauma is already ancient history. But if the therapist has her wits about her, she will keep in mind that, although she can do nothing about hurtful life events, she can do something about the patient's psychology.

What, you may ask, does any of this have to do with culture? The current public concern about the abuse of women, of minorities, and of children is necessary, laudable, vital, and urgent, as are the equally worthy concerns of other groups that such complaints are wrong or overblown. It is part of the cultural evolutionary flux that goes on all the time. But the psychotherapist, probably with great wisdom, stands by and works on with her patient. She analyzes the warring cultural commands in her patient's mind, especially as these cause trouble for him. This is one good reason for the psychotherapist not to join in on something which, at this moment, has taken on raucous, "bandwagon" qualities. She, the psychotherapist, wants to be calmer, more thoughtful, and go beyond immediate response to any problem. And she definitely does not want any part of a campaign that patronizingly defines her patient as damaged goods—as "sick."

The typical psychotherapist, often under assault for being aloof from the thrust and parry of real life, has concerns that are overlooked by the enthusiastic blamers. Worse, the blamers seem intent on achieving the dubious consequence of silencing and censoring those who are more thoughtful. The back and forth of what is right and what is wrong is what cultural change is all about. The psychotherapist is interested in truths that are the outcome of free debate and shrinks from blind enthusiasm and hard conviction.

To her horror, the psychotherapist sees colleagues who, fearing for their professional reputation, decline to see women who, in the diagnostic interview, use the word *abuse*. "If they use the word *abuse* about someone else," they reason, "then some day they will use the word about me—probably to my professional regulatory body." I know of one psychotherapist who will no longer see any women patients at all! Another has a security guard patrol his corridor from time to time with the idea that this might weaken complaints brought against him. Yet another, who I was supervising at the time, terminated the treatment of a pubertal girl because sexual issues—long a problem—began to appear in the transference relationship. The patient lost out on the treatment that she badly needed.

This is madness. It is *1984*. It is the adoption and tyrannical imposition of a thoughtless fault-finding. It is, in its essentials, no different from any racist program. The psychotherapist listens nervously to what the blamers say, but she also waits fearfully to hear from a complementary and reactionary other who she fears just as much. The therapist recognizes this danger because in her patients (and in all persons) every urgent claim has its equally strident counterclaim. In the utterly kind, it takes less work than one might think to, sooner or later, find the utterly ruthless. When one encounters a cultural modality that claims to virtuously speak for the oppressed—ruthlessly speaks for the oppressed—one must tremble in fear of the inevitable opposite ruthlessness: "Those fascist bitches! What they need is . . ." "Too much fucking welfare." And so on. The reaction is identical to the complaint.

> He who fights with monsters might take care lest he thereby become a monster. And if you gaze for long into an abyss, the abyss gazes also into you. [Nietzsche 1886, p. 279].

In her psychotherapeutic posture, the psychotherapist will not define her patient as injured, damaged, or as undeveloped.

Nor will she define the world of the other—the patient's other—as wicked, injurious, or blameworthy. In other words, apart from allowing the patient access to the treatment situation, the psychotherapist will not acknowledge pathology or sickness in the patient, lest the patient's crucial role in his madness be overlooked. Whatever the patient does, it has to do with his own personal settling of accounts, his own self-injurious tactics. One way or another, he who seizes upon a particular life, a particular symptom, or a particular dream, does so purposefully, even when his purposes include a way of life that hurts.

The psychotherapist occupies a crucial cultural role and is determined that the role is a necessary one. She does not want to vacate the field, thereby making it available to the blamers and the reactionaries. She is convinced that she and her kind are a valuable cultural resource, and that she must play that role with great resolution. Without her odd "in-between" stance, the cultural debate, the cultural evolution, the oedipal struggle, would be less than satisfactory.

Clifford Geertz (1973) speaks of "deep play" (p. 433)—behavior that is pursued against all odds, yet is of terrible moral import. Here are some examples that come to mind:

The Kwakiutl ritually giving away their possessions.

Speeding in an automobile.

Listening to music by John Cage or Arnold Schönberg.

Having an extramarital affair.

Adolescents leaving home with no means of support.

Reading Goethe and, at the same time, working in a death camp.

Irrational though these activities may seem (is listening to John Cage irrational? Are the Kwakiutl irrational?), they are pursued with passion because, to do so, corresponds to some moral requirement. All are culturally available modalities that can form one element in potential psychological conflict. Typically, one of the outcomes that is pursued is personal suffering.

Such things do not have to be done personally. It is sufficient to vicariously participate in the achievements of one's children, of one's nation, and its various ideological, political, and athletic heroes.

Such cultural modalities appear in the sphere of psychology as identifications. All psychologists know about identification but, I suspect, many have not realized its centrality in human behavior. That mechanism, identification, is the access route to all behavior. I cannot write these words without identifying with the role of "writer." The culture teaches that role to me. Being a father and being a fool are also skillful cultural enactments. The wimp and the horse's ass are performing a cultural role as sure-footedly as the actor or the dissimulator. Every thought, feeling, and behavior is an identification.

If I identify, I blur the distinction between myself and the other with whom I am identifying. In other words, I must displace, say, being a husband, from all the other husbands I have known, to me. The character "husband," who was over there, is now relocated in me. The psychological word for this is *displacement*. Displacement is always part and parcel of identification. In our individualistic culture, we are inclined to disavow our tendency to blur people together, and to deny, for example, that a woman is, to me, also "Woman." In other words, she is uniquely herself but, at the very same time, she is an archetypal figure.

Such archetypes are ubiquitous and can be referred to as abstractions, as categories, or as generalizations. The good thing about the word *archetype* is that it vitalizes what I am talking about. Psychologically speaking, these images are treated like real-life creatures. We believe in the hero, the seductress, and the weakling. But I feel compelled to remind you that the hero, the seductress, and the weakling do not exist. A close look at any person reveals that he is actually a cornucopia of things, and psychotherapists, being in the business of having a close look at people, are acutely aware that stereotypes quickly disappear.

The most obvious example of this is the "sick" patient who, in my practice, disappears from sight after a few sessions. I assume that the reason for this is that I don't participate in the sickness dialectic, and tend to respond to sickness and symptoms with a curiosity about reasons, purposes, and motives.

Having categorically denied the existence of the archetype, I must reverse myself and say that the archetype is intensely real and is forever present. Persons always particularize and stereotype. A woman (a man, a charlatan, a diva) is always unique and is always a stereotype.

This finding is neither good nor bad. It is the way we humans think and negotiate the world. Hence the futility of banning *Little Black Sambo*. Black Sambo, Black Mumbo, and Black Jumbo are unique characters and are stereotypes. I think they are inoffensive archetypes, just as is the cartoon of a smug Canadian prime minister in this morning's newspaper. The black family in *Little Black Sambo* also embodies and promotes (promotes the cultural law, that is) family parenting values. And the political cartoon captures truths by way of the same technique of caricature and archetype.

When a psychotherapist calls her patient "borderline," she has fallen into the trap of believing in an archetype. The person to whom this label is applied is characteristically irritating, difficult, and demanding. He is enacting a well-known cultural role and thus earns not only the title "borderline" but also the descriptions "stupid," "pain in the neck," and worse. But the use of these labels is little more than joining in on the cavalcade of insults that such a person earns for himself. A much better diagnostic term would be that he suffers from a "difficult-to-deal-with character problem" or "behaviorally offensive personality disorder." This would invite the potential helper to think of a person—enigmatic and problematic like all persons—instead of the all-too-common commentary that can so easily write off the person as "another borderline." Those commentators have come to believe in an archetype.

Carl Jung was a promoter of archetypes. He knew that we need the archetype in order to negotiate a world that cannot be newly discovered at every moment. He advises the psychotherapist that her ambition to only describe is futile because there are real and substantial archetypes that the psychotherapist must find. Jung declines to admit that the archetype is just another descriptive image. Despite the psychotherapist's concern about the substantiality of archetypes, we must not give up on the idea too quickly. Without guidelines—and archetypes are guidelines—we would be lost in an avalanche of unintegrated perceptions.

My complaint about Jung is only that he has idealized and romanticized the archetype. Such evidences of "preciousness" alert the psychotherapist and lead her to realize that Jung is doing what we all are inclined to do. We long for and find a belief system, an icon, to which we can hitch our wagon. Thereby we try to avoid the peculiarity of human behavior, to not notice that we are all remarkable puzzles, and that we are sublime and ridiculous all at once. We forget that the posture of irony keeps us honest.

To Jung, coming to know one's archetypes is a healing and salvational event. He encourages a sort of "find your long lost archetypes" psychotherapy. Jung was convinced that the faltering Christian church had left the Western world bereft and that a new, "scientific" faith was needed. The discovery of one's archetypal world was to give this salvation. Jung was a kind of Wagnerian theologian, except that salvation was not to come from art but from union with the historical, the ancient, and the archetypal.

Rieff (1966) offers a wise and illuminating examination of how theorists revert to "beliefs" and "icons," and examines the place of psychoanalytic theories in Western culture. Although he explicitly critiques only Jung and Adler, Rieff leads the reader into the problems created by the social theorists.

A 5-year-old said, "I'm going to have corn flakes for breakfast." Her 4-year-old cousin said, "Me, too." He said "Me, too" to everything that his older cousin said. He identified with her. Identification is very powerful. Later, in the back seat of my car, the older child said, "I'm going to sleep." She was, it must be understood, making fun. The younger cousin dutifully said "Me, too" and promptly fell asleep. He had suggested to himself, hypnotically, that he would identify with the other child, and did so. It is no different from the biblical Joseph's identification with his father Jacob:

> What he felt was imitation and succession; with slight differences, his father before him had experienced the same. It is uncanny to see the mixture of free will and guidance in the phenomenon of imitation. In the end it is hard to tell whether it is the individual or the destiny that actually follows the pattern and insists upon the repetition. The inward and the outward play into each other, and materialize apparently without act of will into the event which was from all time bound up with and one with the individual. For we move in the footsteps of others, and all life is but the pouring of the present into the forms of the myth. [Mann 1934, p. 551]

The cultural law is strict and, since the process of identification is as powerful as the law is strict, we are creatures of culture more than we ordinarily imagine. And, since our parents and families are the deliverers of the cultural message, we are our parents more thoroughly and more inevitably than we like to know. The psychotherapist is acutely aware of this and realizes that what she is hearing from her patient's lips is, recurrently, the words and actions of his parents. The psychotherapist is faced with persons who are in conflict because they identify with contradictory canons—often modeled on their parents—that are embedded in the Western, or any other, code of values.

The code sometimes needs to be shaken up: we violate it and shake it up when we party enthusiastically, or when we celebrate Mardi Gras. At other times, things get too lax; then we "lay down the law." But the individual is forever caught between irreconcilable demands. And a good thing, too. If we ever came to have clear univocal rules, they would be enforced with utter ruthlessness. No other way would be allowed.

The cultural code, despite its self-contradictions, is ruthless enough as it is. In our own way, we are all uncomfortably fascist at some level. I do not mean that at the level of fantasy or wish we may all be found to be unattractively unwholesome, or that, at the level of action and ideology, we may come off somewhat better. I mean that no one has to look beyond his own heart to see how opinionated and convinced he is of his own preferred ways. The silliness (or is it madness or, perhaps, tyranny?) with which any of us may argue with our spouses should bring home this point to everyone. We argue at those times with the conviction of any ideologue. People who find no nasty, fascist side in themselves worry me. I fear that, like all who are convinced of their own virtue, they may be the most dangerous fascists of all. Obvious fascists are easy to spot. Racists, gender fascists (of either sort), and explicit elitists make up that lot.

The subtle fascists are a variant on the utterly democratic psychotherapist that I have been developing as a model in these pages. As I mentioned in the first chapter, she very slyly believes (and tries to get her patients to join her in this belief) that this makes her (and her converted patients) better than ordinary folk who, in her quietly scornful way, she counts as being the "rabble."

The cultural code is transmitted by all persons to everybody at all times by talking to their friends, to strangers, to their children, and to their colleagues. They are talking about the cultural law:

> "I wouldn't take that from her. If you let her get away with it once, then . . . "
>
> "When she does that, she's showing that she needs your love and understanding more than ever."
>
> "Don't let him watch TV so much."
>
> "You know, of course, that 'all work and no play, makes Jack a dull boy,' so quit nagging him about TV."
>
> "Try to get more exercise."
>
> "Wear black more often. It suits you."

Everyone is talking about rules, values, and preferences. Thus, value assignments are available for contradiction.

Moral regulation is not just a matter of rules against incest and parricide. The oedipal law is about how we dress, and about our posture. It is about how to be a student and how to be a teacher. Everything that we do must be done according to the laws governing the role behavior in question. There are clear-cut rules about how to be a slob or a boor or a genius, including paying the price of being a boor or a slob, and gaining the rewards of being a genius.

Self-help books—an important source of rules about marriage, sex, and child-rearing—are stridently opinionated, cliché-ridden, and are slaves to the latest fashion. But even so, they contribute to the ever-evolving cultural law. They may balance out long-winded, convoluted thinkers like me, who also contribute to the ever-evolving oedipal/cultural program. Self-help, like television, is generally a vulgar and trivial source of cultural values. Their promoters think I am out of touch and neglectful. Do I not care about the mistreatment and abuse that is going on in the world, they ask, while I am fretting over the nature of reality and of truth?

All societies, in addition to having debatable and manipulable rules, share the incest taboo as a foundational cultural demand. I do not mean that the incest taboo is an exhaustive explanation of culture, but only that family structures depend on the incest taboo as one of the key cultural ingredients. And I do not mean that the incest taboo, in contrast to the other cultural injunctions, is univalent in its demands. Like every other cultural demand, the incest law is ambivalent. Sons are required to love their mothers forever. Despite the common awkwardness that sons feel about this, they strive to fulfill it even though (I am making an absurdly reductionistic statement; it is multi-determined just like everything else) it is a violation of the incest taboo. If a man is to abandon sexual interest in his mother and is to love and cherish her (and this is what the culture demands), then even the incest taboo is put forward ambivalently.

Freud's Oedipus complex is trivialized when it is said that boys want to go to bed with their mothers and to kill their fathers. A better way of putting this is to say that boys are sexual and the culture demands that they be sexual. In negotiating the cultural roles available to them and demanded of them, each finds his own way. For all, the incestuous is at least possible, and that forbidden psychological crime is universally committed since, by way of thought or gesture, sexuality is ubiquitous. And, one way or another, that crime is atoned for. Even the boy who makes overt sexual demands on the mother is "solving" the oedipal dilemma, in his case by flaunting the rule and thereby provoking the world to chastise and forbid him.

Even in the unfortunate family in which such an eventuality is consummated, the restraint, that is to say, the guilty knowledge of having committed the unforgivable, is a humiliating ever-presence. To illustrate the incessant psychological stance of the psychotherapist, I will push this line of reasoning further. What if a boy consummates the incestuous act with his mother, is not (consciously) guilty and humiliated, and is, perhaps, smug and dismissive. Did he then simply get away with it? The psychological answer is no. The psychotherapist's assumption is that the violation of the oedipal law can never go unpunished. The law is internal and punishment inevitably follows. Whether that punishment is a symptom or some painful style of life varies from case to case.

The parallel psychological crime of father resentment, or father-murder, is a parallel case in point, as are the roughly similar circumstantial configurations toward mothers and fathers in girls. There are in the literature convoluted theories about male and female sexual development, mostly theories bound up with the question of who has castration anxiety, who has penis envy, who has to change love objects in order to traverse certain developmental milestones, and so on. The theorists who do this have learned that onanistic habit from Freud. What they have forgotten is that human behavior and human development are only predictable insofar as we are capable of sex, hunger, locomotion, and the rest of the biological repertoire. This, the psychotherapist takes for granted.

She finds it to be unthinkable that "meaning behavior," such as a castration fantasy, could be misunderstood so blatantly that a theorist would believe that it must appear as part of a normal or developmental configuration. What the psychotherapist is interested in is not a futile search for general patterns but, rather, how any such psychological posture appears in an individual. In her psychotherapeutic work, she never does anything else. She begins and ends with the assumption that every person is idiosyncratic. She expects forms and manifestations to be unrepeatable and unique every time she finds them.

The generalizations that are made about these concepts are futile. The items that my wrongheaded colleagues select to theorize about, and which they think are "characteristic" of males or females, or of homosexuals, are social roles available to anyone. The only thing that is of psychotherapeutic import is what a particular individual does with the available social roles. To count some as normal or as primitive can only be a form of disguised name-calling.

More than that, every violation of the oedipal cultural code, including things as trivial as not eating one's vegetables and not laughing at father's jokes, is internally and psychologically punishable. The violation of that code is inevitable, eternal, and forever fraught with dilemma and confusion.

The analysis of the conscience-superego ultimately yields a detailed display of the polychromatic and internally inconsistent set of built-in laws that all of us carry around with us. To hope to resolve (make go away) the wretched demands that we all make upon ourselves is to miss out on why such a cultural web of morality is necessary.

The cultural-oedipal code is transmitted by language. The law of God is made up of words. God speaks to man of what is expected of him. In other words, the cultural web is a web of words, a web of signification. When people try to achieve some sort of moral balance, they do so by talking. The talk in the psychotherapist's office is, in principle, attempting to do the same thing as is the talk in the confessional, and the chatter at a cocktail party. Much of the talk is ritualized cliché. The parent talking to the untidy adolescent is enacting something prescripted. We can predict how both sides of the conversation will go. The "strong poet" of Harold Bloom (1973) has a deathly fear of cliché, as does the psychotherapist. For her, saying the same thing more than once guarantees that nothing will change. The same words serve only to perpetuate the status quo.

The film *All That Jazz* is about the genius theater choreographer Bob Fosse. I watched the film one evening in the presence of a professional dancer who had worked with Fosse and knew many of the performers being portrayed. In one scene, Fosse worked with a dancer and held her in various dance positions that follow the language and movements of ballet. I assumed that as he moved the dancer's torso and limbs into various positions he was showing her how he wanted her to implement his choreography. "No, no," said the dancer who was watching the film with us. "He is experimenting. He is trying to find dance positions that have never been tried before. Fosse was terrified of cliché and never stopped experimenting."

So the creative choreographer uses the same model as do all who are interested in change. The psychotherapist is no exception and therefore is never finished trying to destabilize the paralytic world of words in which her patients are entrapped. She does this, first, by way of her demanding silence. To that silence, the patient responds by trying harder, by trying new words, and by experimenting with what else he can say. The therapist, with ever more silence, goads and subverts further.

When she does speak, the psychotherapist is trying to destabilize the crippling linguistic domain in which her patient lives. She may do this by emphasizing, underlining, bracketing, and putting things in "scare quotes." She contradicts, usually gently, but occasionally boldly. And most of all, she redescribes.

There are also more talkative psychotherapists who advise and counsel and reassure. These psychotherapists fear silence and its potential for permitting novelty, the unexpected, and, most feared of all, the unconventional and the never-before-conceived. To the silent, restrained, in-depth psychotherapist this kind of chatter can only be a compendium of the feared cliché, the univalent idea, and the impoverishment of language, of thought, and of life. It forecloses on the possibility of the subtle, the remarkable, and the cherished sin, and replaces it with evil, virtue, and the pathetic.

But the psychotherapist, having condemned, shrinks from too much condemnation. She disagrees with Socrates who believed that only the philosopher possesses the *logos*, that is, reason or the word. In her disagreement, she does not claim that the wordy ones have no access to silence and the unique, but only that they fear it. The reassurers and the advice givers, too, may elude the world of cliché.

Jacques Lacan was the master destabilizer. He is the legendary case of proud obscurity and yet, inexplicably, we are inclined to be interested in the enigmatic texts that he inflicts on us. If this discussion seems like an experiment in reading hieroglyphics, I can only say that any first reading of Lacan is, indeed, obscure. I end this chapter with some suggestions about further Lacan readings. In the next chapter he is referred to in the context of a clinical, and therefore a more practical, context.

Lacan, like every good psychotherapist, recognized the ambiguity of the cultural, oedipal, linguistic world in which all of us reside. His highly unique linguistic vision of the human psyche is a constant onslaught on our usual smug, pat theorizing. On the one hand, Lacan tells us that wellness lies in the achievement of "full discourse," that is, in a richness of linguistic competence. It is as though he is saying that madness is due to a kind of deficit in linguistic skills.

When reading him, one sometimes thinks that reading poetry, doing cryptic crossword puzzles, and studying the obscurities of Lacan are the enriching route to a better life. He likes to imply that the "Symbolic," that is, the cultural/linguistic code, must be imposed, perhaps ruthlessly imposed, upon the subject in question. The "cut" and the creation of a "gap" are examples of how the new linguistic "law of the father" is to be inscribed upon the patient.

But Lacan is a terrible trickster who is in dead earnest about what he is up to. Even as one begins to suspect that his form of psychotherapy is a tyrannical subjugation of the patient to his linguistically brilliant agenda, Lacan undermines our beginning comprehension of him. Suddenly we realize that, for Lacan, language is a slippery business and thus not something that one can impose after all.

Redescription is the ultimate tactic of the psychotherapist; words can change everything. However, no redescription is to be afforded ultimate truth status. Like Lacan, my psychotherapist is convinced that words subvert and call into question. With her words she teaches no truths, apart from the paradoxical truth that there is no truth. Lacan dramatically disperses what we and his patients comfortably believe in, but he does not do this by expecting us to buy into new beliefs. To be linguistically renewed is enough.

To Lacan and to semiologists in general, psychic life begins with the act of differentiation. Before differentiation of concepts or of words, what can there be? Can there be a void without a differentiated fullness? Can there be an edible stuff without an inedible stuff? Good without bad? Here without there? Love without hate? These questions address Freud's old notion of "quality." The assignment of quality always depends on a discrimination or a differentiation. It is always that something is good for this or is good for that. These are value assignments, moral positions on what is to count as good or as bad.

Much debate in the psychotherapeutic literature worries away at an issue about which Lacan, in contrast, is absolutist. Is it, as I have argued, indeed true that psychological life revolves around moral dilemmas that are inevitably inspired by the oedipal/cultural law? Shouldn't more emphasis be placed on preoedipal matters? By "preoedipal" these debaters mean the earlier, one-to-one relationship with the mother. In other words, is there not a stage of development that antedates the infant's entry into the linguistic, rule-structured, culture that I have described? I say no. The child, insofar as he does not reside in a world of culture, a world with linguistically coded values, is not yet a person. The ultimate criterion of personhood is to be a participant, even if only slightly, in a culture. A precultural participation in the world is only that of a human organism who has not yet entered into psychological personhood.

For Lacan, preoedipal issues cannot exist. If, for example, the infant thinks of the mother as a principle of goodness, then the father is the complementary principle of badness. His presence is a challenge to the world, which gives birth to psychological life by denying access to the mother or by insisting on the existence of a differentiated world. She cannot be conceived as good, desirable, and empathic without the complementary awareness of a figure who denies access to her. Without the denying figure, she cannot exist for the infant, since conceiving of her—of her being—is not possible without the complementary conception of her non-being.

In a fundamental way, psychic life is understood by Lacan to be located in the law of the father who says no, an arbitrary no that awakens the child to a life of presence and absence, of good and bad. To Lacan, there is an infinitude of dichotomies both subtle and gross, all endlessly complicated by the dichotomy conscious/unconscious. Lacan affords to preoedipal issues no semblance of equal dignity. In agreement with Freud, Lacan grounds all of psychic life in the vicissitudes of the oedipal law, most explicitly formalized in the incest taboo. So-called preoedipal issues are, to him, merely subsidiary incarnations of the oedipal law. The affirmation that the love of the good caregiving mother is unique and fundamental is merely obedience to a conventional oedipal injunction that demands that mother-love be highly valued, and that mothers themselves should be respected and loved nonsexually. Mothers themselves, it is demanded, are to act lovingly and empathically.

But, states Lacan (again in agreement with Freud), every description of a good empathic mother is to be unpacked in order that the description can be expanded, illuminated, and made more complex. Can only the superman—the *Übermensch*—bear to know the warded-off unconscious elements in a claim of motherly goodness? Can such an oedipal demand—that mothers be seen as good—be analytically deconstructed? To what extent can the "incestuous" love between patient and therapist be deconstructed, without deconstructing, and perhaps destroying, the therapy? When a patient says, "I need a father," is he accepting a conventional oedipal morality? And must it be so? Must one always "need" a father? Or are all psychological positions analyzable? This is Freud's "plague," Lacan's topsy-turviness, and my own suggestion that psychotherapeutic work is always shockingly inconvenient.

The brevity of this comment on Lacan does him a disservice. For more information, see Bowie (1991). I recommend not reading Lacan himself, as he is too obscure, too self-indulgent, too much of a show-off, and too much show business razzle-dazzle. But one work to try is *Seminars* (Lacan 1953–1954, 1954–1955). The *Ecrits* and some of his other works are more difficult.

Lacan makes clear that language is of the essence in psychotherapeutic work. When I complain of colleagues who do not listen psychologically, and who, instead, take the words of their patients literally, I am complaining that they have lost their psychological bearing. They have forgotten that language, and the way our patients use it, is the stuff of our work and, perhaps, the stuff by which one can live a human life.

10

The Therapeutic Mind

If it is supportive, it cannot be psychotherapy; if it is psychotherapy, it cannot be supportive.

—S. Crown, 1988.

My clinical examples have, I hope, given a dramatic portrait of the psychotherapist's behavior. But it is necessary to ask a few more questions about what she is doing. What, for example, are her guiding therapeutic ideas, and why does she do precisely what clinical examples illustrate? This is especially important because what she does is, all too often, odd, provocative, and enigmatic. How does she conceive of such modes of intervention, and what theories does she have in mind? Four overlapping principles come to mind:

1. The therapist is determined that she is not "doing something" to her patient.
2. As far as she can manage it, the psychotherapist lets herself be imaginatively carried away by the stories, dreams, and convictions told to her by her patients.

3. She must keep alive in the back of her mind that self-deception is, for all persons, the order of the day.
4. The psychotherapist, apart from the simple courtesies of day-to-day life, does nothing but make interpretations.

The therapist is determined that she is not "doing something" to her patient. Instead she insists that the two parties to the exercise constitute a dialectic between two subjectivities, with the attendant hardship that comes with an awareness that all is subjective. Observation is, in this mode of thinking, no longer a safe haven for the psychotherapist and, as a consequence, never offers sure footing to either practitioner or theorist.

The framing of the psychotherapeutic situation in intersubjective and dialectical terms carries with it dangers, the most common of which is associated with how the idea of intersubjectivity is to be understood. Most psychotherapists, especially beginning psychotherapists, believe that they offer to patients a decency and concern that their patients have never experienced before. This is not surprising since most psychotherapists have pursued their profession out of a spirit of concern for unhappy people and are by nature consciously inclined to kindness. This is a bitter pill for those of us who want to be the purveyors of "the good." But in the world of psychology, it is unbecoming to take at face value what the patient and what the psychotherapist believe about what they do. Nevertheless, all too often, intersubjectivity has come to carry the meaning of a special closeness or a heightened understanding unavailable in ordinary interpersonal commerce. At its worst, the idea of the therapeutic interaction has become romanticized so that the psychotherapist is believed to have a unique access to and understanding of her patient.

The word *intersubjectivity* conveys nothing of this sort. It refers only to the conceptual framework that best promotes the psychotherapist's work and thought. It is intended to be almost synonymous with "dialectic," and acknowledges the eternal failure of understanding that bedevils even the most worthy of personal interactions. The incorrigible self-deception characteristic of all persons fundamentally subverts all subjectivity, and guarantees that our most sublime interactions are also only partial recognitions of truth. The agonistic character of every dialectic (see Chapter 1) serves to further defeat any possibility that the psychotherapeutic encounter will be transcendent and sublime.

The word *subjectivity* carries numerous burdens, even as it illuminates matters for us in other respects. One of these burdens is that there is a subtle but definite implication of passivity. It deemphasizes action. To refer to "preferred personal stances" partially corrects this, but carries a thin-blooded insinuation that behavior is merely "preferred." Intersubjectivity intends to demonstrate that we are locked into semiotic worlds of our own design that constrain us inexorably. We ought not to fret too much about the failure of words to capture our intent perfectly. Perfectly articulated theory and language would render humans mechanical and sterile.

The psychotherapist's emphasis on subjectivity is subject to other abuses. All too commonly, certain subjective states are assigned higher value than are others. Commonly integration, cohesiveness, and a clear sense of identity are afforded such preference. Uncertain self states and confusion are cast as being somehow faulty or even as primitive and "prestructural" (whatever that means!).

I suggest that the psychotherapist eschews such assumptions. To her, uncertainty and confusion are definitive and resolute subjective stances that are as motivated and purposeful as are integration and cohesiveness. She is inclined to see identity and integration as wholesome sounding banalities. To her, such definite, solid, and stable positions bespeak a state of imprisonment, an enslavement by a semiotic world that allows little flexibility and forbids change. She wants the ego to be open, and, to her, uncertainty counts as a trivial price to pay for the splendid and nerve-wracking benefits of not being locked into rigid positions. In its safest usage, *identity* is what we pursue and may become, rather than being a static existential state. What we may become is never to be thought of as an eventual end point or final resting place. We are creatures of flux, and our identities are not established.

All of us are locked into our rigidities and are forever compelled to struggle when change is at stake. Even confusion and fluidity are, to the psychological theorist, solid and inflexible stances whereby the person under consideration is resolutely confused and resolutely fluid. But we can think and speak of "non-identity" and "nonintegrated" postures, thereby promoting the possibility of change.

As far as she can manage it, the psychotherapist lets herself be imaginatively carried away by the stories, dreams, and convictions told to her by her patients. Although skeptical by nature, and cautioned to such skepticism by her theories, the psychotherapist tries to suspend judgment, to suspend disbelief, and to reside as fully as she can in the truth world of her patients.

To sense the worlds of which she is becoming aware, her suspension of judgment is, when she can manage it, radical. The psychotherapist wants to be immersed in what she hears, to submit to the narratives that emerge. In short, she finds herself enthralled. This impossible feat is accomplished even though, in another part of herself, she knows that narratives are always corrupt, deftly deceptive, and full of projections. The stories that her patients tell her are grounded in displacements that steer the patient away from other, more disturbing truths. Everything told is drenched in value judgments. In a certain sense, every word told to the therapist (just as is every word spoken by any of us) is a paranoid distortion, aimed at self-comfort, excusing the self, and discovering the unsavory only in the other.

All this the psychotherapist does in a state of cool chastity and standoffishness. She is betrothed to reflectiveness and hence loyal to reason and to the avoidance of folly. Even flamboyant psychological symptoms—extravagant paralyses, preposterous panics, and the vulgar self-abuse of depressives—are listened to respectfully and acceptingly. Dreams, which patients, without the psychotherapist's prompting, report with great seriousness, are afforded as much interest by her as is any other communication. When she hears of troublesome relationships, the therapist makes no sounds of caution or of concern. Especially with relationships, she is liable to listen for a dialectic between her patient and the other, rather than judging the other who has been portrayed in troublesome terms. Even the idea that the patient is presenting to her psychotherapist the dialectic between himself and another is treated in a once-removed manner. To the listening therapist this is a report, a story, a narrative, about a dialectic. It is what the patient wishes to present to the therapist as being the state of affairs, rather than being an actual state of affairs. Can an actual state of affairs ever be known, apart from how it is narrated to us by another or by ourselves?

The emotional entanglement of the patient with his therapist—the transference—is the most brilliant arena in which the patient's story can unfold. In that arena the therapist is faced with innumerable opportunities for fearful evasions and excited indulgence. It is all too easy for the therapist to be unwittingly charming and to provoke and incite modest transference love into inflamed transference love. It is equally easy to subdue and to kill the patient's love by way of banalities such as, "This is just something stirred up by the treatment," or "This is just a repetition of your one-time love of your father (of your suppressed love for your husband, brother, teacher)."

Angry transferences are more often subjected to the latter fate. The therapist's annoying remark—not necessarily wrong—is easy to explain away by recourse to "What I actually meant was . . ." What the psychotherapist ought to do when her patient (supposedly) misunderstands her is to hold her tongue. Most of the time anger is a rare and precious commodity and the therapist is well advised to not explain herself for she will, on the one hand, cripple or kill the angry moment or, on the other, display her nervous defensiveness. That defensiveness will lead the patient into maneuvers aimed at comforting the therapist or, less commonly, lead him into scorn and disdain for the therapist's cowardice. The psychotherapist never aims to suppress her patient and therefore her fate is to eternally listen and to believe—at least at first.

The transference is one example of the patient's *object relationships*. There is a danger that this term will lead the observer to think of a discrete person having a relationship with a discrete other. The psychotherapist sticks with her dialectical position and is inclined to say evocative things such as "the other is constitutive of the 'I.'"

Why must the psychotherapist listen so much and so credulously? Partly it is because she wants her patient to relax and to let down his guard. He should never have the feeling that the therapist wants him to achieve a goal or to feel that he must do anything for the therapist. If she mentions a behavior, perhaps a tendency on the part of the patient to be forever rational, reasonable, and organized, she is liable to imply that it is a problem, that she wants him to give it up, that he ought to loosen up.

She must mention typical behaviors despite the inhibiting potential of everything she says. Just the same, the idea she wishes to convey to her patient is that the state of being highly rational is him and, in a certain sense, will always be him. "This is you," she says, and, although she may not say so explicitly, wants always to imply an addendum: ". . . and who is to say that this should be otherwise?" She may even prophesy that, naturally enough, and to their great mutual interest, his response to what she points out will usually be a further, or even an increased, torrent of rationality and organization. If she implies that free associations or a stream of consciousness is the order of the day, her patient is quite likely to make a rational attempt at such nonrational modes of thought and speech.

Another reason for her innocent restraint is that she hopes that it will put her patient into a position wherein he will think. If she takes no sides, advocates no particular actions, and is dispassionately restrained, her patient can neither cooperate nor oppose. He can only think. This is what the psychotherapist wants for her patient. She is eternally terrified of simplicity and reductionism. Like the contradictory mandate given to us by our culture, and even as she eschews final positions, she finds herself standing for a firm position after all: "There are two sides to every issue, and therefore sloganeering—'Hug your children more!' or 'Give them more structure!'—is to become well-nigh impossible."

As she performs her initial task and takes her patient's tales at face value, she becomes aware that many voices are clamoring to be heard. The consciousness that thinks her (that she can be passive enough to let the patient "think her" is precisely what she wants to accomplish) turns out to be made up of swarms of conscious homunculi in action. These are narratives—preferred stories and tales that she is hearing. In her state of receptivity she dare not know yet that there is a contrapuntal world of unconscious homunculi. These "creatures" carry the patient's beliefs, values, and archetypes and are in convoluted and often mutually contradictory interaction with one another. Like the values demanded by the cultural law, the patient's beliefs and values are inconsistent.

The ego, the id, and the superego are highly elaborated homunculi—and very intelligent ones at that. Any conceptual model for mind must, ultimately, be made up of such creature-like structures. If I say of the mind that it is made up of warring factions, then ergo, homunculi. If I say that "generator" and "test" is the most potent model of mental functioning, then ergo, homunculi. We are talking about people and therefore people-like parts and elements are inevitable.

> It is possible to suppose that the character of the ego is a precipitate of abandoned object-cathexes and that it contains the history of those object-choices. [Freud 1923, p. 29]

Such internalized identifications are the stuff of all behavior, because, being creatures of culture, we act in accord with cultural modalities, most often as they have been presented to us by parents and other important persons. It is not even necessary that we should have personal knowledge of our identificatory models. We can just as well identify with historical figures who, for one reason or another, we have chosen as models.

There has always been a widespread interest in reincarnation and in past lives. Those past existences and vaguely remembered images of oneself—images often ardently believed in—are to be taken seriously. The psychotherapist interprets these images as manifestations of identifications deeply present in the mind of those who make such claims. Whether these are called introjects, internal objects, or primary process presences is probably of minor importance. The important point is that they may be visible only with great difficulty or, on other occasions, attain a reality that makes for deeply believed delusions and illusions.

The same thing goes for spiritism and for various forms of "possession." They may be considered old fashioned, and optimists may believe that "enlightenment" will make such beliefs disappear, but I suspect that they are part of any human heritage. In another form they are the archetypes through which we orient ourselves in the world. By way of her credulous listening, the psychotherapist permits these psychological homunculi to become legible.

It is common for theoreticians to think of persons as being rational centers of action. In addition, they are liable to say, this central rationality is contaminated by a variety of unconscious subversive forces, including identifications. This type of formulation portrays Freud's great discovery in terms more modest than is required. What he drew to our attention is that persons are *fundamentally* self-deceptive and self-deluded, and have no pristine exempt-from-conflict core. To conceive of a rational central core, only contaminated by conflict, is to miss the scandalous point that Freud wished to make.

Freud's early formulations of this point already lead us into a catastrophic disequilibrium if we try to know ourselves or another. Lacan has pointed out again and again that in *The Ego and the Id* (1923), Freud has partially recanted his own heretical discovery. During the course of treatment, he now says, the ego gradually conquers the id. In other words, the idea of a fundamental self-deception is modified, critics of psychoanalysis will retreat, and the world will heave a sigh of relief. One must not be deceived. Despite his theoretical pyrotechnics, Freud's clinical writings never falter. When examining and analyzing—be they patients or literary figures—he steadfastly adheres to his claim of ubiquitous human self-deception.

The trickiness of language bedevils critical psychological thought every step of the way. Take, for example, the word *person*. It has, I would say, a solid ring to it. It presupposes a substantiality that the psychotherapist wants to undermine. That substantiality is the reason why so many have opted for the word *subject*. Unfortunately, the psychotherapist is discontent with that term as well. It is better, because it suggests a certain fluidity. But the passivity that it implies creates new headaches. Although the psychotherapist wishes to doubt that the patient is as much an agent of his life as he may think, she is equally reluctant to deny him agency. She wants not to understand her patient as the product of blind forces and, at the same time, she does not want to see him as a voluntaristic free will. As always, she wants multiple descriptions to be applied. The trick is to not get too hung up on words, to refrain from substantializing them, and to try to describe everything many times over. Multiple metaphors and multiple descriptions are our theoretical salvation.

> The belief that regards the soul as something indestructible, eternal, indivisible, as a monad, as an *atomon*: this belief ought to be expelled from science! . . . But the way is open for new versions and refinements of the soul-hypothesis; and such conceptions as "mortal soul," and "soul as subjective multiplicity," and "soul as social structure of the drives and affects" want henceforth to have citizen's rights in science. [Nietzsche 1886, p. 12]

Nietzsche was a forerunner of Freud. He was a radical critic of the idea of a unitary self: "Evil I call it, and misanthropic—all this teaching of the One and the Plenum and the Unmoved and the Sated and the Permanent" (1884, II, p. 20).

This adds up to the third dictum for the psychotherapist to live by: *she must keep alive in the back of her mind that self-deception is, for all persons, the order of the day*, even though the psychotherapist more commonly—at least in the foreground of her mind—lets herself be carried away by the universe to which her patients lay claim.

Carried away though she is, the therapist is dreamily aware of incongruities in her patients' narratives. Even as she pursues her credulous agenda, she notes in her patients' free associations, that is, in the tales to which she is witness, definite patterns, repetitions, and preoccupations. Not that she quickly or bluntly reveals what she sees. Instead, she tries to respect the mask. But, like the artist, she sees much and suffers the fate of all who see too much. It is "inhumane," says Thomas Mann (1936), that the artist should strip away all artifice, all comforting illusion:

> To see things clearly, if even through tears, to recognize, notice, observe, even at the very moment when hands are clinging and lips meeting, and the eye is blinded with feeling—it is infamous, indecent, outrageous. [pp. 106–107]

The psychotherapist's conviction is that truth is a mobile army of metaphors and her ardent hope is that she can escape from the ordinary as she does her descriptive-explanatory job. Familiar language will sometimes work but, more often, she has recourse to novel—perhaps eccentric—language. With a self-deprecating chuckle, she thinks to herself that she must emulate genius and find never-before-known tactics of description. "What else can I aim for," she thinks, "if I am trying to actualize all possible forms of the world?"

The search for the truth, the psychotherapist ruefully acknowledges, is not a question of accumulations of more and more knowledge. On the contrary, the patient's fate, as he increasingly looks inward, is that of the Christian church. Christianity, even as it demanded belief, undermined the idea that belief can be solid or certain. Heller (1965) paraphrases one of

Nietzsche's most subtle arguments (as opposed to his usual frantic ones):

> On the one hand, [the Church pursued] a more refined sense of truth than any other civilization has ever known, an almost uncontrollable desire for absolute spiritual and intellectual certainties; and, on the other hand, the ever-present suspicion that life on this earth is not in itself a supreme value, but in need of a higher, a transcendental justification. [p. 181]

To Nietzsche, this meant that intellectual reflectiveness, sought with unremitting honesty and illuminated by a persistent mistrust of the world, can only lead to the undermining of knowledge. The task of the psychotherapist is the same. Her patient's search for self-knowledge can only lead to increased doubt about all that is claimed to be known. But the patient (and his undermining and disturbing psychotherapist), even as they struggle toward their ambivalent goal, will, like the Church, fight tooth and nail not to know the very thing they claim to seek. Again and again, belief will be invoked.

All too often, this will take the form of elitism. "The therapist and I, special and unique by way of our strangely rigorous assignment, are a cut above the masses who ignore such profundities." Just as often, the patient is left out of this equation and it is only the wise psychotherapist who occupies a place of special status: "Thank God," says the patient, "that I found this remarkable person who has transformed my life."

That elitism has been carried to even greater lengths. Both Nietzsche and Socrates, under the title of the "noble lie," were convinced that special truths were to be kept from the masses, who were incapable of such understanding. Unfortunately, the belief in special knowledge of truth is shared by every tyrant. Even Samuel Johnson, when he debated Bishop Berkeley ("I refute you thus"), was reverting to the argument from blind belief. "It's obvious," he announced, even though it was not obvious to the very person he was debating.

Whenever she can, the psychotherapist tries to unmask such belief-convictions. And, even when she is successful, she will be chagrined to find that the patient still believes that the psychotherapist is, for example, a unique wonder or a malignant persecutor. When we successfully refute our spouses, do they not still pursue their false agendas? When the same therapist looks inward, will she not discover her own foibles and, with a willfulness equal to that of her patient, will she not simultaneously disbelieve what she has just discovered? Self-deluding lies, even when revealed, are inclined to persist.

Science differs from other belief systems in its willingness to call every belief into question and, most important, its willingness to call its own beliefs to account. This is the same questioning stance that the psychotherapist attempts to attain. But the systematic nature of her attempt is too often implicit, rather than explicit, and if, like certain misguided scientists, she claims to discover solid facts and substantial truths, she has lost her bearings. The explicitness of the psychotherapist's doubt is captured by a comment in Freud (1917):

> [Psychoanalysis] has from the start frivolously forfeited the sympathy of every friend of sober scientific thought, and laid itself open to the suspicion of being a fantastic esoteric doctrine eager to make mysteries and fish in troubled waters. . . . Yet I can assure you that the hypothesis of there being unconscious mental processes paves the way to a decisive new orientation in the world and in science. [p. 22]

The psychotherapist's credulity is eventually strained. The patient fails in his agenda of free associations, and becomes repetitive. A full freedom of desire would permit unending fascination, unending novelty, and an endless expanse of thought. Instead, associations flow into patterns and dead ends. It becomes clear that the patient desires specifics. He has an agenda. His desire, rather than being neutral and universal, is limited. Desire seeks:

The good.

The essential.

The true answer.

The dream or the imaginary.

The solid.

The coherent.

The correct theory.

That which intoxicates and satisfies.

All these items are opinions on the intrinsic nature of things and of the world. Each is an echo of the idea that God had a purpose or a thing that he wanted to create, something special, concrete, real, precious, and holy. In fact, the world is not discovered but, instead, is something with which we cope, play, dance, struggle, or have a dialogue. Such forms of essentialism are one of the great theoretical pitfalls awaiting the psychotherapist, because she, just like her patient, longs for solid ground, clarity of theory, and a final answer. The other pitfall, to be discussed later, is the hierarchical notion of developmental stages.

The psychotherapist does not have a direct view of her patient making a naked pursuit of his elusive unconscious agenda. Instead, she sees him enraptured by conscious, self-deceptive goals, but interrupted by unconscious intrusions that inexplicably present themselves. The psychotherapist sees unexpected suffering, supposedly not sought by the patient but, willy-nilly, repetitively apparent. Patterns become apparent, for example patterns such as consistent passivity. The stories told by such a patient depict him almost exclusively as the locus of "happenings" and only rarely as the agent of "doings." Slips of the tongue (and other parapraxes) erupt and contradict what the patient has been at great pains to establish. He is preoccupied by things. Why? Could it be that, if he is not resolutely preoccupied by weakness, might he, to his horror, be preoccupied by power and potency? Why do certain recognizable characters repeatedly appear in the patient's narratives? Are these required archetypal figures who the patient dare not permit to be out of the foreground?

There are numerous issues that can alert the psychotherapist to the unconscious agendas with which the patient secretly undermines the very thing that he thinks he has in mind. A comment made by a psalmist to one of my patients illustrates my point. He was a believer in a number of cultlike practices and was much impressed one day when a psalmist said to him, "You will always be backed into a corner by women!" I had, for a long time, been wondering how to enter into this patient's world of occultism—a world precious to him and not to be called into question by anyone.

Suddenly I knew what to say. "Of course," I said, "all of us are backed into corners by women. What is actually in question is not whether women back us into corners but, instead, in what way are we backed into a corner by women, is it not?" In other words, I pointed out to him that all interpersonal events are discoverable in any life and that being "backed into a corner by women" is one of those universally discoverable things. For the psychotherapist, being backed into a corner is not a discovery made by a palmist but, rather, a well-known and persistent interpersonal posture or role that serves a purpose in the patient's life. For another person, being backed into a corner by a woman could never appear as a conscious thought and, in some cases, the only permissible configuration would be the perfect opposite: "I back all women into a corner." In other words, the discovery that a person is, or will, always be backed into a corner, is a trivial, if not universal, banality.

Anything important is problematic and therefore one could make the same prophecy about anything that matters. Children will always back us into a corner. The nature of truth will always back us into a corner. So will friendship, the law, and the fact of the world's existence. In contrast, how we struggle with these things is of very great interest.

This is well illustrated by the young psychotherapist who tells her patient that he is angry. This statement is, at best, a cliché and, more accurately, is merely the statement of a universal truth. Is not every person, one way or another, angry? The only illuminating comment that can be made to a patient on this score would concern his way of being angry. We are all angry but, more important, how are we angry? Further questions can then come to mind. When angry, am I, on the surface and in my own awareness, the man who is eternally without anger? Am I, then, a person of intensified kindness and goodness? Or, instead of becoming the man of eternal goodness, do I become an odd reclusive fool? Do I shriek and rage and earn for myself the judgment that I am a stupid hothead?

What is in question for the psychotherapist is rarely whether something is there or not there. Her question is rarely an existential one. Generally, she assumes that all persons fully know the range of human mental states. She is interested, instead, in the nature of the person's anger, or the style in which a person is angry, or backed into a corner, or is anything else that is human.

The psychotherapist is much interested in guilt. She assumes its presence *a priori*. Does it appear as conscious guilt? Or does it appear in a more derivative form, for example as low self-esteem? Unfortunately, the phrase *low self-esteem* has become a cliché and has lost its serious psychological meaning. If a person persistently thinks ill of himself, is it not obvious that he feels guilt? And, if he persists in this despite evidence that he is not a wicked sinner, does this not suggest an unconscious belief that he is a sinner? In the modern cliché such an attitude is attributed to the environment, and is thought to be merely a response to environmental attitudes, an attribution that is an oversimplification.

What about the person who, although eager to live a happy and successful life, repeatedly and inexplicably acts against his own interest? I do not refer here merely to the many small ways in which all of us sabotage ourselves, although such behaviors are good examples of what I have in mind. I also refer here to catastrophic, self-damaging criminality, to alcohol and drug abuse, to the undermining of marriage and family, and to the psychological self-abuse of depression or of any other disabling mental state. All are, one way or another, manifestations of guilt or, in another language, of self-punishment.

This analysis of guilt and of anger can be used as a model for the analysis of many other mental elements. To the psychotherapist, love, intelligence, motivation for treatment, and psychological-mindedness are all candidates for qualitative and not quantitative analysis. She assumes that they are universals, and she wants to know how they manifest themselves in particular persons. The nonhierarchical position of the psychotherapist demands that she make no judgment about what form of love, intelligence, or psychological-mindedness is better. This is a theoretical truth that warrants general interest.

My assertion that intelligence is not a discoverable thing that can be found in me or in someone else will be a blow to those who find intelligence to be a precious trait in themselves. Nevertheless, the psychotherapist's assumption is that intelligence, like so much else in a person, is a psychological stance—a posture that serves multiple unconscious purposes. If I portray myself—for my own benefit and for the benefit of others—as intelligent or, perhaps, as an intellectual, I have seized upon it as a culturally available role. It can only be assumed that, over the course of my life, I have found it to be an adequate solution to my personal circumstances. Some would call this my "compromise solution."

For other persons, a posture of "I'm not very bright" has become the solution of choice. And for still others, a quirky type of mind works best. Such a person might be verbally brilliant and a practical dullard. Some are great lovers and others seem not to love at all. Some are loners, and others gregarious. To some people, cool civility is admirable; to others, enthusiastic hugs are to be delivered widely. The psychotherapist views such matters with disinterest and dispassionately. They are, she assumes, none of her business. She is terrified of judgment in her professional actions and is appalled whenever she hears colleagues slip into hierarchical thinking. At her best, she is ever alert to tendencies in herself to think of certain behaviors as sick, pathological, infantile, or primitive. Although she knows that she may unwittingly say this of a behavioral trait, the psychotherapist is concerned that she may make a worse blunder, and generalize such judgmental attitudes to a person. The person—not just the trait—is primitive, infantile, and pathological.

This all-too-common tendency is institutionalized in certain developmental theories. Every theory that postulates stages of development is in jeopardy of promoting some behaviors as mature and other behaviors as immature. The psychotherapist will not participate in this judgmental game. Her mandate is to remain neutral. She advocates no final, preferred, or better way of life and relishes Nietzsche's (1909–1911) observation that "Whoever has attained intellectual freedom even to a small extent cannot feel but as a wanderer upon the face of the earth—and not as a traveler toward some final destination; for that does not exist" (I, p. 638). Therefore the psychotherapist gives no credence to any of the following as positions to be advocated:

Maturity, health.

Freedom, emancipation.

Individuation, integration, cohesion.

Discovery of a blameworthy element in the world.

Linguistic competence.

Finding one's true self.

Finally, *the psychotherapist, apart from the ordinary courtesies of day-to-day life, does nothing but make interpretations*. In a simple sense, this means speaking to her patient of what she sees, but "what she sees" is an *interpretation* of what she sees. In the strange world of psychology (and in much of the philosophical world) interpretation is all that is possible. By doing this, the therapist reveals angles and implications in what the patient has said that he will not have thought of before. In his typical biting style, Nietzsche (1886) underlines my point:

> It is perhaps dawning on five or six minds that physics, too, is only an interpretation and exegesis of the world (to suit us, if I may say so!) and *not* a world-explanation. . . . Most of what today displays itself as "objectivity," "being scientific," . . . "pure knowledge, free of will," is merely dressed up skepticism and paralysis of the will. [xiv, p. 211]

Repetitive and self-injurious behaviors come to the psychotherapist's attention most prominently. They are dealt with as psychological postures that are neither substantial nor essential, but as merely arbitrary and circumstantial. No interpretation made by the patient or by the therapist is permitted peaceful status as correct or as having superior truth value.

Every element in behavior is an identification. There is precious little that any person can do that is not modeled on a cultural role or archetype, especially a role embodied in another person—a parent, a family member, or a teacher. The model can even be a historical figure or an imaginary or literary figure. The point that the psychotherapist wants to keep in mind is that she must constantly try to determine who is "speaking the patient" at any given time. "Is this the voice of his father?" she might ask. "Could this be Macbeth who reports his sleepless night—Macbeth who, at the hands of his own guilt, hath murthered sleep? Or Ulysses? Leopold Bloom? The big bad wolf?" She must not forget, as she listens, that she must listen in two registers, for both the conscious and the unconscious identifications. The manifest will always be the perfect disqualifier of the latent.

As she works, the psychotherapist will increasingly find herself to be abandoning words like *rational*, *criterion*, *foundation*, and *absolute*. Instead, she will begin to have a higher regard for the irrational, the uncanny, and the magical-poetic.

> Mr. Snow was not interested in traditional sexual intimacy with his wife. He liked cuddling, receiving passive oral sex, and, less enthusiastically, mutual masturbation. Sometimes, after touching his wife sexually, he would carefully

wash his hands with soap. His wife was insulted and hurt. Reluctantly, after many months, Mr. Snow began to talk of his displeasure (he meant revulsion) with his wife's genitals, which he insisted on calling her "box."

As he and I struggled with this, it became clear that there was a certain safety in the term *box*. That slang word successfully transformed his wife's genitals for him. Instead of being an indeterminate and mysterious wonder (wonder is my term, and is far too complimentary for Mr. Snow's taste), he had transformed the female genitals into a geometric figure. No more mysterious, smelly, and luscious genitals existed. It was now a sterile sample of right angles and straight lines, and thereby very safe.

Although Mr. Snow did not say so, the word *box* has other implications as well. Pandora of Greek mythology, too, had a box. Her genitals, the story seems to suggest, are in accord with the nonvoluptuous preferences of Mr. Snow. To the surprise of Pandora and of the whole world, the innocent-looking box is a container full of demons, a fearful imagining about the female genitals that is characteristic of many patients. Pandora is Woman, set down upon the earth to punish man for his transgressions. The story was important enough to Greek mythopoetics that Pandora assumes the same punishing form in two mythological versions of her story.

In tandem with his troubling story about his dealings with his wife, Mr. Snow talked of the "looseness" of the female genitals. Were his anal sphincter (his "bum-hole") loose, a lot of indeterminate and messy poop might come out. His rational mind might, in an analogous way, be undermined by these discussions and, he suspected, this was why he was having an increased sense of confusion. To him, confusion was a great tragedy; to me, it was a welcome sign of comfort with the indeterminate. Did his confusion foretell comfort with the female genitals?

The mysterious genitals of Woman. Is it like a dream, full of strange and fascinating nooks and crannies? Is the psychotherapist's interest in dreams a substitute for—a displacement away from—another topic that is more unexpected, forbidden, and puzzling? Is a dream a safer arena for psychotherapeutic contemplation? Do we psychologists talk more about the penis—the safer-to-talk-about penis? Is a dream, like the woman's glorious genitals, a thing different or hidden from ordinary life, apart from immediacy? Can one enter into the woman's genitals just as one enters a dream, and are both these reluctant treasures accessible and yet disturbing?

A woman's genitals are what anchor a woman in her identity as woman, and she identifies with them. To be sexual through the mediation of her genitals means she must glory in, and savor, their amazing powers of pleasure, satisfaction, and reproduction. Furthermore, she must glory in their receptiveness and, although the word is stigmatized, in their passivity. By identifying with that organ, a woman gives birth to herself as an agent of birth and as an agent of receptivity. Distaste for passivity is, to me, bias. Who is to judge and to decide that passivity is to count as unattractive?

By the same token, a man identifies with his penis, also a wondrous organ. What men have is a thing that "sticks out" and can "stick into something." A man, by identifying with his penis, comes to create himself in the image of action, of penetrator, and in the image of pursuer. A boy, although not yet informed about the sexual function of the penis, identifies with the intrusive and active male role as he comes to know it in his father and in the culture's portrayal of Man. Later, he will join that activity with his own sexual performance and the adequate sexual employment of his penis.

If a homosexual man identifies with his penis, he usually identifies with receptive organs as well. Typically these are the anus and the mouth. Heterosexual men, too, identify with mouths and anuses at times: oral and anal reception by men is common.

Women, too, by way of penetrating fingers and tongues, identify with their own potentially intruding body parts, and enter and investigate openings. Our species is imaginative, witty, and various in its sexual tastes, and my focus on the female genitals is of interest largely because its discussion is, more often than not, neglected.

Women identify, too, with the bleeding of the menstruating genitals. Why else would it be that they—overwhelmingly more often than men—make scratch cuts to their wrists? Why else would it be that women, more often than men, cut their fingers with kitchen knives? (I know, of course, that I ought to say that they so cut their fingers because they are the ones who work in kitchens.)

From the Koran: Potiphar's wife was enthralled by her beautiful slave boy, Joseph. Her friends were baffled that the great lady should lower herself to loving a slave. To enlighten them, Potiphar's wife invited her friends to tea, a tea at which she served wonderful fresh pears and apples. To cut the fruit, she made sure that each of her friends had at her place a beautiful, and very sharp, silver knife. As they began to serve themselves, Potiphar's wife had Joseph enter the room so that they could all see him. To the psychologist of gender differences, what happened next, was obvious. All the friends—ladies-in-waiting, hangers-on, and minor nobility—cut their fingers to the bone when they laid eyes on the beautiful Joseph and tried to cut their fruit. The carnage was so great that the whole room was spattered with blood. The sight of the beautiful slave boy had excited in them an awakening of their identification with their own genitals. More specifically, he excited in them an identification with their own bleeding genitals. How wonderfully wise was Potiphar's wife!

By virtue of such identifications, are not men fated to have a special interest in a "stick out" intrusive mode? And are women, in a complementary fashion, fated to a receptive and passive mode of being in the world? The answer is one of those ambiguous treasures that psychotherapists aim always to keep in mind. Men are, indeed, intrusive and, as is the case for women, "anatomy is destiny." Just as true is the fact that men are forever liable to be backed into a corner, that is to say, to be passive. Women are passive and women are potent. All these statements are true even though, according to Aristotelian logic, they contradict one another. A person who would, on the grounds of political correctness, trumpet any one of these statements as exclusive truth is indulging in unadorned sloganeering and propaganda.

My analogy of the female genitals, the dream, is a quantum of discourse as surely as is any rational statement. A dream's enigmatic form is, however, due to the fact that it is a puzzle or a rebus and, as a consequence, it requires decoding. This is no different from the decoding of a mistake, a slip, or a parapraxis (*Fehlleistung*). Every mistake, no matter how stupid, is also an urgently successful fragment of discourse. In the stupid and wonderful world of psychology, a blunder (verbal or nonverbal) is also a wildly successful announcement. In Lacan's felicitous phrase, "the unconscious is structured like a language," and its manifestations are a rich and decipherable form of speech.

The double speech to which I refer is a product of the inexorable legalities that the culture bequeaths to us. The patient's unconscious speech, in radical disguise, is hidden because his moral economy finds those speech opinions to be unworthy and unbecoming. The parapraxes of speech and behavior—often thought to be psychological catastrophes—are common and purposeful in everyone.

We must read Freud's cases or Freud's dream analyses in *The Interpretation of Dreams* to recognize his determination that dreams, parapraxes, and commentaries on the woman's genitals are all multilayered and ambiguous. It is clear that the clouded speech intended by the dream is anterior to its interpretation and to its decipherment:

> It may well be that dreaming is a single whole, wherein dream and interpretation belong together and dreamer and interpreter only seem to be two separate persons but are actually interchangeable and one and the same, since together they make up the whole. Whoever dreams interprets also; and whoever would interpret must have dreamed. Your Excellen-

> cies . . . have lived under luxurious circumstances of unnecessary division of labour, so that when you dreamed, the interpretation was the business of your private soothsayers. But at bottom and by nature everybody is the interpreter of his own dream, and only out of sheer elegance does he have himself served with an interpretation. I will reveal to you the mystery of dreaming: the interpretation is earlier than the dream, and when we dream, the dream proceeds from the interpretation. How otherwise could it happen that a man knows perfectly when an interpretation is false? [Mann 1934, p. 892]

These are great truths spoken by two of the greatest of psychologists—the biblical Joseph, speaking in the words of Thomas Mann. Not that these master psychologists are idiosyncratic creatures who speak final truths. On the contrary, they know as well as does the modern psychologist, that truth is sought but never found. I assume, for example, that Joseph is wrong and also right when he claims that the dreamer knows when an interpretation is false. But the biblical tale demands that he speak as he did.

> Mr. Snow had more to say. When I, his therapist, am vague, odd, indeterminate, and, perhaps, tempting, then I am the female genitals. "You stink, you asshole," he announced.
>
> I thought to myself that he needed to cleanse himself of me, just as he had cleansed himself of his wife's secretions and smells. "So," I said, "I suppose you must now wash your hands of me?"
>
> Thereupon ensued a long, complex, confirmatory dialogue. His rationality is, he said, a "clean-up" measure. His joy in crisp sparkling shirts, ties, and suits, is a product of the same clean attitude that he so diligently fosters. My humor always buoys him because it refreshes and distracts him from darker (smellier? dirtier?) elements. "Thank God for Dr. W.'s sense of humor!
>
> "I am very sensitive to smells. I get all worked up when there are smells in a room. A few days ago, my son's girl-

friend laughed because my son had made a smell, and I couldn't believe that she would laugh. And yesterday I thought there might be a smell in this office, so I tried not to breathe through my nose. I actually considered walking out of your office."

I asked a question: "Why is it, Mr. Snow, that the smell made by another is offensive, whereas one's own smells are not? Indeed, may not one's own smells even be pleasurable?" The question is rhetorical. It aims to undermine Mr. Snow's attempts to live in a nonpsychological world, and to illustrate that it is not logical to be offended by this smell or that. Instead, he may want to think about his flamboyant (can so rational a man be called flamboyant?) reaction to smells, and to contemplate a psychology of smelling.

"I wouldn't touch that comment with a ten foot pole."

"Perhaps you would wish to wash your hands of it?"

"When I do a business case study, I immediately notice that it is, to begin with, vague and disorganized. I love 'solving' such studies and getting the right answer. Unfortunately for me, there often is no right answer. Because of that, I find myself doing something that *does* have a right answer: I correct the grammar. Grammar has strict rules that can be applied and I love commenting on the use of the ablative case and on gerunds. And why on earth, I ask you, do people put periods outside of the parentheses when there is a completed sentence inside the parentheses?"

Clearly, Mr. Snow finds the female genitals or the metaphor of the female genitals wherever he turns. And, wherever he finds it, there is a way of rendering it geometric, rational, and submissive to clear rules.

The psychotherapist wants to be right and to know and pronounce the truth. She wants this for many reasons but, in her (somewhat ridiculous) psychological self-revelatory way, she emphasizes that she wants this because of her pride, her vanity, and her recalcitrant wish to aggrandize herself. With wistful sighs she reminds herself that if her convictions are only relatively valid, there is no reason to stand up for them courageously. And yet, despite having no actual grounds for doing so, she tries to fight for her determined, indeterministic position. Ultimately, she fears, there are never adequate reasons for changes in belief (and change in beliefs is what psychotherapeutic change is all about) but, when she can, she struggles on anyway. The re-creation of a life, of one's person, can only be judged for what it is worth afterward.

What she is trying to do is to clear a space for living by demolishing idols, a sort of proscription, rather than a prescription for how to live a life. She want to sweep cobwebs out of corners, so that the distortions that prevent creativity are less influential. She has a persistent faith in the potential creativity of all people. Her work is, she thinks, a sort of destroying of a house of cards. She tries, like Ludwig Wittgenstein, to eliminate philosophical puzzles. She is also self-reflectively aware that she must not make an idol out of "tearing down idols." The idea that the psychotherapist has in mind is that she is never looking for essences.

Often, she thinks of herself as an event in her patient's life that leads him into an awakening, just as a great novel can awaken. Or can it? Surely, one might hope, Melville's Ahab, Dostoyevski's Raskolnikov, and Conrad's Kurtz are cautionary characters who can inspire us to lead better lives? The psychotherapist can only respond with another of her wistful sighs. "If only it were true that someone knew how to find a 'better' life, whatever that elusive thing might be." But must we not protest at this black commentary? What about a fine friend? What about my great and wise teacher? What about Bach, Mozart, and Ella Fitzgerald?

"No, no, no," says she. "This is a terrible and disturbing truth. One can never think that a man's responsiveness to great art is a measure of his character and his worthiness—his 'wellness.' Else how could he pursue serious culture in the morning and drop a bomb in the afternoon?"

I define psychotherapy narrowly as an exclusive and resolute search for self-knowledge. I advocate no support, advice, or counseling. But this is a minority position. Wherever I turn I hear calls for nonanalytic measures. Many psychotherapists believe that patients who are sicker or more disturbed warrant measures other than an inward search. This is, I believe, based on two errors. First, there is an apparent concrete belief that certain patients are, indeed, sick—hence, fragile, weak, and vulnerable. According to this logic, psychotherapy is a strong medicine that can break through or undermine weak defenses or weak psychological structures. But the notion of sickness is an hierarchical assumption that is fraught with nonpsychological and prejudicial bias—a bias that leads to the less-ambitious treatments that are advocated when "support" is recommended. Indeed, I am inclined to argue that these supposedly sicker patients, were they indeed sicker, would be more in need of an ambitious treatment than are those whose lives are less contaminated by suffering and self-undermining catastrophes.

Were this merely the misapprehension of some practitioners, the problem would be less worrisome. But the unwarranted hierarchical assumptions that mislead the uninformed psychotherapist have become institutionalized. This is particularly pernicious in the case of the numerous theories of development that plague our field. I have tried to undermine the influence of these theories (Warme 1994). All such theories promote the idea that certain behaviors and modes of thought are mature and that others are primitive or infantile. The theories of psychosexual development, of narcissistic development, and of self and ego development all share this prejudicial attitude toward behaviors that are merely variants on what people do.

The second error is the concretization of psychological terms. When a noun is used as a psychological term, there is always a risk that the psychological action in question will be treated as a thing. For example, if we say that an individual has a weak ego, all we mean is that he has adopted a posture that our culture labels weak. A man who relies on others for decision making, and weeps when he is expected to decide for himself, is easy to categorize as having a weak ego. The same goes for those who have poor judgment, who make judgments that are not in accord with social norms. Similarly, those who act impulsively are given the diagnosis of poor impulse control. Any one of these three examples is considered to be a sign of a weak ego.

But there is no thing that is weak. In fact, there is no such thing as an ego. It is only used because it has become a language habit. This habit invites us to believe that there is a thing to which the noun refers. The noun is merely a metaphor for a hard-to-pin-down piece of psychology. It would be useless to legislate that, in psychological theorizing, nouns are to be forbidden. Our language uses nouns in this way all the time, and any hope for a perfect language is as futile as is the quest for psychological perfection.

The leitmotif of this book has been the insistence that psychological phenomena can only be adequately captured by way of multiple descriptive metaphors. To say a person's ego is weak is not to be taken literally because it is only one of a host of metaphors that can be applied. For example, one could say of the patient who is said to have a weak ego that he is a self-injurious fool. Who else would indulge in the avoidance of decisions, make poor judgments, and perform stupidly impulsive acts?

Some will be horrified that I invoke these new, somewhat judgmental descriptions. They are, indeed, judgmental, but the earlier descriptions are judgments, too; the judgment was that the person in question is a victim of a structural weakness in a part of his psyche, the ego. One can clearly see that both metaphors limit our ways of conceptualizing what has gone on, and that reality is best served by the use of many exhaustively descriptive metaphors.

The idea of support can only be invoked if the theorist has concretized and taken literally the metaphor of weakness. It means that the theorist declines to apply other metaphors to the psychology of her patient. If she falls into this trap, she will decline to communicate hard truths to her patients and, furthermore, will never learn that it is possible to convey awkward and inconvenient information with tact and with good effect.

That psychotherapist, although full of good intentions, will patronize her patients with praise and advice, and will use self-disclosure to show her patient that he is no worse off than is she. Finally, her interpretations will be less than forthcoming since she will avoid the unconscious always or whenever she (patronizingly) thinks that her patient will "not be able to take it" (Winston et al. 1986).

The intensive psychotherapy that I advocate for all patients is single-mindedly subversive, although subversive with kindness, humor, and philosophical wistfulness. For some practitioners, it is a therapy for the few, and for some, it is a therapy only to be found in formal psychoanalytic treatment. I disagree. To me, psychoanalytic treatment (and any other intensive insight promoting therapy) is not captured only by the traditional formal method. The essence of in-depth treatment lies elsewhere. The therapist is doing her insight-oriented analyzing task if she does the following:

1. Attains some version of neutrality or disinterest in her attitude toward her patient.
2. Thereby becomes curiously psychological in her stance vis-à-vis her patient.
3. Intervenes only by way of interpretations intended to promote insight.

The only intensive psychotherapy or psychoanalysis that I can conceive of does not depend on frequency of meetings, on the use of the couch, or on the formal title "psychoanalysis," although I wish that time and economics would permit every applicant for psychotherapy to attend five times weekly and to use the couch.

I am demanding a lot from the psychotherapist. Apart from the educational psychotherapists (who have no choice but to train and persuade) all therapists should be resolutely interpretive of what is unconscious. To me, it matters not a whit whether the psychotherapy is brief, a single interview, or four years of five times weekly analysis; the reappropriation of what is warded off is the psychotherapist's sole task. What is sauce for the goose is sauce for the gander, and no patient in psychotherapy should be deprived of the benefits of self-knowledge.

11

Despisèd and Rejected

He is despised and rejected of men; a man of sorrows, and acquainted with grief: and we hid as it were our faces from him; he was despised, and we esteemed him not.

—Isaiah

The Christian ideal has not been tried and found wanting. It has been found difficult; and left untried.

—G. K. Chesterton

Why bother doing psychotherapy with persons with major mood disorders? After all, the usual medical opinion on this matter is that this is a biological disorder that warrants a biological treatment. Since such persons have neurochemical abnormalities, it is said, the potent and effective drug treatments that are now available are the most logical form of intervention.

There are two objections to this line of argument. First, despite what is so often said, no one knows just what these so-called illnesses are. Whether they are called mood disorders, affective disorders, or manic-depressive illness, they are merely descriptions of certain kinds of behavior. The clear and resolute awareness that we are describing patients allows us to describe further and to redescribe. Redescription is the central tactic of the psychotherapist. Elaborate description is a sound and dependable procedure, whereas diagnostic statements are piteously liable to abuse. Here is the faulty logic into which diagnosticians can slip and which leads me to make my complaint.

Persons with certain severe symptoms—intensely sad mood, sleep difficulties, and appetite disturbances—can be grouped together into a recognizable syndrome that can be called "mood disorder." But what causes people to be in such a state? There must, we assume, be a cause. It is answered that it is because the patient has a mood disorder that he is in such a state. One can now see the faulty thinking. Certain symptoms are to be classified together and given a syndrome name; that syndrome name is then, suddenly, transformed into the cause of the symptom state.

The logic is undoubtedly wrong but, when used properly, it is a legitimate medical tactic. Syndromes are grouped together in the hope that a disorder can be identified but, in the odd form of thinking that I have pointed out, the name of a syndrome has come to count as a true illness and as a cause of certain symptoms. Were mood disorders named properly, for example, "Burton's syndrome," no one would make the logical error of saying that Burton's syndrome causes intense sadness as well as appetite and sleep disturbances.

No specific neuro-physio-biological abnormalities have ever been discovered and reputable textbooks do not claim otherwise: "The causal basis for mood disorders is not known" (Kaplan et al. 1994). In medicine at large, syndromes are typically accompanied by clearly identifiable physical or physiological changes. In the mood disorders we discover emotional, sleep, and eating changes that are thoroughly nonspecific since every person can have them. Nevertheless, students are required to conscientiously record as telling symptoms these elements of ordinary life.

The second objection to the biological position concerns the rhetoric that emphasizes the superiority of drug treatments. The results of drug treatment are about the same as the results of psychotherapeutic treatments. The new, better, drugs are freer of side effects but, my colleagues tell me, their effectiveness is about the same as that of the older drugs.

Although I am concerned about the overuse of drugs, I am also concerned that my skepticism may be overblown. The prevailing opinion is that depressive disorders are best treated with psychotherapy *and* with the appropriate drugs. But such a fair-minded opinion does not satisfy me as much as you might think. Partly, this is because of the very high incidence of the largest category of mood disorder—*Major Depressive Disorder*—which is said to afflict 15–25 percent of the population. Such an incidence makes me think of a variant on normality rather than of psychopathology.

There is another mood disorder which afflicts only about 1 percent of the population, nowadays known as *Bipolar I*. These people have both serious depressions and serious episodes of mania. I am less sanguine about the psychotherapeutic treatment of these patients. Is such a doubt due to the fact that manic patients are less likely to faithfully attend their appointments—or to come at all? Or is the doubt a consequence of more innate, more recalcitrant elements in their manic depressive way of life? Certainly, it would be unwise to deprive these patients of lithium (or newer drugs). Nor does it contradict the use of electroshock treatments, even though it is viewed with abhorrence by much of the public. None of these cautions mean that psychotherapy is contraindicated.

Do drugs, perhaps, work more quickly than psychotherapeutic methods? It is hard to know. There are many claims about the marvelous quickness and effectiveness of the antidepressive drugs. Yet, such enthusiasms can also be understood as the common credulity of our magic-hungry species for relief from the miseries that are part of every life. Dramatic anecdotes abound in psychotherapeutic circles as well and, one suspects, magical hope prompts credulity there, too. As Ferenczi and Rank (1925, p. 52) pointed out, "splendid cures . . . were effected, sometimes in a few days or weeks."

Among psychotherapists there are exchanges of stories about patients improperly treated by negligent biological psychiatrists; upon entering psychotherapy, they promptly recover. In biological circles there are reciprocal judgmental stories told about patients misled by fruitless years of psychotherapy for problems easily managed by the administration of appropriate drug treatment. Patients, too, tell both kinds of story. Therefore, in the case of psychotherapists, I propose that we say that their remarkable results are due to the "Prozac effect"; for the biological psychiatrists, I make the analogous proposal that their splendid outcomes be attributed to the "psychotherapy effect." Here are two stories from a psychotherapist's case records, both of which illustrate the rapid psychotherapeutic improvement characteristic of the "Prozac effect."

> Mr. Cousineau, a 40-year-old tool and die maker, entered therapy upon the urging of a psychiatrist-friend. He had been seriously depressed for nine years and had seen numerous psychiatrists, had been hospitalized six or seven times, had been treated with many drugs, and, a few months before his psychotherapy began, received electroconvulsive therapy.
>
> The psychotherapist, who had a special interest in the treatment of major depressive disorders, saw Mr. Cousineau three times weekly using the couch. The therapist, although she had no special warrant for optimism about this case, had a determination that this man, like any other patient, had the right to receive the benefits of a resolutely analytic approach to his problems. She therefore worked with him without using any supportive measures apart from her single-minded interpretive strategy. The patient himself, although very impatient about the ineffective drug treatments, continued to take his lithium medication lest he precipitate an even more ominous mental state. He had been

warned that there were great dangers in discontinuing the drug.

The patient spoke for six days in a stereotyped way about his stupidity, his harmful effects on his family, and about the futility of the treatment that was being attempted. This style of his was in keeping with the psychiatric records, going back nine years, that the psychotherapist had in her possession. She spoke little, but on one or two occasions in each appointment made brief comments on what she was observing: "You take great pains to convince me of your inferior status. Every word you utter aims to establish that you are the 'wretched one.' . . . It has been your fate for the last nine years to be exclusively understood by yourself as stupid, burdensome, and without value."

In the seventh appointment Mr. Cousineau reported that he had had wild dreams all night long. This was unusual because he did not remember having dreamed for many years. When he awoke his depression had vanished. In fact, he said, he had been depressed for longer than the nine years in which he had been a psychiatric patient. He recalled being depressed even as a teenager. But, he added, after being free of depression for a few hours that morning, the depression had returned.

During the following weeks the intensity of his depression gradually waned and, after seven weeks, was gone, never to return. At that time, Mr. Cousineau discontinued his lithium medication without the drug treatments ever having been discussed with his psychotherapist. She was, she reports, simply uninterested in the topic and, since her patient had another psychiatrist who prescribed the drugs, she left the matter in the hands of her patient and the other psychiatrist. Had her patient asked for her advice regarding her drug treatment, she would simply have analyzed the motives that prompted him to cast her in the role of having a drug expertise that she neither had nor claimed to have. Mr. Cousineau claims that he was fortunate indeed to come under the care of a person as skilled, concerned, and humane as his psychotherapist. He is of this opinion still, although he understands with wry amusement that this is also part of his aggrandizement of her (nine-year follow-up).

A second patient was considered by his therapist, Dr. Able, to have had an indeterminate outcome. However, from my point of view, the facts of the case suggest that considerable improvement had taken place. The therapist, as will become clear from this case report, had a mischievous style that sometimes made even me uneasy. More important is the therapist's ideological fervor that, in my opinion, made her an automatic enemy of nonpsychotherapeutic methods. I am convinced that drugs and biological theories have been overused in recent years, and that opinion of mine undoubtedly made this therapist choose me as a supervisor. My concern about her was that she wanted to transform the advocates of psychopharmacological methods into enemies that she and her patients should denounce together.

This is how Dr. Able reported that case to me. The patient in question had eighteen hospital admissions for treatment of depression and for manic episodes during the three years prior to his work with Dr. Able. He had received every imaginable drug treatment and, expectably, had been given electroconvulsive treatments as well. Because he was a man of some wealth, he had made trips to two centers outside of Canada for consultative opinions, neither of which led to any new formulations of his problem nor to any new therapeutic strategies. Dr. Able said scornfully that those consultants had referred to the patient as a "rapid cycler." She was sure, she said, that such nonexplanatory epithets had been hurled at the poor man in Toronto as well.

The patient in question would only agree to meet with Dr. Able once weekly. He was, in fact, reluctant to come at all because he was convinced that psychotherapy was a waste of time. Nevertheless, because his psychiatrist had insisted on it, he came for his appointments, albeit with an attitude of sulky, stubborn determination. For a year he met regularly with his therapist but, for both of them, the meetings were experienced as awkward and profitless. The patient could think of nothing to talk about and ventured to speak only of small fragments of his personal life. Mostly he talked of his "biological affliction" and of his incredulity at Able's skepticism about that explanation of his unfortunate style of life. He also talked extensively about his various medications, including many details about his visits and phone calls to the psychiatrist who prescribed and advised about drugs. At the end of that first year he insisted that Dr. Able should discuss seriously with him whether there was any value in continuing. "What would you do, Dr. Able, if you were in my place?"

Dr. Able's answer was a comment mischievous enough that it somewhat unnerved me. But I must also admit that it made me wonder whether I was too stuffy for my own good, and for that of my patients. "Mr. Raynor," she said, "if I were you I would fall to my knees, fold my hands in supplication, and beg my therapist to take me into psychotherapy. I would plead with her to allow me to come five times weekly. Furthermore, I would leap onto the psychoanalytic couch, not because it guarantees any therapeutic advantage but just in case it affords such an advantage. That, Mr. Raynor, is what I would do."

The patient was, she told me, nonplussed. He complained that he did not understand why Dr. Able should speak so forcefully in favor of intensified treatment. "I have no sense—as you well know—that the psychotherapy does any good. Only my medications keep me going."

"Mr. Raynor," said his therapist (and I imagine her doing so angrily, almost ruthlessly, and with great satisfaction), "are you not aware that we have been meeting for one year and that since you began you have not been hospitalized?"

Without any need for begging and pleading, Raynor began psychoanalytic work a few months later. On the first day he reclined on the couch (prior to this he had sat in a chair) and, after about twenty minutes of awkwardness, began speaking enthusiastically. I have trouble reproducing the words that Dr. Able attributed to the patient but, in effect, this is what she said. Lying on the couch led the patient to feel a comfort in speaking that he had never felt before; he was filled with thoughts that he wished to discuss; he was eager to proceed. For the next eighteen months the psychotherapeutic work was carried out in a straightforward fashion. A dramatic improvement in his depression took place within a few weeks. At the end of that time Raynor announced that he felt able to carry on alone, and the therapy ended.

Two years later, Dr. Able met her patient at a social gathering. Raynor stated that during the year immediately past, his manic depression had been worse than ever before. Upon questioning it was revealed that, nevertheless, he had no further hospitalizations. When asked why, considering how much his therapy had helped him, he had not arranged to meet again with Dr. Able, he answered, "I never plead or beg for anything from anyone."

Dr. Able invited Raynor to come and to meet with her and Raynor agreed to do so in the fall. He did not call and she did not hear from him again.

This case had an indeterminate outcome. If we are determined to demonstrate to the psychiatric establishment that they are precipitate in their biological (mis)understanding of such patients and wish to prove our case, we must be as modest as possible about what we claim. The only thing that can be claimed with regard to this case is that, just as when they are treated with potent antidepressives, some patients have rapid and dramatic improvements.

Another issue arises from the case of Mr. Raynor. The radical change in his behavior took place when he began using the couch. Does this mean that lying on the couch is the cause of his sudden improvement? And why do we psychotherapists ask our patients to use the couch? No one knows the answer to this question, although it has been said that the reclining position permits regression to take place. The word *regression* is, however, difficult to be clear about, most of all because it can be thought of either as a good thing or as a bad thing (Warme 1994).

I think the reclining patient is, so to speak, addressing the wall. This is not as silly as at first it may seem. The psychotherapist herself, from time to time, may address the wall, for example, when working with a teenager or with a person made anxious by psychological talk. Looking at the wall, she may speak in the third person about the patient who is seated across the room: "I wonder what the devil Mr. X is worrying about today? It's weird. Usually I can talk to him about the sissy game that he plays around his wife. In fact, usually he knows that he does it to cover up his annoyance at the nicey-nice stuff that goes on whenever there is trouble in the house."

To keep the dialogue "cool," the therapist creates a distance between herself and the patient, first, by talking to a part of the room rather than directly to the patient, and second, by talking *about* the patient rather than talking *to* the patient. Such a tactic is nothing new; this is what the therapist does with the majority of her patients. She aims to remain in the world of ideas—including emotionally laden ideas—and of the imagination, and to combat her own tendency to lapse into the less-favored state of concreteness, that is to say, the state of *literalis terminalis*.

Less frequently, patients are intellectual, abstract, and aloof from the thrust and parry of "real life." With them, the psychotherapist may find that the couch is used in the opposite way. This must not be seen as a problem or as a reason to ask the patient to sit up. That the couch facilitates the patient's defensive intellectualizing helps to illuminated the patient's way of life just as it does with the patient for whom the couch makes things concrete and frightening.

The typical way in which the therapist works is to treat everything that the patient says as a narrative rather than as concrete truth. Rather than saying, for example, "You are, in contrast to yesterday, bitching about everything today," the therapist says, "Today the cranky one has arrived in this office; yesterday, another man, the kind man, was here." The second dialogue is more digestible than the first and more direct.

Exactly the same thing holds for reclining on the couch. There is, when the patient is lying down, a certain "once-removed" quality to what is going on and, for patients like Mr. Raynor, reflective talk becomes easier. But this is not always the case. Some patients, just to keep our task complicated, are thrown off balance when they use the couch. Therefore, my recommendation to therapists is as follows: Every psychotherapy patient should be offered the opportunity to recline on the couch, and for many this will facilitate their work. A smaller number will be found to reflect upon themselves better when sitting in a chair. I am told that, occasionally, a patient may opt to walk up and down the room. However, I have never had untoward consequences from the use of the couch, no matter what the patient's diagnosis.

Dr. Able, who had a special interest in the treatment of major depression and mania, told me of six other cases that she had worked with. Those other six cases, she reported, had remarkably successful outcomes. The course of their treatments (not the details of their personal psychology—just the externals of their progress) was very similar. Within a few weeks or months all of these patients stopped speaking of their biological disorder, of their depressions, and of their drugs.

When Dr. Able's lack of interest in such matters became clear (she insisted that she was not for or against the drug treatments but, rather, was simply bored by the subject) the patients seemed to lose interest in these matters as well. They talked instead of their personal lives, of their reaction to their peculiar and peculiarly attentive therapist, and of their remarkable self-definitions as depleted and weak. Those who had manias talked of the inflated self-definitions characteristic of those periods. Most had discontinued their medications of their own accord within a few months, although a few continued with them for up to a year.

Dr. Able's work with these patients, along with my own work with such persons, has made a dramatic impression on me. It confirmed for me what I had always believed: first, any person who wishes it, no matter how serious their disturbance, ought to be given the opportunity to work psychotherapeutically; and second, there is no simple biological causation of mental disorders.

Dr. Able reminded me about the 2,500-year-old story of a Chinese sage who met a young peasant who watered his fields in a primitive and time-consuming manner. The sage asked him: "Don't you know that there is a contraption called a draw-well, a kind of machine that would enable you to water a hundred such little fields in one day?" The peasant answered in this way: "I have heard my teacher say: He who uses machines, conducts his business like a machine. He who conducts his business like a machine, will soon have the heart of a machine. He who has the heart of a machine, has lost all certainties of the spirit. He who has lost the certainties of the spirit, must need sin against the meaning of life. Yes, I do know such machines as you speak of, but I also know why I shall not use them."

These clinical examples illustrate the intimate link between notions of madness and the kind of language that we use for madness. The language of illness is only one way of approaching the problem of mood disorders. The language of psychology is just as powerful, so one way of approaching the psychotherapeutic process is to see it as the conversion of the patient to a new linguistic universe. For example, the words that I now write upon this page are my attempt to convert the reader to a different linguistic universe. If this is so, my attempt could be understood in different ways, depending upon the language used:

> I am inviting you to relinquish archaic theoretical formulations.
>
> By using repetitive and hypnotic techniques I am, in a clever and sneaky way, brainwashing you.
>
> I am manipulating you and charming you with cute, tricky arguments.

I am putting forward a point of view for the interested audience to observe.

All of us have sets of slogans in accordance with which we organize our worlds and with which we justify our actions and our beliefs (Rorty 1989). With this "final vocabulary" we recognize what is to count as virtuous behavior, decide on the villainy of our enemies, explain away our own shortcomings, and manage to justify just about everything that we ourselves do. We also have a final language with which to discuss illness, especially mental illness.

Such final vocabularies are precious to us and are hard to change. Philosophers like Rorty have noted how reluctant we are to change our final vocabularies but psychotherapists have some additional things to say on this score. Final vocabularies are hard to change because each person has personal motives, to a great extent unconscious, for thinking and speaking as he does. These motives are unique and different in everyone, and are seized upon in response to the unique attitudes and beliefs that individuals have created for themselves.

Allegiances to prevailing final languages are demanded by systems of values—superego injunctions—that impel us to think according to certain of the social conventions, which are also the social roles and archetypal behaviors with which we identify. These precious and laboriously acquired language preferences make alternative language patterns hard to introduce.

The psychotherapist is uneasy about using the vocabulary of illness with regard to her patients. Since the well-being of her patients is at stake she is interested in experimenting with languages that may serve her better than does the illness language that is so prevalent. She may well explicitly raise doubts about that language, although not, as you might expect, because she feels that she has a better language. What she has in mind is simply a *different* language, and her great interest is in why a particular patient might so resolutely commit himself to a language of sickness.

She wonders, too, why society has analogous linguistic preferences. This point has caused some of my critics great concern. In essence, their complaint is that, for me, illness has an almost mystical nature and that I am calling into question the obvious. Obviously our patients are sick. Although I deny this, that complaint has led me to the assertion that such a view of illness or "madness" addresses the fact that one of the essential things about human life is that it is not mystical but, rather, a mystery.

Other patients, although fewer in number, are deeply committed to a final vocabulary about themselves that strongly avoids any implication of sickness, victimhood, or affliction. They prefer to speak of how they must stand on their own two feet, how they have made their own bed and must therefore lie in it, and that they must be mindful of past errors and henceforth choose more wisely. The psychotherapist will once again wonder whether other languages are possible and why the language of self-determination and free will are so moralistically preferred by them. What motives drive them to be so self-reliant, she asks? And if they are driven, are they really as self-reliant as they believe? Could they, perchance, be so self-determining that they could stop single-mindedly seeing themselves as self-reliant?

Sometimes psychotherapists fall into the same kind of unidimensional thinking. Here is a victim protocol that one therapist gives to patients: "Take the power in your life now. And as you do that, just repeat to yourself, 'I am now 100% accountable for what I attract into my life.'"

As the psychotherapy progresses, patients will, in their regressive or transformative way, elaborate such vocabularies with greater vigor. Those who think of themselves as sick and afflicted may pronounce upon their sick and afflicted state more vehemently. Those determined to be self-reliant may become more indignantly self-reliant. Since their psychological economy depends on these precious views of themselves, patients will oppose and be offended by the gentle liberties that the psychotherapist takes with regard to all final vocabularies—indeed, to all final positions, opinions, and beliefs.

The dialogue with a depressive patient may go something like this: The therapist has voiced mild skepticism about the patient's repetitive assertions that he suffers from a disease and that he has a chemical imbalance. "It's just common sense that it's a disease" is the argument typically made by such persons. Recourse to common sense is how we defend our final vocabularies. "It's only common sense," we say, "that children need structure and consistent discipline." Or, "It's only common sense that children need us to be empathic and, when they are difficult, they need our love more than ever."

The psychotherapist, too, can understand mood disorders in the same biological commonsense terms, especially since she is likely to reside in, or in association with, a medical/occupational world in which that particular brand of common sense is popular, influential, and taken for granted. And yet, being adventuresome, curious, and concerned that seriously depressed persons be understood in the most illuminating terms possible, she insists on exploring vocabularies that might lead to better help than is currently available.

Statements such as these are easy to make about depressive patients since they are often interested in participating in psychotherapy and, in my experience, often do well. If only the same could be said for manic patients who, much of the time, won't come to psychotherapy regularly enough to make such treatment feasible. On infrequent occasions I have done satisfactory therapeutic work with manic patients, but most are elusive candidates for what psychotherapists have to offer.

The psychotherapist, when at her best, does not participate in these final positions. She knows what the patient means about his commonsense positions, but she has doubts nevertheless. As Rorty says, she worries that she may have been born or educated into the wrong language tribe. She wants badly to hear about vocabularies other than manic-depressive illness and mood disorder. Perhaps, she wonders, she is not observing a manic-depressive illness but, rather, is witness to demonically pursued manic and depressive ways of life. And most of all she wants to experiment with a motivational language.

"He must have reasons for living his life as he does. I wonder what his motives are for debasing himself?" When depressed, the patient himself is the agent of his own self-abuse and self-denigration. When elated he convinces his anxious family (and all of the anxious persons in the world who must deal with him) that they must intervene and regulate his life. He convinces them that they should think of him as inadequate and as lacking judgment. They therefore judge him to be an inferior and sickly individual.

"If I agree that he is sick," thinks the psychotherapist, "I will be a full participant in the final vocabulary to which he so desperately clings. This vocabulary is the guarantor that he will remain unwell." She ultimately wants to have a detailed knowledge of her patient's motives for his deeply held final vocabulary. All too often, this is exactly what the patient does not want to know. The therapist is, as tactfully and patiently as she can, pursuing the unconscious.

"Maybe," thinks the therapist, "what I am observing is not a matter of scientific facts but, rather, a morbid yet poetic achievement." She wants to try out new languages, such as the language of poetry, because she suspects it may be a readier route to the unconscious motives that she seeks to elucidate. She is participating in a dialogue that undoes, or unglues, the final vocabulary of the patient.

> Mrs. Harris had seen two psychotherapists, both of whom advised her husband to have her hospitalized in a psychiatric facility. On both occasions she refused hospitalization and also refused the drug treatment that was offered to her. Eventually, by virtue of considerable shopping around, she found a therapist who, despite misgivings about her potential for suicide, agreed to see her.
>
> As a child, she and her family had moved into a new home. The previous tenants had left behind an old piano and, in the piano bench, she found sheet music. Since she was taking piano lessons at the time, she played the music she had found. Her family disliked the classical music that

> she now began to play, since they had more popular tastes. Mrs. Harris was extremely troubled by this turn of events since, to her, this meant that her family failed to recognize fine art, a taste that she seemed to have developed spontaneously.
>
> Later, she had a similar experience when a friend's family took her to the theater. Once again her parents reacted in a way that indicated to her that their tastes were "low brow." Later still she realized that her mother flirted in a vulgar way with the teenage boys who visited the home. She herself, Mrs. Harris realized, was much more appropriately modest than her own mother.
>
> Mrs. Harris resolutely, repetitively, and inexplicably described herself as the inferior and despicable "low brow" for the first two years of her psychotherapy. Only then did a modification—her recognition of her own hand in the creation of her depressive fate—begin to appear in her narrative.

Although not usually so slowly, so go the narratives of most depressed patients, narratives that are a posture of unfulfilled potential by way of an identification with the imagined inferiority of others. The other is thereby relatively elevated.

A new vocabulary for depression would no longer talk about depressive disease but, instead, would talk about depressive character styles or about a person's "inferiority propaganda." Such persons resolutely define themselves as inferior and elevate others and see them as powerful or better. In essence, they are donors of well-being to others.

Furthermore, such patients raise in comparison a different life that they claim would be better than the one they have. There is a great discrepancy between that imagined better life and their actual life. And in that discrepancy lies their depressive character style. To them "life is elsewhere."

If this is a character trait rather than a disease, then we must have a different and more ambitious attitude toward depressive and elated ways of life. There are, the psychotherapist says, many ways to live a life. She tries hard not to urge that the patient's life should change, although she is puzzled, worried, and concerned that someone should live his life in such a painful way. She advocates no "health" measures or symptom relief but, rather, is ready to enter into a dialogue with the patient should he desire it.

Besides, she is cheered by reading that the rates of manic-depressive illness are much greater in geniuses such as Lord Byron, Shelley, Melville, Schumann, Virginia Woolf, Coleridge, Aldous Huxley, Alexander Graham Bell, Einstein, and Matisse (Jamison 1993, Ludwig 1994). Such information allows her to be more thoughtful and less nervous about her depressed patients.

In her therapeutic work, two ideas eternally intrude into what she is doing. First, she assumes, with great resolution, that the patient is competent. Second, she attempts to position herself "in between."

> In between—it is the dwelling place of Thomas Mann's chief characters, the residence too of anxiety and disquiet, of irony and humor, of tragedy and comedy; that is to say, the accustomed place of man. [Heller 1958, p. 13]

The psychotherapist is content to allow herself the disquiet that follows upon such an uncertain locale. Therefore, if the patient speaks of wellness, she is led more deeply into her disquietude; if of disease, she thinks of another style of life; if despairingly, she thinks of hope. Her interventions with the patient may clarify and simplify matters but not necessarily, since they may, instead, lead to confusion, to increased complexity, to greater density, and to subtlety. Despite Freud's remark to the contrary, for the psychotherapist, a cigar is never just a cigar. Typically, the patient's reports and narratives become more compelling and show less of the banality so usual in stereotypical neurotic behavior.

> It still strikes me as strange that the case histories I write should read like short stories and that, as one might say, they lack the serious stamp of science. [Freud 1893–1895, p. 160]

The psychotherapist is troubled by suicidal threats and suicidal behavior, yet she is inclined to respond differently to such crises from the way in which most helpers respond. To understand this difference, and before saying just how she does respond, it is necessary to make a few theoretical remarks about the depressive style of life.

What goes on between therapist and patient can be conceptualized in many ways. The most common way is to say that patients are sick and the therapist takes care of the sick patient. The greater the degree of disturbance, the greater the degree to which the helping therapist intervenes, helps, takes over. In extreme cases the helper—in this instance someone medical—takes over the patient's bodily functioning including his eating and breathing functions. This is the *in loco parentis* model. The helper, like a parent, takes over the patient's functioning for him. The patient is clearly understood to be disordered and the parent-like helper protects, corrects, and functions for him.

This model, more common in the past than it is now, has unfortunate consequences. In effect, therapists who use this model consider themselves to be healthy objective observers of the patient, and especially of the patient's illness. Troubling in such a circumstance is the idea that the therapist understands what is real whereas the patient is liable to distort reality. Such assumptions are partly based on the idea that psychotherapists have often had some treatment themselves, and, having been thereby "cured," have a purer vision of reality than they had before their own treatment.

This is at considerable variance with reality as it is now philosophically understood. Instead of a singular reality it is more common to speak of a plurality of realities. Each of us lives in our own personal array of preferred realities, not to speak of another array of warded off realities. Therapists are not viewed as having any privilege with regard to particular realities. Psychotherapists are exceedingly uneasy about leading patients into conventionality and into the common and conventional views of what is to count as reality. They are therefore inclined to remain as neutral as possible about these socially designated realities.

The objective real illness model is now less popular with psychotherapists. It is, after all, only one of many models available for comprehending the therapist–patient dialogue or dialectic.

The model that we use must have the capacity to emphasize the interpretation of all interpersonal stances. Within the psychotherapeutic situation per se, it must permit the interpretation of all that transpires including, especially, the mutual interaction of patient and therapist, that is, the transference and the countertransference.

Here is what happens when one uses the first model, the model of the objective therapist who observes and treats/manages an objective illness/problem. The patient states that he intends to kill himself. The therapist attempts to prevent this by way of explanation, persuasion, and by invoking consequences. If this does not work, the therapist may enlist family members or other guardians, and, eventually, may hospitalize the patient. In extreme cases constant observation and monitoring of the patient is introduced. This is the *in loco parentis* model.

Unfortunately, there is little evidence that such modes of intervention reduce the incidence of suicide (Linehan et al. 1991). There is even evidence that the use of a rescue model may increase the incidence of suicide (Hendin 1982, Meissner 1986, Searles 1967). If it is indeed the case that suicide is not reduced by using the *in loco parentis* model, explanations ought to be offered as to why this is so.

Those who focus on the transference-countertransference elements in the potentially suicidal situation do, indeed, have an argument to make on this score. Although they are convinced that they have a worthwhile explanatory position, they are nevertheless uneasy about what they themselves have to say because, first, a person's life may be at stake and, second, because they fear professional or legal repercussions if they use a model that is less well known and a suicide takes place. But here is their argument nevertheless:

Suicidal threats and suicidal behaviors are part of an interpersonal configuration that certain patients prefer to locate themselves in; they compellingly enact a linguistic and behavioral game in which they threaten suicide, and the psychotherapist intervenes in ways designed to prevent suicide. The analytic or linguistic model helps the therapist to level certain complaints about such a turn of events. The psychotherapist (who very much wants to use a strictly analytic model) points out that, since the patient is attempting to coerce a psychologically vital scenario, attempts to prevent suicide are liable to lead the patient to redouble his efforts to kill himself. Then, the therapist is liable to redouble her protective actions, and so on. In this vicious cycle, says the psychotherapist, the possibility of suicide is increased rather than decreased.

Suicide, she says, is not a disorder in the usual sense of being a tangible or objective problem but is, rather, dialectical. The therapist must be extremely cautious about committing herself to rescue attempts for fear that she will do more harm than good. She is mindful of the fact that no one has certain knowledge about whether patients are less likely to commit suicide when she deals with them psychotherapeutically, or contrariwise, whether they are less likely to do so when they are dissuaded or prevented from killing themselves. She wishes there were airtight research data available concerning this issue, and is worried about how ethics committees will respond to proposals for studying this matter. Being as egocentric as any other person, she is inclined to think her model better but, when at her best, smiles ruefully about her own egocentrism.

So what does she do when she applies her therapeutic and linguistic methods with her suicidal patient? What she does is to operate, as much as her courage will permit, according to a few difficult psychotherapeutic principles:

1. She will insist that this suicidal inclination is part of an interpersonal strategy that she and her patient have embarked upon. She will include herself as part of this dangerous dialectic, and will point out that as a mere mortal, and a humane one, she will be inclined to give

protection. By way of her continued interpretive behavior, she will let the patient know that her primary goal is the reinterpretation, rethinking, and redescribing of what is going on.

2. She will refrain from guaranteeing that she will not actively intervene to prevent suicide. She will indicate by her actions that she wishes not to get into the game of no-you-won't-kill-yourself versus yes-I-will-kill-myself, but will also cautiously make it clear that she may well become frightened and shift to a protective role.
3. She will resolutely (but not urgently) point out that suicide is, among other things, a regressive or flamboyant example of the patient's ordinary characterological style. She will, like every psychotherapist, connect everything to everything. In other words, she will liken the suicidal behavior to all of the patient's other self-injurious, self-demeaning, and self-insulting behaviors and speech. She will do this with regard to the patient's current life, the transference-countertransference situation, and the past.
4. She will interpret as well as she can the identificatory aspects of suicidal behavior. The patient, for example, is enacting upon himself a punishment deserved by someone else, or is volunteering to suffer a deadly fate in place of a loved one. All too often the suicidal act is seen by the patient as a strange form of justice for imagined crimes. The psychotherapist will, despite her anxiety, work at the best level of analytic wisdom that she can manage.
5. Whenever the psychotherapist finds herself "knowing better" than the patient or protecting the patient, she will point this out so that he will see that the aggrandizement of therapist and diminution of himself is maddeningly persistent and pervasive, and the therapist is also prone to define the patient downward. She, the therapist, may even chuckle self-deprecatingly about her own vanity.

My colleague, Dr. Shmuel Hazanovitz, after reading the preceding paragraphs, said this:

> I believe that the nonprofessional reader will be struggling at this point with the following sentiments: "Why the hell does the patient feel suicidal while he is in the good hands of the psychotherapist? Isn't there any hope for him? Why is that? No possible light at the end of the tunnel? How so? Aren't they going hand in hand toward the light?"
>
> You have to let me be cruel with you here because both of us know that against these kind of questions, Nietzsche's broad perspective about the truth can only serve to soften our heads and make us mad.

Despite the above counsel, therapists tend to avoid taking on patients with serious depressive disorders. Some psychotherapists react with depression of their own in the face of the eternal pessimism and gloom of such patients. The distracting and inconvenient problems of hospitalization, drugs, and suicide only add to the disinclination of therapists to take on depressed patients.

But I suspect that there is yet another important reason why fewer of these patients are treated psychotherapeutically. The current rhetoric insists that depressions, especially serious depressions, are biological, and that drugs are therefore the intervention of choice. Therapists should keep in mind that the evidence from biology is meager. Finally, evidence from outcome studies is unconvincing with regard to which forms of treatment are preferable. More and better research, especially in areas as critical as suicide, is necessary.

> Mrs. Allan, age 85, who had been a widow for ten years, developed a friendship with a man eleven years her junior. This quickly developed into an intense and intimate relationship that caused her children and other relatives great worry. The man concerned was in a manic state and, as a couple, they began a whirlwind of social activities. Together,

they shopped, went to restaurants, and visited friends and relatives.

Such an active life was unusual for Mrs. Allan, who had always been a homebody and, in fact, had always been scornful of those who lived an active social life. Moreover, she had been a woman embittered about life and critical of frivolity, leisure, and celebration. Men were commonly judged to be lechers and, when circumstances gave her the opportunity, women were denounced as "whores." All in all, she had been thought of as difficult and curmudgeonly.

Her good friend, Mr. Bates, led her on a great round of entertainment but, in his typical manic way, he alienated people constantly, started quarrels, and, when he did not get his way, launched lawsuits. Mrs. Allan seemed oblivious to the foolish behavior of her partner and was obviously smitten and enthralled. Despite the protestations (and humiliation) of her family, she giggled happily when her friend announced, in vulgar terms, that he was now the head of the family.

After six months—happy for her and unnerving for her family—Mr. Bates recovered from his mania, became somewhat depressed, lost interest in Mrs. Allan, and broke off their relationship.

Mrs. Allan, over a period of a few weeks, became seriously depressed, and required hospitalization in a psychiatric facility. During the next few weeks she had many unexplained physical complaints and, although an intolerance to her drug treatment was suspected, no certainty on this score was possible. Her mood lifted for brief periods but she was largely unimproved.

After two weeks the patient began experiencing attacks of panic, sometimes when she was out of the hospital visiting her family. The family suspected that their unhappy mother was tormented by shame and humiliation but, when asked about the attacks, Mrs. Allan gave another explanation. On each of the four occasions witnessed by the family, she, during the attack of panic, described an intense remembering of the death of a family member. On the first occasion, she remembered—almost relived—the death of her father when she was 7 years old. She recalled that only she and her mother were present even though there were ten children in all. Somehow, she said, she had been designated to play this special role at the moment of his death. As she told this story, her extreme anxiety gradually and completely subsided.

On the occasion of the second and third anxiety episode, Mrs. Allan's son, as he had done on the first occasion, once again successfully "talked her down." These episodes were rememberings of the death of her mother and of a sister, this time events from her adult life and, once again, the act of telling the story relieved the panic.

The fourth attack of anxiety was a disturbing surprise to the family. Once more, her son listened with therapeutic intent to the memory that partnered the current panic. It concerned her presence at the deathbed of her brother Andrew when he was 17 and she was 12. But no one had ever heard that Mrs. Allan had a deceased brother named Andrew. At first, the family was inclined to disbelieve the story. When Mrs. Allan had recovered and it became clear that there had, in fact, been such a brother, she was asked why she had never before told anyone about him (she had a sister who had died in childhood but whose death had been talked about). Her reply was, "I forgot." She had, throughout her adult life, forgotten!

But, as it turned out, these words reminded the family of another story. Mrs. Allan's firstborn child, a son, had died at the age of 3 months. This child was never mentioned, but, when the story became known, a daughter asked why their eldest sibling had never been mentioned. To this question Mrs. Allan gave the same reply: "I forgot."

A few days after she had told, during her anxiety attack, of her forgotten brother, the patient got a piece of unwelcome news. A man who she had known for a large part of her life, but who she had not seen for several years, suddenly died. A few hours later Mrs. Allan had the first of a series of major convulsions that lasted for several days. She was unconscious for a week but then, seemingly, recovered quickly and completely. One week after she regained consciousness, she left the hospital, no longer depressed.

Her family quickly became aware that Mrs. Allan was forgetful, emotionally labile, and showed other evidence of brain dysfunction. Clearly, they thought, the series of major seizures had had a morbid effect on her brain. Then, ten days after leaving the hospital, she became manic and, with that onset, there were no more signs of brain dysfunction. At first she was cranky and demanding but, when told that she was manic, she hesitated, seemed briefly puzzled, and then broke into a broad grin. "I'm manic!" she agreed, and then added "Just like Frederick!" (her gentleman friend's name).

Mrs. Allan's mania required a further period of hospitalization. Gaily, she announced to all and sundry that she was manic-depressive, distributed checks and money to family members, and behaved in a flirtatious and sexually inappropriate manner.

The hospital staff were unimpressed or uninterested in the psychological events that had been reported to them by Mrs. Allan's son, despite his sense that these matters had profound importance in his mother's life. Although gracious and patient when he spoke to them, they had no time or conviction that their pharmacological program needed to be supplemented by any psychological illumination of the events that he had reported to them.

Mrs. Allan's recovery was thereafter said to be uneventful. The family worried that she might still be unwell because her happier-than-expected frame of mind persisted. It was strange to them that their difficult mother had become an affectionate and cheerful woman. To them, this suggested abnormality rather than a true or permanent change for the better. Like many psychotherapists, they doubted that our elders can change, either as the result of psychotherapeutic intervention or as a creative response to a life crisis. I want to say they are wrong, but, being a psychotherapist, I am not permitted such dogmatics and may only say that human life is always enigmatic.

About two months later, Mrs. Allan had one more panic attack. Once again, her son "talked her down." And, once again, she had been thinking about a death. Like every psychotherapy patient she repeated and reworked psychological tasks. Each reworking was subtly different. Once more Mrs. Allan spoke of her dead and forgotten brother Andrew. But on this occasion she spoke angrily of her mother. That mother had always been idealized by her and comments made by Mrs. Allan's about her mother always created her in the image of a saint. Suddenly things were different. "My mother was so stupid," she said, and then went on to tell of her mother's insensitive and selfish behavior at the time of her son's death.

Mrs. Allan had changed. She was, as a favorable byproduct of a life crisis, a kinder and more generous-spirited woman. Perhaps, too, she was better when, for the first time that anyone knew, she had criticized her mother. Who can complain about such an outcome? But let me sound a complaining note nevertheless.

Might the realignment of her life have been quicker, surer, more thorough, and more enduring if she had spoken to a psychotherapist? Do the elderly deserve the ear of the therapist just as much as the young? Should major neurobiological catastrophes lead us into abdication of our psychotherapeutic responsibilities? Should we not recognize and respond to the outrageous, marvelous, madness that, for better or worse, can appear in any person?

On the other hand, I could say that Mrs. Allan did have a psychotherapist after all. Her son did listen and speak and think with her about what was going on. A few weeks after her criticisms of her mother, another psychologically intense conversation with her "psychotherapist" son took place. By the time he told me of this latest conversation, I had begun to feel like a performer in Freud's story of "Little Hans" (Freud 1909). In that story, a father acted as psychotherapist to his own son and sought advice from Freud as the process went on; Mrs. Allan's son acted as psychotherapist to his own mother and sought advice from me.

One of the ways in which Mrs. Allan had, throughout her life, made herself unpopular, was her harsh and unforgiving criticism of family members. On numerous occasions, these criticisms were so harsh that daughters and sons felt they could no longer associate with her. Once, she made vicious anti-Semitic remarks to a daughter-in-law, as a consequence of which that son did not speak to her for six months. On another occasion, she made accusations about a granddaughter that were disturbing in their cruelty and strange in their unrelatedness to anything that Mrs. Allan could have known of that granddaughter.

Her psychotherapist-son was aware of these events but did his best to see the positive side of things. "She was awful the first time," he said, "but, in the second mess she got herself into, she apologized about the granddaughter remarks and, after a few months of alienation, she and the granddaughter's family made it up."

Because Mrs. Allan had apologized, her son assumed that she had, at age 85, "mellowed" and, when yet another piece of nastiness came to pass, he hoped for the best. He phoned his mother to discuss a new episode of alienation with yet another daughter-in-law. Christmas was coming and he hoped to make peace before that holiday. "Just one more thing to do," he told his mother. "Why don't you just phone Jack and Sara, tell them you're sorry, and the whole thing will be over." To his surprise, Mrs. Allan once again pleaded ignorance. She did not know what she should apologize for.

"Sara threw me out of her house," she said. Her son was flabbergasted. Apparently, she had leveled a string of unkind accusations that had left son and daughter-in-law in a state of fury and they had, indeed, told her to leave their house and had driven her home. Plenty of nasty words were exchanged.

But the son did not give up on his peacemaking mission. Cheerfully he tried to cajole her into some insight, into some perspective, and into a state of 85-year-old wisdom. "Forget it," he said. "You know how you are. Every once in a while, you get critical with women and say too much. It's no big deal. Just phone Jack, tell him you're sorry, and the whole thing will be over. Christmas is coming and everybody will be able to relax and forget this thing." The psychotherapist-son felt hopeful that this tactic would work because, during some recent conversations, his mother had surprised him by her psychological sophistication. Her critical thoughts about her own mother had suggested to him that she could well have made a bit of a realignment of her psychological world.

Unfortunately, whatever realignment had taken place did not apply during that telephone conversation. Mrs. Allan shrieked out in unhappiness. "I am not a witch. She (the daughter-in-law) threw me out. What do you mean I do this all the time? My sisters were horrible. I don't remember saying anything to A or to B or to C. This is terrible. I am not a terrible person! I'm not! I'm not!" By this time, Mrs. Allan was weeping convulsively, and was shatteringly depressed. Her son tried to calm her, but failed.

This phenomenon has been called by some a paranoid defense against depression. Mrs. Allan had available to her only two antithetical ways of being in the world. When I pointed this out to her son, he agreed. "When my mother hates someone, she feels fine and moreover, is a highly sophisticated and psychologically astute person. In a funny way, she is quite content to have an enemy who, I guess, she is quietly denouncing. We are always surprised at how calm she can be when there is a kind of horrifying situation of hatred festering in the family. Eventually, she gets over it but hardly ever apologizes, except that one time.

"I'm not sure, but I have a suspicion that when she gets over her hatred, she is getting ready to have a depression. She worries about everyone, demands reassurance about everybody's financial situation and her own financial situation, and is full of complaints about her health." To what Mrs. Allan's son has said, I will add this: she oscillates between the paranoid position and the depressive position.

Yet another hospitalization was required. While in the hospital Mrs. Allan spoke of another event that her doctor son had assumed she had forgotten. Many years before, one of her sons had a severe and crippling stroke. During the acute phase of his illness, he had been unconscious for several weeks. Mrs. Allan had taken his ring, removed a precious stone from it, and had the stone set in a ring of her own. In place of the stone that she had taken, she placed a smaller precious stone of her own. When the family remonstrated in horror, Mrs. Allan brushed aside the objections. "He doesn't know the difference," she asserted, "and besides, he is such a dopey that he doesn't need such a big stone in his ring anyway."

The family, accustomed to their mother's arbitrary habits, let the matter pass. They were saddened when their now-handicapped brother had a partial recovery and realized that his ring had been plundered. Mrs. Allan, despite being told of this, insisted on keeping the jewel, and scorned the concern of the rest of the family. They considered her incorrigible and dropped the matter.

During the current hospitalization she herself raised with her son, my informer, the question of the stone that she had stolen. Tearfully, she explained that it was absolutely necessary that she take possession of it and offered as explanation a farfetched cock and bull story. Her son stated that the explanation was totally untrue. Her explanation was of interest nevertheless. The interest lay in Mrs. Allan's need to explain, a guilty awareness that contradicted the family's assumption that she was oblivious to what she

> had done, She obviously had known that what she had done was wrong. Silently, the guilt had festered in her all through the years. She was, according to her son, a pathetic sight as she made her futile excuses, accompanied by bitter tears.
>
> A few months later, Mrs. Allan died. Her family assumed that she had died of shame and self-horror. Did she deserve to have psychotherapy?

This fragment of psychotherapy is from the treatment of a typically difficult case. Rather than using as my illustration another depressed patient, this woman had the ungainly label of "borderline" applied to her. It would have been next to impossible to find a therapist to work interpretively with this woman because of her lack of "psychological-mindedness" and because of other so-called deficits. The psychotherapist always suspects that when this happens, the rejection is due to unacknowledged fears and disapproval in the diagnostician. The psychotherapy protocol that follows demonstrates that this young psychotherapist, despite his chatty manner, adheres strictly to a nonsupportive, interpretive style of work.

> Dora Field, a 22-year-old biker, was pressured to attend our clinic by an outside agency because they feared she might kill someone during one of her dangerous rage attacks. At the time of her assessment, she screamed and shouted at the examining resident and at the staff psychiatrist who attempted to intervene. Miss Field lived on welfare in a group setting. At the age of 5, because of physical violence in the home, she had been removed from her parents by the local Children's Aid Society. Her natural mother died when the patient was 6 and her father's whereabouts were unknown. She had lived in numerous foster homes until the age of 18.
>
> The audio recorded material that follows is part of the tenth meeting of a precontracted, twenty-session, brief therapy. Do not be distracted by the excessive talkativeness of the psychotherapist who, in his youthfulness, was trying

to make sure that his patient did not miss his point. Better to note how single-minded he was in pursuing the unconscious motivations of his patient.

The therapist had canceled the previous meeting on short notice. For the first twenty minutes the patient had talked cheerfully about her friends and about various happy events.

Michael is the patient's boyfriend. He has a 3-year-old son, also called Michael. Little Mike's mother is Jane, but she has disappeared leaving the child in the care of a relative. The therapist begins to intervene by interpreting the patient's reaction formations against anger, especially against anger that he suspected must have been aroused by the missed appointment the previous week. In this vignette the patient also reports, for the first time, a detailed transference fantasy. As the patient's anger becomes clarified, the therapist completes and consolidates the interpretation by reconstructing the patient's excessive claiming of responsibility.

Patient. And I told him I wanted a friendship ring before I got any ring at all, right? (laugh) You know. 'Cause then I'll always have it, right? So he said "OK." So we were looking through, uh, the *Consumer's* book. And, uh, I was looking at all the rings and I said, "I want this one," right? This one caught my eye. So I said, "That's the one I want, right there" (laugh). "The one with the two diamonds and the two hearts in it." So I got it (laugh) and then we were looking . . . cause he said he wanted to get me a new stereo cause my stereo that I have, right, has got to be thrown in the garbage. But it's, like, eight years old; there's no needle left on, right, on either side. All the needles have broken off it, eh? Well, not broken, but they're just, they don't play the records, they go across the records, right? So. We didn't get a new needle for it because it was so old, eh? It doesn't look like it's eight years old but it is. You can tell just by the sound of it, right? Cause it crackles and everything (laugh). Like it sounds like it's gonna explode, right? But we were looking at stereos and he asked me which one did I like. And I said "that one." It's a black one. And there's a white cover for the needle? It's really nice.

Therapist. Now, the last few times we've been meeting, the topic has been you being nice to people. Sometimes when they didn't deserve it, right? That's sort of been the story. In almost every session. Now, today, you're talking about many nice things, and that means that I'm sitting here wondering to myself whether there are other things that have been going on, perhaps things that aren't so nice. And that you, in your usual way, feel that it's very important to try and talk about the nice things. Now I was trying to think—were there any things that you mentioned that weren't so nice? Uh. There are only two things that I heard. And I was listening hard; I was trying to listen to whether there were any negative things that you talked about. One was that I was away last week, and you were very disappointed about that. You give . . .

Patient. (laughing) Yeah, I was. I'm not embarrassed. I was, I was really . . .

Therapist. What; am I . . .

Patient. (laughing)

Therapist. Am I supposed to say "Bingo!" now I hit the nail right on the head? I guess I did, eh?

Patient. Yeah, I was . . . I flopped down on the chair (laugh) and I just looked at Michael and I said, "Guess what. You don't get to meet the doctor." And he said, "Why?" I says, "Well cause he had to go to court today." (laugh) I was . . . I moped all day (laugh).

Therapist. Were you annoyed at all? You were a little sad . . .

Patient. I wasn't annoyed. I was just disappointed. I couldn't get mad, it didn't matter what happened (laugh). I was just so disappointed. And then, all of a sudden, I just forgot about it, it was like (laugh), you know, it was here today and gone tomorrow type of thing.

Therapist. Well, that's typical of you.

Patient. (laugh) Yeah, well. If you put it that way, yeah (laugh). I'll agree with that (laugh). (short pause) But, I moped around and enjoyed it, so.

Therapist. Well, you know, I'm aware that right now I'm playing an important role in your life because this problem of your anger has worried you for years and years. And your anger hasn't been mild anger, you've had bouts of tremendous anger, where you almost thought you might kill somebody someday. And I don't think you've ever had a chance to sit down with somebody and try to tackle this problem of your anger before. And I know that you're worried about it. That's why our meetings are very, very important to you, and that's why I say that I think I'm playing a very important role in your life right now. So, when you say that you felt very disappointed I know what you're talking about. I don't think it was just sort of, "Oh well, you know. Missed an appointment. I'll see him next week." It was more important than that. In a way you were wanting to show me to Mike. And I stand for something that you're hoping is gonna make a big difference in your life. So you probably were very disappointed. Now whether you were annoyed or irritated or angered cause I wasn't gonna be here . . . ? Well, if you say you didn't feel annoyed I have to take your word for it, and I guess that would be very very much like you. To try not to be annoyed. Which is part of the problem of your anger. That it's either anger that's so strong that it's almost murderous, or no anger at all—zero—especially with me. The other examples of not being annoyed at me were those two weeks in a row that I was late, remember? And, uh, as you said to me, it really annoys you; you hate it when people keep you waiting. But not me? Me—I get off the hook.

Patient. (laughs)

Therapist. And I think that's probably connected with this problem of your anger. That you deal with it by not getting angry when one would expect at least some annoyance. You're really quite tangled up with this thing. A puzzle to understand that. Do you ever think about this when you're not here?

Patient. Yeah, I think about this on the way home or when I get home. If I was sitting by myself staring out the window, I'll think about it. And in my mind I'll picture you and I talking . . . but on my way down here was strange. I was thinking, as usual, right? You know (laugh), no one to talk to, right? And I saw this little vision in my head. OK. I was walking down here, was across the street from this building? As I was walking, I was looking all around me and then, I don't know, something hit my head and I just, you know, I don't know, something hit my head and I just, you know, I was just thinking about it, right? And I walked in here and I was all of a sudden in tears (laugh). I was taking a real temper tantrum, right? And I sat down and you asked me, well, what's my problem, right? And I told you, and then I got up and I started hopping around the floor (laugh) like, jumping around and smashing things, right? . . . that I would smash anybody, but, that's not the point, right? (laugh) I just grabbed whatever I could and I smashed it on the floor. And all I could say, all I remember saying to you was, "I'm gonna kill her, I'm gonna kill her, I'm gonna kill her!" (laugh) OK? But I think the reason why I have that little picture in my head is because . . . OK, just before I left, Mike's cousin called him, right? And this lady, Lisa, was talking to Mike and apparently . . . OK, do you remember the name Jane?

Therapist. You did mention the name Jane.

Patient. Well, she's the mother of Michael's little boy, right?

Therapist. Right.

Patient. But see, Michael sort of, like, ". . . get out of my life." Like, he was in, OK, he was in a place, it was a nut-house. 'Cause she spun his head around . . . she's a little, two-bit tramp . . . And I don't want to see her, because I will kill her. Apparently she's been seen three times here in Toronto. [Here follows a long, rambling and furiously angry complaint, which is unclear, but seems to imply that Jane neglects little Mike.]

Patient. (continuing) . . . But I told—when Mike told me about that, I mean, I flew right off my handle (laugh). My broom handle, right? Like, I just went "vroom" in the air, cause like one minute I was all happy cause we were getting little Mike, right? And as soon as he mentioned Jane it was like . . . you could see flames in my eyes. Like, all I saw was red. Nothing else but red. Like I'm not so angry now because I know that if she comes near me, like, I will kill her. If I don't use my hands I will use a bat, and I told Michael that. I said, "When I take little Mike to the park . . ."

Therapist. I'm still not clear what you're so mad at her for.

Patient. Because she's nuts. (laugh) When she had him [little Mike] she would get home and go outside and not attend the kid at all. She ignores him. Like, the kid'll say, "Hi, Mummy." You know! Jane would look at him as if she didn't even own him, right?

Therapist. You told me this before, I remember now.

Patient. You know. Any mother that ignores her son, to me, that's no mother at all. And I would give anything in the world to just rip her head off. (bitter laugh) You know. And now that I've got the chance, I'm gonna go out and I'm gonna do it.

Therapist. Now, you better think a little bit. Why are you so touchy about this subject of neglected kids?

Patient. Because I know what it's like to be neglected. (laugh)

Therapist. You're darn right that's the reason. And you . . .

Patient. And I don't like it! I despise a lot of things in this world, and that is one of them.

Therapist. And you still carry with you a lot of bitterness and resentment about being neglected. Now . . .

Patient. Yeah, that's right.

Therapist. I want to go on a little bit. See, you had a daydream before you came here. In the daydream . . .

Patient. Well, the daydream was when I was on my way down here.

Therapist. . . . you come in here and you act like a little child.

Patient. And I took a temper tantrum. (laugh)

Therapist. And you took a temper tantrum.

Patient. Well I started to cry and scream and holler at you, telling you that I wanted you to help me, right?

Therapist. Right. A neglected child. And the question that you were asking in the daydream, I think, was whether *I* would pay attention to a neglected child. Would I pay attention to you, would I take you seriously? Or, if you're a "pill," or if you have a temper tantrum, whether I will neglect you the way you have been neglected in the past, when you were a kid. That's what it's about. It's you, still trying to struggle with this terrible rage and disappointment that you must have felt when you were a kid. And you're still struggling with it in the relationship with me, because in a way you turn me into a parent, and that's why you want to bring Michael down to show me. You wanted to say to Michael, "Look Mike, I've got a good parent now. I had a lot of disappointments when I was a kid . . ." and if I miss an appointment or if I'm late for our appointment, that causes trouble for you. Because to you it raises the possibility that I'm neglecting you. And then you'd be in that state of rage and fury . . .

Patient. But I'd be mad at myself though, I wouldn't be mad at you (laugh). See, I take it out on myself and I blame myself.

Therapist. I wouldn't be surprised if that's true. Yeah, you wouldn't . . . you have trouble getting angry at me because you're still busy trying to turn me into something perfect. So you won't get angry at me, you'll take it out on yourself instead.

Patient. Yeah. (laugh)

Therapist. As though it's your fault.

Patient. I'm good at that! (laugh)

Therapist. It's *your* fault if *I'm* late.

Patient. Well. More or less, yeah. (laugh) Like, I should've been here 10 minutes earlier! (laughing) Right? I do that. Like, if I'm waiting for someone and I know that they were there, right, I'll start freakin' out, like, (good-natured yelling:) "I should've been here!" And I'll scream and holler and pound on the floor, right. And I'll walk around and I'll be cursin' and swearing and saying, like, "Why wasn't I here?!" Or, if someone *was* there, and if someone knew they were there and didn't bother telling me, decides to tell me the next day, I'll tell ya, I'm twice the time bomb. Because I go nuts. (laugh) I go, like literally nuts, eh?

Therapist. Let me tell you another . . .

Patient. 'Cause I get right, like, there's nothing can stop me, you know what I mean? (laugh)

Therapist. Now. There's more to this story; it's even more complicated. Here's another complication. When you talked about getting angry at Jane, you compared yourself to a witch. You said, "I came right off my broomstick." Now, you see, that's an idea about yourself. What you're doing is, you're thinking of yourself as a witch. A witch is a very bad woman. And that's one of the reasons why you're so quick to blame yourself. Because you have an idea that *you're* very bad. And when you come in here and you say to me, "I'm gonna kill her . . . if I have a baseball bat, I'll crush her skull with a baseball bat!" . . . in a way you really believe that you're like a witch. That you're really a terrible person. And that, too, is exactly what you must have thought when you were a kid. When you were neglected and shunted around and never had a chance of having a home of your own, you must have thought it was because you were bad. So at times you couldn't even blame people. You don't say bad things about your foster parents to me. You're very generous when you talk about them; you say nice things about them mostly. And I think it's this business of thinking that it's your fault.

At the time of the six-month follow-up interview, Miss Field reported no anger "attacks" since the psychotherapy ended. She has lost twenty-five pounds, a process that had begun during the psychotherapy. She claims that her relationship with Michael is a happy one and that they plan to marry. In addition, she has obtained employment as a chambermaid, the first job of her life.

This improvement was real and gratifying to all concerned. But, five years later, Miss Field was heard from again. She was in great distress because, having had two children of her own in the interim, they were being taken into child care. She wanted to see the therapist again. He offered her ten sessions, which she came to with some limited success.

12

Mourning the Graven Images

> Behaviourism is indeed a kind of flat-earth view of the mind . . . it has substituted for the erstwhile anthropomorphic view of the rat, a ratomorphic view of man.
>
> —Arthur Koestler

A malaise has come to afflict the field of psychotherapy. I am inclined to call it a vulgarity, a profanity, an outrage. The media and the enthusiasts trumpet this corruption and, incomprehensibly, professional psychotherapists in increasing numbers take parts of that rhetoric unto themselves.

Since I am a psychotherapist, I must quickly alert and, perhaps, try to befuddle the reader. The critical voice that you have so quickly heard is not the expected voice of the psychotherapist because, in her odd psychological place, the psychotherapist is ordinarily found to be poised "in between." In this instance, this means that, in her professional world, she hovers eternally between critique and, contrariwise, the accordance of honor to every position. She is, you see, determined that the subject who knows does not exist. Therefore, it must be clear that complaints such as mine are an indulgent pleasure and a kind of psychotherapeutic wickedness. All of this should become clearer in the following pages even though psychotherapists, in their work, typically wish that things would become *less* certain and *less* clear.

Were psychotherapy a fashionable frivolity—and, in view of its increasing debasement, the intelligent public is beginning to believe so—this would only be pathetic. But, since most who seek psychotherapy do so because of grave worries about themselves, my concern is not idle. Indeed, if one pauses for only a moment, one must realize that he who pursues psychotherapeutic treatment does so because his very life or, at least, the life of his soul, is at stake. I have never known a patient who came for help frivolously.

Since psychotherapy is a serious business, its practitioners should be informed about matters psychological. By this I do not only mean that they should study academic psychology or read Freud—although they should—but, instead, mean that they should know something of the great thinkers of the Western intellectual tradition. It is not that every psychotherapist needs to read Socrates and Aristotle, and about Moses and about Christ. Nor is it obligatory that they should be scholars of Augustine, Chaucer, Shakespeare, Dostoyevski, Proust, Kierkegaard and—yes—of Freud.

But the great thinkers of the past should not be neglected either, lest we hitch our psychological thinking to the passing and the fashionable. It would be tragic if the psychological insights of the past should be overlooked, especially since they have undergone the severest of tests—the test of time. I don't expect the psychotherapist to be a thoroughgoing scholar but should she not, at the very least, be modestly informed?

The old and the wise are no longer recognized as counselors. Warriors, clergymen, and family doctors now rarely count as serious experts to whom we can turn with our psychological woes. Therefore, my critique is directed, first, at psychiatrists, psychologists, and social workers—the most professional of the psychotherapists—and, second, at the host of self-proclaimed psychotherapists that has sprung up in recent years.

Here is my complaint. The media inundate us with behavioral advice that is claimed to be a sure route to mental health. We are instructed to express our feelings, communicate, share, be authentic and to trust (this assumes that a person can trust upon command and requires a majestic indifference to the fact that the trusting will trust willy-nilly and the mistrustful will do the contrary). Furthermore, we are to be empathic (a wonderful word gone bad) and to give solace by way of comforting caresses and embraces, usually called "hugs." But God help me if my professional regulatory body finds out about such embraces! None of these sentiments are in and of themselves unattractive. But the implication that such sentiments and actions can be mandated strikes me as barbarically naive. Most of the time it could only lead to falseness.

I would add that these are all "motherhood" statements. Upon closer scrutiny, however, one becomes aware that this is a motherhood rhetoric with a subtle but powerful extra dimension. The propagandists for all of these simplistic romanticisms deliver another, less palatable, message. If we, their audience, do not comply with their opinions we are considered to be, at best, uncooperative fools and, at worst, hurtful enemies of progress—whatever that is! These advocates scorn those of us who are uncertain about how life should be lived. They do not comprehend that there are many ways to skin a cat and many ways to live a life. In *Thus Spake Zarathustra* (1884) Nietzsche said, "They . . . have discovered themselves who say 'This is *my* way; where is yours?'—thus I answered those who asked me 'the way.' For *the* way—that does not exist" (III, p. 11). We real psychotherapists (do I need to draw attention to my ironic intent? Have I not already pointed out that I know that the subject who knows does not exist?) and our thoughtful fellow thinkers find much of what these propagandists say to be mere blathering, except that we also fear them as fascists who cleverly hide their fascism behind a screen of love.

Like all good enthusiasts, they know that the best rallying cry includes the incarnation of an external devil who, on this occasion, is us, the cautious skeptics who wickedly ruminate about the fact that the unsavory and the sinful can be found in all of us. The fool-killer comes not only for the obvious fools. She comes for all of us. Ask not for whom the bell tolls, says the psychotherapist, it tolls for thee—and for me.

I fear that my psychoanalytic colleagues will be offended if I say that they, too, are tempted to participate in the rhetoric of mandated kindness and join in on the longing to identify some version of "normal" behavior. Here is how some of them go along with the popular but misguided fashions that I am complaining about. Psychological unwellness is, they say, due to incomplete development. Patients are fixated at, say, the oral, anal, phallic, or oedipal level. They are symbiotic, enmeshed, unintegrated, fragmented. When they are at their unkindest, certain colleagues will say of patients that they are infantile, primitive or, most distastefully, "borderline." I must say that I was grateful to find an ally in a witty young woman who paraded outside a psychiatric hospital wearing a T-shirt that said, "Borderline is HELL."

Such insulting commentaries on patients are made with surprising earnestness and sobriety. The comments are rationalized by, first, recourse to normative standards and, second, the development of elaborate developmental theories that, to me, are merely vehicles for making unattractive and judgmental pronouncements about unhappy people.

In my book *Reluctant Treasures* (1994), I have critiqued the various developmental theories that I claim are all-too-often used to rationalize misguided psychotherapeutic methods. I argue in the book that these theories put forward standards of health and of maturity that are mere apings of the thin-blooded standards put forward by the self-help industry.

These various theories seem to be happily embraced by certain practitioners who have not noticed the blatant mutual contradictoriness between major theorists. This problem is of especial importance because some of these influential theorists are, in other areas of their work, among the most subtle and sophisticated of our writers. Because he is, in my opinion, of great theoretical importance to our field, I am particularly chagrined that Jacques Lacan falls into some of these traps.

Briefly said, it turns out that one group of theorists claims that people are born in a state of chaos (fragmentation, "psychosis," autism, etc.), and that good experiences, parenting, and/or psychotherapy will lead the child into normality, coherence, and maturity. Such ideas are, I am sorry to say, central to the works of Melanie Klein, Margaret Mahler, Heinz Kohut, and Jacques Lacan.

In perfect opposition to this are the ideas of equally well-known theorists such as Donald Winnicott, Eric Fromm, Wilhelm Reich, Jürgen Habermas, and other members of the Frankfurt school. To them, the child is born in a pristine state and is corrupted and tarnished by bad parenting and by a pernicious culture. Once again, a benevolent world, including the worlds of parenting and of psychotherapy, can have an ameliorative or "emancipatory" effect.

I like to distinguish three kinds of development, only one of which is innate. The only hard-wired development that I know of is physical, such as growth, puberty (but not adolescence, which is psychological), and aging. There are, second, historical phases in a human life, such as adolescence, marriage, having children, and taking on an occupation. These phases are of much greater interest to the psychotherapist, but, to her, that interest is not in the fact of particular phases but, instead, in the way in which a phase is negotiated. It is a matter of quality and not of quantity. Adolescence is less tied to puberty than is usually thought. In normal deviations from the typical, and in accidents of nature, adolescent behavior takes place even though puberty has not occurred. In other words it is, in large measure, a social phenomenon.

The third evolving stream is moral development. This, more than either of the other two, is the great interest of the psychotherapist. To her, moral dilemma is paramount. All behavior is, she insists, a compromise or a product of, moral dilemma. Change, too, is nothing more nor anything less than a change in moral stance.

The psychotherapist refuses absolutely to adopt any description of the ideal person. Instead, she aims for an impossible-to-achieve open-mindedness. There once was a time when we were prejudiced against some of our best people—the Jews. But not now. Now we are prejudiced against those with "poor object relations." Until recent years, it was futile for a homosexual to apply to a psychoanalytic institute to train as a psychoanalyst. As one committee member said of applicants, "They have poor object relations."

Psychoanalysts should be the guardians of theory and should act as our consciences so that we will keep our psychotherapeutic focus on the complex, the enigmatic, and the disturbing in human psychology. In the past they have, after all, been ardent theoreticians and have taken great pains to remind the world that good intentions illuminate only the most superficial layers of the human spirit. But I see in many analytic publications an increasing tendency to forget what psychoanalysis worked so long to establish. Now I hear from that discipline naive talk of empathy, of "real relationships" (whatever that could mean), and of fragile, damaged, and defective patients. Apart from cringing at an arrogance that defines other persons in such demeaning terms, I wish to decry the failure to remember and to remind themselves of the eternal human inclination to self-deception. Instead, many psychoanalysts, particularly young psychoanalysts, have reverted to a pre-Freudian conception of patients as suffering from some form of mental degeneracy.

In contrast to the injunctions of these, the misguided tempters, a precious (equally misguided? stubborn? enlightened?) group of colleagues make this kind of argument. The wellness of our souls is attained, we say, by following another kind of injunction—perhaps the command of the Delphic oracle: "Know thyself." Is this trite? If I say that Freud's central thesis is that change depends on insight, would that be convincing to those who have never examined Freud closely enough to know him as one of this century's authentic great spirits? As Richard Rorty (1993) points out,

> We observe that Freud's ideas have, within a remarkably short space of time, gained the same sort of reception as Plato's and Christ's. Freud has become one of our moral teach-

> ers. We live in a time and place in which the everyday language of moral deliberation—the language in which Ann Landers writes her columns and in which our leading intellectuals write their diaries—owes more to Freud's division among id, ego, and superego than to Plato's division among intellect, spirit, and appetite. . . . So we think it enough to note that Freud's narrative . . . has partially superseded both Plato's narrative of the ascent from the cave and the Christian eschatological narrative of a return to our supernatural home. [p. 25]

I would argue that knowing oneself is a more potent prescription for enriching the spirit than it at first appears to be. To strengthen my position I typically conjure up as allies the philosopher/psychologists—and that includes the novelists—that I referred to earlier.

"Become who you are" Nietzsche's *Zarathustra* has taught us (1884, IV, p. 1). This point struck Alexander Nehemas powerfully enough that, in *Life as Literature* (1985), his splendid book on Nietzsche, he titled a chapter, "How One Becomes Who One Is." To invent oneself was, to Nietzsche, the greatest goal in life. He created the world-figure "Nietzsche," who we all know but who bears little resemblance to the strange isolated man with bad headaches who wrote Nietzsche's works.

By quoting a philosopher, I once again give away the network of alliances that I am trying to establish. But if I am to illuminate what constitutes or determines psychotherapeutic change, should I not be quoting from research findings? Should I not be able to concretely pin down something that has come to be solidly established after many years of psychotherapeutic developments? Should there not be data that could be summoned and graphs that could be displayed?

Unfortunately for them, those who want science to give such answers cannot, on this occasion, have their way. Instead, it is more likely that the philosophers and the poets will light our way as we try to grasp just what happens when a person changes. And, as they have their way, the reader will have to tolerate their intrusive voices as I struggle to make a case for the idea that poets will speak psychological insights that no single person can speak alone.

In attempting to study scientifically the results of psychotherapeutic treatment—what is ordinarily called "outcome research"—the researcher must establish what is to count as a successful outcome. This is no mean feat and, for a scientist, is probably an impossible feat. Why should this be so? Do we not know what it is for a patient to be better? In fact, should not "betterness" be obvious?

Well, it is *not* obvious. Every conceivable "good" outcome can only be a value judgment or a consensus opinion. Consensus is simply public opinion regarding what should be counted as a good outcome. There is no tyranny more dogmatic than that of consensus. Among the many forms that it takes are religious doctrines, positivism, capitalism, socialism or, even worse, a sort of television talk-show morality. It is hard to know just what it is that we might consider to be an objective healthy outcome.

Freud thought that, perhaps, the ability to love and to work might count as a criterion of cure or of wellness. Others have opted for happiness, for creativity, or for (in the jargon) good object relations. Few of us would doubt that in the ordinary world these states might often be counted as desirable ones, but this does not mean that these constitute health standards or requirements.

In contrast to these rather bourgeois sentiments, other commentators might well claim that the ability to love and work, happiness, creativity, and good object relations are not for them. These so-called healthy outcomes, they might argue, are merely matters of taste. Just because it is common to value these things, does not mean that they constitute a standard for which one ought to strive. Such normative standards, they would insist, merely raise banalities to the status of an arbitrary health "requirement." And, they would surely add, such scandalous banalities condemn much of the unique and interesting to the category of psychopathology. Normative behavior is precisely what the psychotherapist is not interested in.

Nietzsche's statement that a person should become who he is can be set beside Thomas Mann's (1934) wistful commentary in the preface to *Joseph and His Brothers*: "Compare yourself, recognize what you are" (p. vii). Mann read Nietzsche and wrote about him, but it is nevertheless striking that he should have used words so similar to Nietzsche's as he tried to capture what a person might strive for. And what a strangely vague mission both these geniuses assign to us.

Mann was impressed enough by the mischievous philosopher to, in effect, paraphrase him again. "No one remains quite what he was when he recognizes himself" (p. vii) says Mann, and then says it yet again: "After re-description one no longer stands where one did when one began" (p. vii). Both are reminding us of what Socrates said:

> It is the greatest good for a human being to have discussions every day about virtue and other things you hear me talking about, examining myself and others, and that the unexamined life is not worth living for a human being.

A proposal that claims that "the unexamined life is not worth living for a human being" is one that the psychotherapist is eager to endorse. Just the same, it is an endorsement that, in the final analysis, she will not give. Although her life as a psychotherapist is devoted to this proposition, to helping her patients to develop insight, and theoretically attractive though it may be, she dare not embrace Socrates's conclusion wholeheartedly. She is assiduously wary of absolute belief systems, even when she herself finds them sympathetic.

Ultimately, she is only willing to say that Socrates is correct insofar as self-examination is highly important for some people but, as a psychological theorist, she would also say that, for many other people, self-examination is uninteresting or is judged to be unimportant. Indeed, some would say that self-examination is, at best, self-indulgent and, at worst, disturbing or destructive.

Insight is the route to change for many people but it must be kept in mind that there are many ways in which people comfort themselves and ease their sorrows. For those who believe that self-examination is disturbing and destructive, change for the better is to be accomplished by avoidance of the negative and the pursuit of the positive. The psychotherapist typically reacts with distaste to such preferences but, properly, she must acknowledge that preferences vary and that only at her own theoretical peril does she judge.

I say this in full awareness of the fact that I have already judged—and judged harshly—those who disagree with me. But on this more tolerant occasion I refer to the preferences of those who are in a state of suffering and, for them, their choice is paramount. But for psychotherapists I have a different expectation. If they fail my tests, I indict and condemn.

Some readers will be wondering what all the intellectual fuss is about and whether these comments are going to degenerate into the scholastic quibbling of an enthusiast or an ideologue. But being fed up, I fear, is the required fate of those who deal with the psychotherapeutic zealot who, in keeping with her awareness of human diversity, is determined to enrich her understanding from every possible source.

The theoretical psychotherapist that has taken form on these pages seems to me to have taken on elitist qualities because, as is by now clear, she scorns the obvious, and prefers to associate herself and her calling with the poets and the muses. Fortunately, she also has the good sense to be amused by her own pretensions.

The zealous psychotherapeutic theorist therefore rules that, despite Mann and Nietzsche, self-reflection is never to be mandated. By the same token, developmental theories of personal change, that is, theories of "personal growth" and the advocacy of so-called mature behavior, are out of order. Although she knows and shares in the public attitudes toward what is called mature behavior, she simultaneously maintains that, privately, theoretically, psychologically, and analytically, she is uneasy about those attitudes, even as she discovers them in herself. As a psychotherapist, she is convinced that she must shy away from advocacy or any institutionalization of, or predetermined certainty about, what constitutes health or maturity.

Strangely, many metaphors of change are just as potent in their affirmation as they are in their antithesis. To change for the better can mean to grow up or, contrariwise, to achieve child-like innocence. Although for some it is a benefit if they "wake up," on certain occasions the opposite is true. Sometimes it is an improvement when a person who is relentlessly industrious finally relaxes and, literally, falls asleep on the couch! How peculiar that falling asleep, sloth, and passivity might be legitimate contenders for the status of worthwhile psychotherapeutic change.

For some persons the development of a sense of trustfulness may be a welcome relief; for others a measure of mistrust makes life safer and more successfully negotiable. And what about thinking for a change, or not thinking so bloody much? Either may turn out to be a good thing. What about talking more—actually addressing issues—and talking less—reflecting rather than endlessly chattering?

These changes may seem trivial but it is all we have got. It is not, I submit, a minor thing if a person comes to be quieter and less talkative. It can reflect a change in the way that person's soul is forged. The metaphor of psychological development may sound more scientific but it is, first, too limited a term to capture the kaleidoscopic possibilities in change and, second, typically concretized and literalized into a real or "nothing but" explanation.

The psychological stance of every person depends on his or her moral balance, and change cannot take place without an attendant or antecedent shift in that moral balance. All aspects of behavior are invoked on moral or moralistic grounds and, in effect, we are forever saying to ourselves "do not do this" or "do not do that." The psychotherapist always wants to know what her therapy can contribute to her patient's impoverished reserves of moral intelligence. Most of all, she does not want to fall into the trap of believing that a person's moral standards are a simple product of what they have been taught. Every moral decision, she wants to say, is as fraught with dilemma, confusion, and richness, as is any prudential decision. Nietzsche, yet again: "It is the price of fruitfulness to be rich in internal contradictions" (1888, p. 488).

To say that the superego is a mere internalization of the parents, of the cultural law, is a banality, albeit a Platonic claim. Freud (1914) complicated this assumption by pointing out that morality has many sources, including the child's own imaginative morality play, and an idealization of the child's own "perfection."

How, indeed, can a child be creative and invent his own morality? How can a person, supposedly doing novel work in a doctoral dissertation, do so with so little experience of life? Can a person in her twenties really say something new about Shakespeare? The answer, implausible though it may seem to some of us, may be that, yes, they can. Take, for example, the case of Emily Dickinson. Having lived in isolation and, in particular, in isolation from men, she nevertheless wrote this:

> Wild Nights! Wild Nights!
> Were I with thee,
> Wild nights should be
> Our luxury!
>
> Futile the winds
> To a heart in port,
> Done with the compass,
> Done with the chart.
>
> Rowing in Eden!
> Ah, the sea!
> Might I but moor
> Tonight in Thee!

How could Emily Dickinson have known these urgencies, these desires? We know perfectly well that she could, but knowing this makes it no less remarkable. Do you and I know moor, heather, and billow? I believe that we do and, although you and I may have seen these things, Emily Dickinson certainly did not.

> I never saw a moor,
> I never saw the sea;
> Yet I know how heather looks,
> And what a billow be.

When the patient approaches his psychotherapeutic ending, is this not another occasion upon which a riches of metaphor can lead to change? Is not a stereotyped and self-injuring attitude toward farewells one of those things that may become different? For example, is ending not a death? And cannot death lead to the intensification of life and the intensification of the therapy and, not to forget the psychotherapist, might not her efforts be intensified, modified, and rejuvenated? Could an analogy be made with death and rebirth? Was there not a Flood and didn't Atlantis sink beneath the waves? Didn't the world regenerate after the Flood and do we not expect to rediscover Atlantis one of these days? Death and Rebirth. If my mind loosens, associates, links, and connects—I am, after all, a psychotherapist—can I not conjure with my ending/terminating/dying patient, the Deluge, the Euphrates, the Nile, and, instead of merely mourning, contemplate . . . Regeneration and Rebirth?

Such linkages and associations, too, are an element in change. The psychotherapist, to the best of her ability, strikes new and different chords and sounds new correspondences. Her mind drifts widely into a mingled past and future, reality and mythology. If ending is death and Christ is in the grave and Joseph is in the pit, then cannot there be a rising again from the dead, an emergence from the pit, a regeneration of the buried seed? This odd psychotherapist of mine—does her ego dissolve its boundaries and flow into domains external to herself? Where is it mandated that she should be herself and no other? So much for the unimaginative ones who claim that she, and her patients, should be integrated, individuated, and realistic.

Identification with the therapist is an inevitable consequence of the intense involvement between the practitioner and her patient. On every occasion upon which the therapist speaks, the patient can do nothing with her words unless he identifies with her. He must, if he wants to grasp her view of him, become her. This he may do momentarily or eternally or, perhaps more accurately, he will always identify with her momentarily and eternally.

At the best of times our patient will gradually apprehend and make his own—identify with—the many aspects of his own being, of his own self. But, just as his identifications with the therapist will, at their best, be plastic and fluid, so his self-identifications will also not be static, and he will identify with all that he is.

In identifying with the therapist, the patient does what Shakespearean characters do so brilliantly. He, like Hamlet and Lady Macbeth, begins to talk to himself and to change. It is the "talking cure." He reflects and observes and interprets. What he interprets and how he interprets is both an aping of his own therapist and a multidetermined resolve not to interpret as did his therapist. She, in turn, interprets her patient's way of interpreting the world and, in true Shakespearean fashion, the patient begins to interpret his own way of interpreting the world. Harold Bloom (1987) says:

> Chaucer, rather than Marlowe or even the English Bible, was Shakespeare's central precursor in having given the dramatist the crucial hint that led to the greatest of his originalities: *the representation of change by showing people pondering their own speeches and being altered through that consideration.* We find this mode of representation commonplace and even natural, but it does not exist in Homer or in the Bible, in Euripides or in Dante. [p. 54, my italics]

Bloom believes that Shakespeare's portrayal of Lear on the heath is "the most remarkable representation of a human transformation anywhere in imaginative literature." There can also be plenty of drama in the psychotherapeutic situation but, ordinarily, change is subtle. Nevertheless, it is a subtle change that matters. Is it, perhaps, akin to the change in Molly Bloom in the last lines of James Joyce's *Ulysses* in which, after a day filled with seamy moments, she speaks to herself wistfully, wisely, and tragically. Or is she just different?

> How he kissed me under the Moorish wall and I thought well as well him as another and then I asked him with my eyes to ask again yes and then he asked me would I yes to say yes my mountain flower and first I put my arms around him yes and drew him down to me so he could feel my breasts all perfume yes and his heart was going like mad and yes I said yes I will Yes. [Joyce 1922, p. 644]

Her reflectiveness is the very change that we seek to understand and to emulate but that, for the maddeningly noncommittal psychotherapist, has no implication of maturity or health.

Curiously, self-reflection is both the method and the goal of psychotherapy. Ironically, it comes to pass that, by way of reflectiveness, we become more reflective. This is the peculiar, profound, and modest "cure" that we can offer to our patients. Since symptoms speak, our hope is that words will come to speak those symptoms and that, in the powerful way of language, things will become present in their absence. Rather than failing, our patient will speak of deserving to fail; rather than saying this to himself scornfully and insultingly (such cruel speech is a symptom), he will speak with bemusement, fascination, curiosity, and resignation.

The final word must go to Nietzsche, the arch-psychologist. Without the nowadays stridently called-for "niceness" but, rather, with his own more typical abruptness, he announces his own, and the psychotherapist's, imminent silence. It is Zarathustra's last, most vital lesson: "Now, do without me!" (quoted by Steiner 1958, p. 4).

References

Auden, W. H. (1927–1932). The witnesses. In *W. H. Auden: The Collected Shorter Poems 1927–1957*. London: Faber & Faber, 1966.

Bhabra, H. S. (1995). Empathy is all—all about us. *The Globe and Mail*, February 1: A1.

Bloom, H. (1973). *The Anxiety of Influence*. Oxford: Oxford University Press.

———. (1987). *Ruin the Sacred Truths*. Cambridge: Harvard University Press.

———. (1994). *The Western Canon*. New York: Harcourt, Brace.

Bowie, M. (1991). *Lacan*. Glasgow: Fontana.

Cayley, D. (1992). *Ivan Illich in Conversation*. Toronto: House of Anansi.

Crown, S. (1988). Supportive psychotherapy: a contradiction in terms? *British Journal of Psychiatry* 152:266–269.

Denby, D. (1994). Queen Lear. *The New Yorker*, October 3: 88–96.

Dilthey, W. (1894). Ideen über eine Beschreibende und Zergliedernde Psychologies. In *Wilhelm Dilthey's Gesammelte*

Schriften, vol. 5, pp. 139–240. Leipzig, Berlin: Teubner, 1921–1934.

Erikson, E. (1963). *Childhood and Society*. New York: Norton.

Ferenczi, S. and Rank, O. (1925). *The Development of Psychoanalysis*. Trans. C. Newton. New York: Nervous and Mental Disease Publishing Co.

Freud, S. (1893–1895). Studies in Hysteria. *Standard Edition* 2: 1–335.

———. (1905). On psychotherapy. *Standard Edition* 7: 257–268.

———. (1909). Analysis of a phobia in a five-year-old boy. *Standard Edition* 10: 3–149.

———. (1911). Letter to L. Binswanger, May 28. In *Ludwig Binswanger, Sigmund Freud: Reminiscences of a Friendship*, trans. N. Guterman, pp. 32–33. New York: Grune & Stratton, 1957.

———. (1913). Totem and taboo. *Standard Edition* 13: 1–162.

———. (1914). On narcissism. *Standard Edition* 14: 67–102.

———. (1917). New introductory lectures on psychoanalysis. *Standard Edition* 15 and 16: 3–496.

———. (1923). The ego and the id. *Standard Edition* 19: 3–66.

———. (1926). The question of lay analysis. *Standard Edition* 20: 179–258.

———. (1930). Civilization and its discontents. *Standard Edition* 21: 59–145.

Geertz, C. (1973). *The Interpretation of Cultures*. New York: Basic Books.

Gopnik, A. (1994). The great deflator. *The New Yorker*, June 27 and July 4: 169–177.

Harlow, H. F. (1958). The nature of love. *American Psychologist* 13: 673.

Heller, E. (1958). *Thomas Mann: The Ironic German*. New York: Paul P. Appel.

———. (1965). *The Artist's Journey into the Interior*. London: Secker and Warburg.

Hendin, H. (1982). Psychotherapy and suicide. In *Suicide in America*, ed. H. Hendin. New York: Norton.

Husserl, E. (1929). *Cartesian Meditations,* trans. D. Cairns. The Hague: Nifhoff, 1960.

Jamison, K. R. (1993). *Touched with Fire: Manic Depressive Illness and the Artistic Temperament.* New York: Guilford.

Joyce, J. (1922). *Ulysses.* London: Penguin, 1986.

Kaiser, H. (1962). Emergency. *Psychiatry* 25: 97–118.

Kaplan, H. I., and Sadock, B. J. (1991). *Kaplan and Sadock's Synopsis of Psychiatry*, 6th ed. Baltimore: Williams & Wilkins.

Kaplan, H. I., Sadock, B. J., and Grebb, J. A. (1994). *Kaplan and Sadock's Synopsis of Psychiatry*, 7th ed. Baltimore: Williams & Wilkins.

Kaufmann, W. (1980). *Discovering the Mind*, vol. 3. New York: McGraw-Hill.

Kazin, A. (1994). Jews. *The New Yorker*, March 7: 62–73.

Koestler, A. (1968). *Arrival and Departure*. New York: Bantam.

Lacan, J. (1953–1954). *The Seminar of Jacques Lacan, Book I. Freud's Papers on Technique*, chapter VII. New York: Norton, 1988.

———. (1954–55). The dream of Irma's injection. *The Seminar of Jacques Lacan, Book II*, chapter XIII. New York: Norton, 1988.

Leavy, S. A. (1980). *The Psychoanalytic Dialogue*. New Haven: Yale University Press.

Linehan, M., Armstrong, H., Suarez, A., et al. (1991). Cognitive-behavioral treatment of chronically parasuicidal borderline patients. *Archives of General Psychiatry* 48: 1060–1064.

Lipsey, M. W., and Wilson, D. B. (1993). The efficacy of psychological, educational, and behavioral treatment. *American Psychologist* 48(12): 1181–1209.

Luborsky, L., Singer, B., and Luborsky, L. (1975). Comparative studies of psychotherapy. *Archives of General Psychiatry* 32: 995.

Ludwig, A. M. (1994). *The Price of Greatness*. New York: Guilford.

Mann, T. (1934). *Joseph and His Brothers*, trans. H. Löwe-Porter. New York: Knopf, 1981.

———. (1936). *Stories of Three Decades*, trans. H. Löwe-Porter. New York: Modern Library.

Marmor, J. (1979). Short term dynamic psychotherapy. *American Journal of Psychiatry* 136(2): 149.

McCarthy, T. (1981). *The Critical Philosophy of Jürgen Habermas*. Cambridge, MA: MIT Press.

McKinney, W. T. (1989). Interdisciplinary animal research and its relevance to psychiatry. In *Comprehensive Textbook of Psychiatry*, ed. H. I. Kaplan, and B. J. Sadock, 5th ed. Baltimore: Williams & Wilkins.

Megill, A. (1985). *Prophets of Extremity*. Berkeley: University of California Press.

Meissner, W. (1986). *Psychotherapy and the Paranoid Process*. Northville, NJ: Jason Aronson.

Menninger, K. (1959). Hope. *American Journal of Psychiatry* 116: 481–491.

Nehemas, A. (1985). *Nietzsche: Life as Literature*. Cambridge: Harvard University Press.

Nietzsche, F. (1884). *Thus Spake Zarathustra*. In *The Portable Nietzsche*, selected and translated by W. Kaufmann. New York: Viking Press, 1954.

———. (1886). *Beyond Good and Evil*. In *The Basic Writings of Nietzsche*, translated and edited by W. Kaufmann. New York: Modern Library, 1968.

———. (1888). *The Twilight of the Idols*. In *The Portable Nietzsche*, selected and translated by W. Kaufmann. New York: Viking Press, 1954.

———. (1888). *The Will to Power*, trans. W. Kaufmann, and R. J. Hollingdale. New York: Vintage (1967).

———. (1909–1911). *Human, all too human*, trans. H. Zimmerman, and P. V. Kohn. In *The Complete Works of Friedrich Nietzsche*, ed. O. Levy. New York: Macmillan.

Ornston, D. (1985). Freud's conception is different from Strachey's. *Journal of the American Psychoanalytic Association* 33: 379.

Rapaport, D., and Gill, M. (1959). The points of view and assumptions of metapsychology. In *The Collected Papers of David Rapaport*, ed. M. M. Gill, pp. 795–811. New York: Basic Books, 1967.

Rieff, P. (1966). *The Triumph of the Therapeutic: The Uses of Faith After Freud*. New York: Harper & Row.

Rorty, R. (1989). *Contingency, Irony and Solidarity*. New York: Cambridge University Press.

———. (1993). Centers of moral gravity: commentary on Donald Spence's "The Hermeneutic Turn." *Psychoanalytic Dialogues* 3(1): 21–28.

———. (1994). Towards a liberal utopia. *Times Literary Supplement*, June 24. N4760: 14.

Searles, H. (1967). The "dedicated physician" in the field of psychotherapy and psychoanalysis. In *Countertransference and Related Subjects*, pp. 71–88. Madison, CT: International Universities Press, 1979.

Smith, L. P. (1931). "Afterthoughts." In *The Oxford Dictionary of Quotations*, ed. A. Partington. Oxford: Oxford University Press.

Spitz, R. (1946a). Hospitalism: a follow-up report. *Psychoanalytic Study of the Child* 2: 113. New York: International Universities Press.

———. (1946b). Anaclitic depression. *Psychoanalytic Study of the Child* 2: 313. New York: International Universities Press.

Steiner, G. (1958). *Language and Silence*. New York: Atheneum, 1986.

———. (1974). *Nostalgia for the Absolute*. Toronto: CBC.

———. (1989). *Real Presences*. Chicago: University of Chicago Press.

Suter, R. (1989). *Interpreting Wittgenstein. A Cloud of Philosophy, a Drop of Grammar*. Philadelphia: Temple University Press.

Warme, G. (1994). *Reluctant Treasures: The Practice of Analytic Psychotherapy*. Northvale, NJ: Jason Aronson.

Winston, A., Pinsker, H., and McCullough, L. (1986). A review of supportive psychotherapy. *Hospital and Community Psychiatry* 37(11): 1105.

Index

About the Author

Gordon Warme was born in Toronto and educated at the University of Toronto, the Universität Heidelberg, and the Menninger Clinic. He is a practicing psychotherapist, senior consultant to the Psychotherapy Centre of the Clarke Institute of Psychiatry, and supervising and training analyst at the Toronto Institute of Psychoanalysis. Dr. Warme has been president of the Canadian Psychoanalytic Society, visiting professor at Ben Gurion University in Israel, and founder and director of the Toronto Child Psychotherapy Program. He is the author of *Reluctant Treasures: The Practice of Analytic Psychotherapy*.